NOVISSIMA DESCRIPTIO.

TRIONALE

Vaigatz

IOV
GHO
RIA

OB

DO

OB

DO

RA.

Obafl. Zolota morch

Puftezora

A Viatsko

CHIN

TVMEN

Cama fl.

bash

NAGAIA.

Shakashuck

Yoldaf.

ARTA

R

Baghtiar

Sherachuck

Mare
Caspium

Mangusta

Zlata, Baba, id eft aurea
vetula ab Obdorianis et Ion
gorianis religiofe colitur. Ido
lum hoc facerdos confulit;
quid ipfis faciendum quoue fit
migrandum, ipfumq; dictu
mirum certa confulentibus
dat responfa certique e-
uentus confequuntur.

MOY   ED

A

Obafl.

Siber

Kitaia
Lacus

TVRK

A Mangusla shayfura am uf
iter habent, fine ullis fedibus cum fumma
aquę penuria A Shayfura ufq; Bogar par
itineris interuallum latrocinijs infestum.

the MOSCOVIA of Antonio Possevino, S.J.

UCIS
Series in Russian
& East European
Studies

Number
1

MOSCOVIA

ANTONII
POSSEVINI
SOCIETATIS IESV.

ANTVERPIÆ,
Ex Officina Christophori Plantini,
Architypographi Regij.
M. D. LXXXVII.

Original Frontispiece to the Antwerp edition of *Moscovia*, 1587.

P. Antonius Possevinus, S. J., from *Galerie illustrée de la Compagnie de Jésus,* Vol. VI, by A. Hamy, S. J., Paris, 1893.

the MOSCOVIA of
Antonio Possevino, S.J.

translated,
with Critical Introduction
and Notes by

Hugh F. Graham

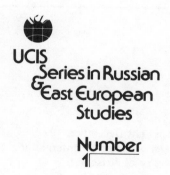

UCIS
Series in Russian
& East European
Studies

Number
1

University Center for International Studies
University of Pittsburgh

Library of Congress Cataloging in Publication Data

Possevino, Antonio, 1533 or 4-1611.
   The Moscovia of Antonio Possevino, S. J.

   (UCIS series in Russian and East European studies; no. 1)
   Includes bibliographical references.
   1. Catholic Church—Doctrinal and controversial works—Catholic author.
2. Catholic Church—Relations (diplomatic) with Russia. 3. Russia—Foreign
relations—Catholic Church. I. Title. II. Series: Pittsburgh. University. University Center for International Studies. UCIS series in Russian and East European
studies; no. 1.
BX1780.P5813   327.45'634   77-12648
ISBN 0-916002-27-6

Additional copies are available from:

University Center for International Studies
Publications Section
University of Pittsburgh
G-6 Mervis Hall
Pittsburgh, PA 15260
USA

TABLE OF CONTENTS

INTRODUCTION

The *Moscovia* is a narrative composed by Antonio Possevino, S. J. relating his experiences in Muscovy in the years 1581-1582, where he was sent as the personal emissary of Pope Gregory XIII to arrange a truce between Ivan the Terrible, the Grand Prince, or Tsar, of Muscovy and Stefan Batory, the King of Poland. Since Possevino was instrumental in achieving the truce, the *Moscovia* recounts a considerable success for Papal diplomacy in a region to which the Papacy had heretofore failed to penetrate. However, the Pope had expected much more to emerge from Possevino's mission. When Ivan the Terrible sent a courier, Istoma Shevrigin, to Rome in February, 1581 to ask for Papal assistance in bringing the war between Poland and Muscovy to a conclusion, the Pope and his chief advisors hoped that their intervention might lead to the establishment of regular diplomatic relations between Rome and Moscow, the adherence of Muscovy to a "League of Christian Princes" to attack the Turks, which was a dream cherished by all sixteenth-century Popes, and, above all, to the creation of channels of communication which would open the way to uniting the Muscovite church with Rome on the Pope's terms. Since none of these objectives was accomplished, the *Moscovia* is also a chronicle of developments symptomatic of the declining ability of the Holy See to control the course of events in Europe. It may be well to sketch the background to the dispatch of Possevino to Poland and Muscovy.

Many of the profound changes that were taking place in Europe during the sixteenth century were caused by the rise and spread of Protestantism and the corrosive effect it was exercising upon traditional institutions and loyalties. The Holy See had initially been slow to react to Luther's challenge and had underestimated the danger to the Church's position posed by the explosive forces which Protestantism was releasing into society. Its failure had allowed Protestantism to make rapid and substantial gains; only gradually had the Papacy become aware of the need to combat the diffusion of the new religious movement. The Church's response assumed a variety of forms: the Conciliar movement, regeneration, and reform of clerical morals, restructuring the educational apparatus at all levels, revitalization of existing religious orders, and the appearance of a new one, the Society of Jesus. Catholic rulers, conspicuously the Habsburgs, were exhorted to oppose the spread of Protestantism in the lands under their jurisdiction. All these activities were known collectively as the Counterreformation.

Another danger to Papal hegemony came from the militant presence of the Ottoman Empire in the Balkan peninsula and Hungary. To combat it the Popes strove sedulously to create an alliance involving all or most of the European rulers, but their plans were continually frustrated by the increasing atomization of the European community. A growing awareness of the extent of these two dangers aroused Papal curiosity concerning Muscovy, in which the Popes had maintained a sporadic and unproductive interest for a number of years. Pope Gregory came to believe that one way the Papacy might recoup some of the losses it had recently sustained through defections to the Protestant cause was to extend its religious dominion to regions which had not previously been under the Church's jurisdiction, an idea which had been given fresh impetus by the gains the Jesuits had scored in America. The Pope further calculated that the adhesion of Muscovy, about the extent of whose power and resources he had formed inflated and inaccurate views, to the alliance against the Turks would appreciably increase the prospects for the expulsion of the latter from Europe. In the sixteenth century Muscovy had emerged from the isolation which had formerly surrounded it: the moment was opportune; only a suitable pretext was required.

Muscovy was known to possess a large Christian population communicant with the Greek rite. Lacking concrete information, the Pope and his advisors confidently assumed that its rulers had accepted the mandates of the Council of Florence, which in 1438, in ordaining the reunion of the Greek and Latin churches, had compelled the former to recognize and acknowledge the Pope as the Leader of all Christendom. The Muscovites, however, had decisively rejected the Florentine Union; the *Moscovia* is filled with instances of the difficulties Possevino encountered because he was laboring under the erroneous assumption that they subscribed to it. The prospect of bringing millions of Muscovites formally into the Catholic fold was tantalizing. Poland, now a bastion of the Counterreformation, had since 1578 been waging a highly successful war against Muscovy, yet Ivan's overture to the Pope, which ignored the Polish king, a firm supporter of the Jesuits, met with a quick and positive response. No assertion that the Pope and his advisors were fully aware of the political motives that underlay the Tsar's action can obscure the fact that they were prepared to sacrifice the gains for the Catholic cause made by the Polish king to the dream of converting the Muscovites. The Pope's interpretation of what constituted the Church's true interests illuminated a further and more fundamental problem. Simply stated, Grand Prince Ivan and the other rulers of the sixteenth century, as they felt their way towards the new concept of a sovereign independent nation-state functioning as the basic unit in the organization of Europe, were more in tune with contemporary developments (however much they might differ from one another in outlook, approach and method) than the Papacy, which continued to be indissolubly wedded to the mediaeval principle of ecumenicism. Possevino fully shared the Pope's views; perhaps that was among the reasons why he was chosen as his emissary. Possevino had, however, other qualifications to recommend him.

Antonio Possevino was a splendid example of the zeal and devotion the Society of Jesus could inspire in its members. In view of his prominence during the early years of the Order, it is surprising that no recent biography of him has appeared.[1] His mission to Muscovy has fared somewhat better.[2] Possevino was born in modest circumstances at Mantua in 1533 or 1534. Early manifesting his scholarly capacities and his religious calling, in 1550 he was sent to Rome, where he attracted the attention of Cardinal Ercole Gonzaga, who made him his secretary and tutor to his nephews. Entering the Jesuit Order in 1559, he rose rapidly. He embarked upon further studies in Rome, but his skill as a diplomat had become known, and such talents were precisely what the Church needed as it sought to intensify the Counterreformation. In 1560 Possevino was sent to Piedmont and Savoy, where he vigorously upheld the cause of the Church as he refined and sharpened his abilities as a debater in contests with Protestant leaders. Ordained priest in the Order in 1561, he was immediately sent to France, a major theater of religious controversy, where he worked for the Church loyally and devotedly in a variety of capacities for the next 12 years. In 1573 he was recalled to Rome to serve as the General Secretary of the Order, a post he held until 1577, when a situation developed calling for his delicacy as a negotiator. The Church had become convinced that King John III could be influenced by his Catholic wife to bring Sweden back to the fold. Possevino was sent to Sweden, and his sojourn at the Swedish court constituted his initiation into the complex politics of the Baltic area. He made two journies to Sweden, in 1577 and 1579, and although he acquitted himself ably, it proved impossible to restore Catholicism there. The next year Possevino was selected to undertake the challenging and responsible assignment of mediating between Poland and Muscovy. The proximate cause of his mission was the Livonian War, about which it will be necessary to say a few words.

Muscovy's quest for security and a maritime outlet permitting sustained and greater contact with the rest of Europe had drawn the attention of her Grand Princes to Livonia, a territory which roughly comprised that of modern Latvia and Estonia. The formidable band of military zealots known as the Livonian Order, affiliated with their more powerful counterparts to the southwest, the Knights of the Cross, had long proved capable of maintaining Livonia's autonomy under the nominal suzerainty of the Holy Roman Empire, but in the sixteenth century the situation began to change. The knights, no longer infused with religious enthusiasm, had grown luxury-loving and unwarlike. They were increasingly at odds with the townsmen, who were jealous of their commercial privileges; Protestantism was making substantial headway among all segments of the population, and the native peasants were growing restive under the increasingly heavy exactions demanded from them.

Muscovy had long enjoyed regular trading relations with Riga, the chief city and port of Livonia, and thus Ivan was fully informed of these developments. He came to the conclusion that a propitious moment now existed for Muscovy to annex Livonia, although he realized that such a move on his part was bound to provoke a response from Poland, Sweden and Denmark. Having decided to use force and aware of the seriousness of the step he was contemplating, he undertook systematic preparations to strengthen his own position. He captured the Khanates of Kazan' and Astrakhan' in order to secure his eastern flank and, not daring to attack their enclave, he employed every means at his disposal to establish good relations with the Crimean Tatars, who were vassals of the Ottoman Sultan. After these preparations had been made, Ivan invaded Livonia in 1558. The invasion was initially successful and Muscovy acquired control of much of the countryside, but Ivan failed to take the chief towns, and the attack soon aroused the other Baltic powers against him. The struggle continued in a desultory fashion until 1577, when Ivan launched a major drive to bring the prize firmly within his grasp. He almost succeeded, but developments in Poland which he could neither have foreseen nor forestalled were to have a disastrous impact upon his fortunes.

The death of King Sigismund-Augustus in 1572 brought about an interregnum, while various forces vied for the Polish throne, but by 1576 Stefan Batory, Prince of Transylvania, had prevailed over all his rivals. In his person Poland acquired a ruler of energy, resourcefulness, daring and proven military capacities. Batory's policy was to drive Muscovy from Livonia and carry the war into the enemy's territory. He lost no time putting his plans into operation and invaded Muscovy on a broad front in 1578. Severely weakened by the long struggle in Livonia, protracted internal disturbances, and ceaseless Tatar raids, Ivan was unable to resist Batory's onslaught, which portended final disaster for Muscovy. His situation was desperate, but Ivan showed himself equal to the challenge when he appealed for Papal mediation.

Ivan knew that the Pope could not resist the possibility of obtaining Muscovite participation in a crusade against the Turks, and as a careful student of Byzantine history he was aware that former Popes had on occasion sacrificed their best interests in the hope of achieving Church Union. He thought that Pope Gregory might be even more willing than his predecessors to respond because of his alarm at the inroads Protestantism had made among the ranks of the faithful. He dispatched Shevrigin to Rome bearing a carefully-worded message. He made no promises, but he knew that the mere appearance of a Muscovite in Italy would arouse old enthusiasms. The alacrity of the Pope's response proved that the Tsar had calculated correctly.

The first task that Possevino was obliged to perform once he had started on his mission was to mollify ruffled feelings in Poland, where some took the view that the Pope had betrayed them. The diplomat proved more than equal to the occasion, for in a series of conversations he succeeded in making a very favorable impression on Batory and winning the King's support for his undertaking. Possevino's position at the Polish court might have been more awkward if the people of Pskov had not rendered him unexpected assistance. In August, 1581, following up his series of successful campaigns, Batory decided to take Pskov, the gateway to the rest of Muscovy. He ordered Chancellor Zamojski, the Commander-in-Chief of the Polish armies, to invest the city, confident that it would quickly surrender. Matters turned out otherwise, for the fortifications were very strong and the besieged put up a determined resistance. Ivan was sufficiently encouraged by this check to the enemy's ambitions to quibble over the Polish demands which Possevino brought with him to the Muscovite command post at Staritsa, a fortress on the upper Volga, which he reached in late August. Returning to the Polish camp in early October after lengthy discussions with the Tsar, Possevino informed the King and the Chancellor of the stance their opponent had adopted. They indicated their intention to continue the siege of Pskov throughout the winter if necessary, although, as Possevino himself discerned, the difficulties of conducting it were steadily mounting. Possevino was told to inform Ivan of their determination in his request for further negotiations. Ivan decided to send delegates to a neutral place, and thus the way was prepared for Possevino to undertake the mediation which was the ostensible purpose of his journey.

The *Moscovia* is Possevino's version of the activities he engaged in while on his mission to Muscovy. He understandably tried to stress the importance of the role played by the Pope in making peace and to emphasize his own contributions to the negotiations. He glossed over or omitted incidents that would present him in a bad light, for beneath the calm and controlled exterior that many years of diplomatic experience had taught him to display lay a proud, hot-tempered and passionate nature. Unlike many other visitors Possevino was not content with merely reporting a mass of undigested facts; he was a trained and discriminating observer, possessed of a curious and inquiring mind, who subjected the data he accumulated to scrutiny and analysis and drew conclusions from them. His natural abilities were favored by the position he occupied; he enjoyed access to leading men in Muscovy, including the Grand Prince, and thus his account constitutes an important source for sixteenth-century Russian history. Possevino's religious prejudices may be anticipated and discounted; what remains is the perceptive analysis of a mature and experienced man of affairs, who was endowed with a considerable degree of tolerance on all matters save dogma. Possevino's delineation of Ivan deserves special mention. He presented a rich composite portrait of the Grand Prince, and even in the religious disputations he held with the Tsar, he was willing to give his opponent a measure of his due. It is no madman that appears in these pages, but an antagonist worthy of the best efforts of one of the most able diplomats in Europe. Possevino's lack of command of the Russian language is not important; his narrative provides valuable insights into the character of the complex and enigmatic Tsar. To illustrate these points it will be appropriate to comment on some salient features of the *Moscovia.*

Chapter I contains Possevino's observations on the extent of the devastation and depopulation that had taken place in the parts of Muscovy through which he travelled. It is compelling testimony to the country's lack of recuperative powers, one reason why Ivan had to bring the Livonian War to an end. Possevino showed considerable interest in the types of fortifications found in Muscovy, and displayed a real grasp of tactics and strategy. His description of the fortifications of Pskov helps to explain why the city was able to resist the Poles. In commenting upon the attractive appearance presented by the Kremlin in Moscow Possevino unconsciously revealed his pride in his native land. An Italian architect had designed, and Italian workmen had helped build the Moscow Kremlin; it reminded him of home.

Possevino saw how the Tsar's authority ran unchecked and unchallenged throughout Muscovy. He believed that the principal ingredient Ivan had employed to achieve his uncontrolled dominion was fear, an emotion he found ubiquitous, produced by the application of capricious terrorism directed against individuals and entire families alike. He substantiated his conclusion with examples, drawn from his own knowledge, of the hypersensitively suspicious nature possessed by the Grand Prince. In short, he was describing the state of mind pervading Muscovy in the wake of the *Oprichnina,* although he did not allude to it specifically, nor can it be determined whether he was familiar with the details of its organization. *Oprichnina* was the term used to designate Ivan's device of dividing Muscovy into two separate territorial units, one administered by leading members of the old Boyar aristocracy with which Ivan was often in conflict, and the other under the direct control of himself and his chosen lieutenants. In the latter, acts of violence were frequently perpetrated against those whom Ivan deemed to be his enemies. Completing this portion of his commentary Possevino provided a list of the Tsar's chief advisors; with certain exceptions they were all individuals whose rise to prominence coincided with the existence of the *Oprichnina*.

Possevino furnished information on the new system of land tenure instituted during Ivan's reign. The Grand Prince desired to create a new class of serving-men (*Pomeshchiki*) to counterbalance the influence of the hereditary nobility, and he needed many men to fight in the army as the result of his ambitious foreign policy. He rewarded the members of this new group with grants of land, but he saw to it that they could never aspire to the independence the older nobility had enjoyed by instituting a system of life-tenure based on the satisfactory performance of military service, reserving his right to approve the transmission of allotments within a family, and prohibiting the alienation of holdings. Possevino also noted the rapidity with which the institution of serfdom was spreading in Muscovy. The system had been in the process of development for some time, but it too received powerful impetus as the result of Ivan's policies. The Crown was obliged to place increasingly severe restrictions upon the free movement of the peasantry because its greater need for revenue compelled it to increase the number and extent of the exactions made upon the peasants and because the government had to guarantee a dependable supply of labor to satisfy the wants of the new class of serving-men and free its members for continuous military service. This was the beginning of a system that was to have profound economic, social and political consequences in later Russian history. Among the further observations found in this section are allusions to the effect that the Grand Prince continued to be the chief merchant and trader in the country, that no clear line of demarcation between the Privy Purse and the Public Fisc had yet appeared, and that Ivan had enjoyed success with the reforms he had initiated in the 1550's to increase the accountability of provincial officials to the central government. The version Possevino obtained from an eye-witness as to the reasons why Ivan killed his own son possesses a certain psychological verisimilitude that commands respect.

Possevino could not refrain from quoting in full the grandiloquent speech he made to the Tsar on the achievements of the Jesuit Order. It contained an odd play on words, perhaps unintentional: refusing the sable skins (*pelles*) Ivan had given him on his departure the priest declared that he and all the other members of the Order would gladly sacrifice their skins (*pelles*) for the glory of God. Ignoring the speech (not the only occasion on which he showed a nice ability to discriminate between the significant and the irrelevant) Ivan intimated that he would be highly offended if the envoy scorned his gifts. His feelings were dictated by his strongly-developed sense of protocol. Possevino described the elaborate ceremonies performed at the reception of foreign dignitaries and was shrewd enough to recognize the great importance the Muscovites attached to protocol. He advised the Pope to instruct future delegations scrupulously to discharge all ceremonial functions in which they were invited to participate.

In the concluding portion of Chapter I Possevino began his assessment of the chances for successfully disseminating Catholicism in Muscovy. His survey reveals two divergent strains in his makeup, that contributed to the ambivalence characteristic of his approach to many of the problems which confronted him on his mission to Muscovy. He combined within himself the visionary idealist, who was in constant danger of overreaching himself in his enthusiasm, and the practical man, who offered sensible suggestions concerning details, attention to which might spell the difference between success and failure in a strange and foreign environment. They included such items as the proper equipment and clothing to take on the journey, how to avoid being bitten by bedbugs, and what tip should be given to the attendants who saw to an envoy's needs.

Chapter II is addressed directly to the problem of disseminating Catholicism in Muscovy. Possevino made a careful assessment of the difficulties involved, which he recognized were very substantial. His description of the structure of the Muscovite Church was sober and factual, and if certain stock remarks (references to Orthodox priests are usually followed by such statements as "if priests indeed they be") are left aside, reasonably free from animosity. His strictures on the lack of educational institutions in Muscovy were no more than a reflection of the prevailing reality. Possevino was virtually the only Western visitor who liked Muscovite ikons. He found them attractive and reverent, and regarded them as overt expressions of the deep religiosity he believed he saw in the common Muscovite people, to which he more than once paid a sincere tribute.

In this chapter Possevino manifested an ambivalent attitude towards the Greeks, the confusing implications of which he did not seem to be aware. At one moment he would harshly attack them; once he went so far as to exult that such traducers of the Truth had fallen into Turkish servitude, but immediately afterwards he would call upon Ivan to maintain the proper Greek form of worship in the Muscovite church. He did not differentiate clearly between the Greeks of antiquity who, he believed, had practised a pure form of Christian worship and their degenerate successors who had, in his opinion, fallen away from their model. Assuming Muscovite acceptance of the Council of Florence he failed to heed Ivan's categorical statement: "I do not believe in the Greeks; I believe in Christ" (p. 69).

After observing the Tsar on numerous state occasions Possevino came to the conclusion that Ivan was consciously striving to create the image of a potentate who combined in his own person the attributes of both king and high priest. Such a concept, however meaningful to inheritors of the Byzantine tradition, was foreign and repugnant to one of Possevino's background. This led him to believe that the Tsar was deliberately indulging in all the ceremonial pomp the envoy witnessed in order to enhance his authority and deceive the people. Possevino had once written a refutation of the arguments advanced by Macchiavelli in *The Prince* and thus he can scarcely be blamed for having acquired a certain cynicism, but in this case his sophistication misled him; a genuine, if somewhat hysterical, strain of religiosity formed an essential part of Ivan's temperament.

On undertaking his mission Possevino, in his lack of information on the actual state of affairs in Ivan's realm together with his burning zeal to spread the faith, was led to entertain the most sanguine and optimistic fancies of a successful outcome, but upon his arrival he soon began to appreciate the nature, extent and complexities of the problem. He was not afraid to criticize previous Popes for failing to investigate matters more closely. Passing the problems in review, he noted (with grudging approval) the strong attachment the Orthodox felt for their ritual, and the influence of the Protestant colony in Moscow. Next, indulging in a flight of wishful thinking, he speculated that Ivan might be moved to grant Catholics full freedom of worship and religious activity in Muscovy. Ivan was never prepared to do more than allow Catholic priests to attend to the religious needs of their foreign communicants. They would never have been permitted to proselytize among the Muscovites. This section again illustrates the blend of the visionary and the practical man in Possevino. He dreamed of the vast increase in the numbers of the faithful that would result from "reuniting" the Muscovites with the Church, while at the same time making the logical deduction from what he had observed that the Church should not try to labor in Muscovy, which (in the military parlance Possevino sometimes affected) was not likely to succumb to a frontal attack, to the neglect of Lithuania, as it contained a large population with close ethnic and religious ties with the Muscovites, upon which much more persuasive influences could be brought to bear since the country was under the control of the Polish king.

Possevino chose to interpret the cordial reception the Tsar gave him as a sign that God had inclined Ivan towards a more favorable view of Catholicism, although he knew perfectly well that political considerations had occasioned it. He drew attention to the difficulties of language and communication, and he was one of the very few to comment upon the ramifications of this problem. His remarks illustrate how little was known or understood concerning Muscovy elsewhere in Europe, for Possevino was obliged to explain that all books and pamphlets which anyone might wish to present to the Muscovites should be in their language and printed in the Cyrillic characters of the alphabet the Muscovites used. He reported the ludicrous and pathetic fact that no Muscovites could profit from the copy of the Confession of the Faith composed by Pope Pius IV he had brought with him for their edification because it had been translated into a mixture of South-Slavic languages and written in Latin letters, which the Muscovites were unable to read. The incessant difficulty Possevino had with interpreters, which he vividly described, undoubtedly was one of the reasons why he observed somewhat testily that Seminary curricula should include study of living languages. The foregoing considerations led Possevino to devote his concluding remarks in Chapter II to the effectiveness of education as a means for disseminating Catholicism in Muscovy. It was a subject he understood well, and he strongly believed it was the best way to achieve his objective.

Chapter III is Possevino's version of the disputations he held with the Tsar in Moscow, after the conclusion of the Truce of Iam Zapol'skii, on the subject of religion. It was the moment he had long been waiting for; he regarded his other activities as preliminary or contributory to it. He had made elaborate preparations for the confrontation, and he hoped that the role he had played in bringing about the peace settlement would dispose the Tsar favorably to the substance of what he intended to say. Ivan, on the other hand, would just as soon have avoided the discussion. However necessary he had considered it to accept the Truce of Iam Zapol'skii, he could not regard the loss of Livonia with equanimity, since he had devoted so large an expenditure of time and resources to acquiring it, nor could he view Possevino's mediation as a triumph for his cause. He had not the slightest intention of taking anything Possevino might say on the subject of religion seriously, but he felt obliged to accord the Pope's envoy a hearing on the topic, if only to avoid criticism from neighboring Catholic rulers, with whom he was anxious to maintain good relations, who might interpret his refusal as a discourtesy to the Pope. Here was Ivan's motive for permitting the disputations to proceed, but it is fascinating to observe, as the debate progressed, how the Tsar yielded to his instinctive love of theological controversy and became a passionate participant in the encounter.

Possevino's narrative can be compared with the official Muscovite version. The two are completely independent of one another, but their content displays many striking similarities, as well as the expected differences. In the Muscovite version Possevino appears clumsy and inept; sometimes stubborn and rash, sometimes timid and deferential, he was easily bested in argument by the Tsar, who exposed him as a man who did not know his Bible or even simple matters of liturgy. Possevino's own account portrays him as an imposing and dignified figure, always in full control of himself whatever the provocation, as he made a measured and orderly presentation of significant major issues. Such divergences as these were, of course, to be anticipated; of interest is the comparative agreement between the two versions concerning the Tsar. Ivan was depicted as a man with a passion for quoting Scripture and an intense lover of argument, who would lose his temper and get so carried away as to become at moments incoherent, but with equal suddenness resume a calm and courteous demeanor.

The fundamental point that immediately appeared from the disputations was that each participant was equally sincere and fully convinced of the correctness of his position but neither one could enter into a genuine exchange of opinion with the other. In these circumstances no progress was possible. In the first (and liveliest) debate Possevino devised what he thought was an ingenious way to put forward his case for the primacy of the Pope without offending the Tsar. He asked Ivan whether he considered himself entitled to obedience from his subjects because he was the legitimate successor of St. Vladimir of Kiev, who had introduced Christianity (adopted from "schismatic heretics," as Possevino never tired of pointing out) into Kiev in 988 A.D. In previous interviews with the Tsar's advisors Possevino had tactlessly gone out of his way to emphasize that Italy had known Christianity 1200 years (an exaggeration) before Muscovy; here he incorrectly referred to St. Vladimir as Vladimir of Muscovy; Ivan thought he meant Vladimir Monomakh. Possevino intended to take advantage of Ivan's assent to this proposition and declare that the Pope was far more deserving of obedience because he was the Successor of St. Peter, who was in turn the Successor of Christ. However, his ploy succeeded only in arousing the Grand Prince's wrath, for Possevino had failed to realize sufficiently that one of the major causes of the severe internal disturbances that had afflicted Muscovy during Ivan's reign was the Tsar's abiding conviction that his authority was under attack and his person in danger from his own subjects, for none of whom a claim to preeminence such as Possevino was trying to advance for the Pope could conceivably be made.

Possevino had expected the kind of reasoned and systematic exposition of theoretical positions he was accustomed to engage in with opponents who were, like himself, trained in theology, homiletics and dialectics. He had planned to proceed in an orderly way from the minor to the great central propositions of the faith, and to crown his presentation with a careful, intellectually-wrought appeal to Ivan to submit to the authority of the Pope, both because it was intrinsically right and because Metropolitan Isidor, by accepting the canons of the Council of Florence, had bound the Tsar to do so. Ivan would then state his reservations; Possevino would dispose of his objections, and agreement would amicably be reached. He was thus totally unprepared for Ivan's colorful and slashing style of debate, and for the nature of his rejoinder. He regarded the four questions concerning the appearance and the habits of the Pope, to which Ivan suddenly diverted the conversation, as irrelevant trifling, unrelated to the important issues. He assumed that the Tsar had been tricked into bringing them up by the local Protestants. No matter how useful the questions may have proved to turn the argument away from potentially embarrassing subjects, Ivan had not submitted to the dictation of the foreign commercial colony in Moscow and he had not raised them idly. The questions he asked were based on the report Shevrigin had made on what he saw in Rome and they were addressed to issues of vital concern to the Muscovites. Possevino, as has been seen, had himself noticed the very high regard the Muscovites entertained for details of ritual observance, but his commitment to his cause prevented him from making proper allowance for their attitude in formulating his presentation. For example, shaving beards was expressly prohibited by the highly authoritative Church Council (the *Stoglav*, or Hundred Chapters) which Ivan had convoked in 1551. Carrying a Pope who wore a cross on his feet in a chair for the people to reverence was likewise genuinely offensive to Muscovite religious sensibilities; the astonishment expressed by the assembled courtiers was unfeigned. Possevino was resourceful enough to return clever answers to the Tsar's questions, but they failed to have any effect. He further complicated matters by seeking to use these answers as a means to insinuate his demand that Ivan acknowledge the primacy of the Pope. By doing so he was in effect asking the Tsar to surrender a portion of the complete control Possevino himself had recognized Ivan possessed over the Muscovite church, and to confess he was not fully sovereign in his own land. This was the equivalent of requesting Ivan voluntarily to compromise the autocratic power he had devoted his whole lifetime to acquiring. It is small wonder that he failed in his objective.

According to Possevino, at the brief second meeting between the two contestants Ivan tendered the priest an apology for any offense he might have given him. The Muscovite version contains no allusion to an apology. It has the Tsar tell Possevino with a kind of grim satisfaction that he had warned the priest any discussion of the faith between them was bound to lead to rancor and animosity. At their third meeting Possevino professed to be startled when Ivan suddenly told him he had decided to grant his request to attend service at the Cathedral of the Virgin Mary, because he thought he had made it abundantly clear that he would refuse to do so. Possevino had often visited Muscovite churches and monasteries; he objected solely to being present at a service, because it would be celebrated by those who, in his opinion, held their office unlawfully since they had not been confirmed by the Pope. Not understanding Possevino's distinction between visiting a church and attending a service, Ivan might have made an honest mistake. Possevino declared that by refusing to enter the Cathedral he had outwitted the Tsar, who had deliberately contrived the whole scheme in order to humiliate the Pope's representative. The Muscovite version of the incident states that Possevino had formally expressed a wish to attend service, but when he was told, on arriving at the Cathedral, that he must wait for the Tsar, he lost his temper and walked away in a huff. It is impossible to determine the truth of the matter. Ivan might well have enjoyed taking advantage of the opportunity to have Possevino hear the Metropolitan, following the custom of the Easter service, pronounce anathema against the "Latins," as one of the enemies of Orthodoxy, prior to offering prayers for the conversion of such people, but it is also entirely possible that Possevino's resentment at what he took to be an affront to his dignity got the better of him.

Chapter IV consists of a treatise which Possevino states he conveyed to the Tsar at the latter's request. It was written in Latin, and it is uncertain whether Ivan had it translated, but if he did so, the material he found in it would not be calculated to advance the Catholic cause in Muscovy. Entitled "The Chief Points on which the Greeks and the Muscovites differ from the Latins in the Faith," it stubbornly insisted that the Greeks and Muscovites were one, in spite of all the efforts Ivan had made to disabuse Possevino of that notion. Possevino had the same purpose in mind in composing the treatise that he had at the disputations,--to persuade the Grand Prince to accept church union and acknowledge the primacy of the Pope. If Ivan took the trouble to look up the citations Possevino had given from the Church Fathers to buttress his arguments, he would have experienced difficulty in identifying some and would have discovered that others failed to substantiate the positions they were supposed to support. Possevino hoped that he would please the Tsar with his willingness to be accommodating on items of liturgical practice, to compensate for the rigidity he was obliged to display on matters of dogma.

The second part of this chapter consists of a catalog of "Errors" in belief of which Possevino judged the Greeks and Muscovites to be guilty. They ranged from the assertion that the Greeks (the ringleaders whom the Muscovites uncritically followed) did not consider fornication and usury to be sins, to the stark statement: "The most egregious and palpable error held by Greeks and Muscovites alike is their assumption that they can achieve eternal salvation outside the Roman Catholic Church" (p. 92). This contention is, of course, a matter of opinion; the previous allegations were simply not true. In 1592 Gabriel Severos, a Greek in charge of the Orthodox church in Venice, assailed Possevino for the serious and unfounded charges he had made against Orthodoxy. Possevino wrote Severos a courteous reply,[3] and although he did not go so far as to apologize for the opinions he had expressed, he made no further attempts to elaborate upon them, and he tacitly abandoned them when he later incorporated his views on the best way to deal with Greeks and Muscovites into his own compendium of Church matters.[4] A modern Jesuit scholar highly sympathetic to Possevino has stated flatly that the views expressed in this portion of the *Moscovia* were unworthy of their author and should never have been published.[5] Possevino fell into such error through his incautious reliance on writers whom he hastily consulted as he was preparing to undertake his mission. The authorities he used either possessed no firsthand knowledge of these topics (this holds true for so great an authority as St. Thomas Aquinas, whom Possevino quoted with approval and deference) or else were motivated by a hostile spirit entirely political in origin. This was above all true of the Poles; a good example was Sakran (Jan z Oświęcima) of Kraków, whose naive and unfounded strictures on the Muscovite religion were occasioned not so much by his zeal for the faith as by his hatred of the chief enemy of the Polish state.

Possevino handed Ivan a second treatise, Chapter V, which he had prepared after he arrived in Moscow and learned that the English merchants in residence there had given the Tsar a book which purported to show that the Pope was Antichrist. It contained his refutation of this charge; when Possevino conveyed it to the Grand Prince at their third meeting to discuss religion, Ivan observed a trifle sarcastically that Possevino was very fond of giving him things to read.[6] Again, if Ivan had ordered the work translated and read it, he would have been considerably annoyed at its highly tendentious tone and surprised at some of the historical allegations made in it. Possevino too could be carried away by his enthusiasms. In his desire to illustrate the wickedness of the English for forsaking the Church and attacking the Pope he began the Chapter with a diatribe against Henry VIII. He portrayed the king as a man whose lust for women had led him to abandon his wife (Catherine of Aragon, whom Possevino inadvertently called the sister, instead of the aunt, of the Emperor Charles V). The priest was aware of Ivan's marital problems, and knew perfectly well that in both cases each ruler was anxious to produce a male heir in order to secure the succession for his respective dynasty. Possevino's attack on Henry implied criticism of Ivan; such an approach was not likely to win the Grand Prince to acceptance of his views.

In this treatise Possevino claimed that the Pope possessed the right to judge the character and merits of temporal rulers. If he found them wanting, he was fully entitled to take whatever steps he deemed necessary to depose unworthy monarchs. Possevino had already called upon Ivan to make religious submission to the Pope; now he was urging the Tsar to subordinate himself to a political leader who would reserve the right to scrutinize his conduct and perhaps call for his removal from office. The impression this presentation would make on the mind of a Prince like Ivan can only be imagined. He was a ruler who had not shrunk from decimating the population of entire towns if he conceived even the slightest suspicion that a conspiracy had formed against him. Possevino the diplomat appreciated this, but he was overborne by Possevino the churchman. That the priest would submit such treatises to the Tsar is clear indication that he considered the religious issue paramount, for by making such trenchant observations he ran the very real risk of losing even the few concessions his diplomacy had been able to win from the Grand Prince.

Chapter VI serves as a case-study for sixteenth-century politics and diplomacy. It tells a great deal about the negotiating techniques utilized by the Poles and the Muscovites, and compares and contrasts their methods. Possevino narrated this chapter in the more remote third-person style that befitted this formal subject. The Polish king had intimated his intention to continue the siege of Pskov no matter whether negotiations got underway or not. In response, some of Ivan's advisors demanded an all-out effort be made to relieve the city and prosecute the war, but they were unable to persuade the Tsar, who had come to the conclusion that peace was what his exhausted country required. Accordingly the negotiating teams arrived and took up residence in and near Kiverova Gora (a hamlet adjacent to Iam Zapol'skii, the place that had been selected as the original site for the parley) in the middle of December, in the depth of a severe winter; the conditions under which they had to work were graphically described by Possevino. The Muscovites easily adapted themselves to the situation; between sessions they functioned as merchants and traders, to the amazement of Possevino, who feared that these arrangements would lead them to neglect their proper duties, although he was not above enjoying the food they regularly sent to the dismal smoky hut which served both as his lodging and the headquarters for the conference. Both sides employed all the tested devices of diplomatic manoeuvre: the appeal to general principle in order to forestall the opponent's demands or delay answering them, the proposal of maximum conditions in order to cover a strategic retreat to a more acceptable position, the ultimatum, or threatening to quit the conference, a device to which the Poles resorted more frequently than the Muscovites, in order to force the antagonist to back down, and the technique of introducing irrelevant issues (which the Muscovites were fond of using) in the hope of obtaining concessions as the price for abandoning them.

The siege of Pskov, which was seldom alluded to directly, had its effect on the negotiations. When the besieged discomfited the besiegers, as they did on more than one occasion, of existing Seminaries, and called for the founding of new ones, in which Muscovites might somehow be enrolled.

Labor in the field of education might be one solution to the problem, but it was a long and risky process with no guarantee of success. The *Moscovia* as it stands contains but the barest hints of the possibility of another solution, much quicker and more efficacious, with which Possevino was becoming steadily more intrigued. In the course of the successful Polish campaigns, which had amply justified the expectations the King had entertained of them, Batory had become convinced that it lay within his power to conquer Muscovy and make himself the ruler of a large Central European state composed of Poland, Lithuania, the Baltic region, and Muscovy. The formation of this state would precede a new crusade against the Turks of which Batory would be Commander-in-Chief. The achievement of this grandiose objective would carry with it unparalleled opportunities to effect church union on Papal terms, since the Jesuits and others would then be free to work without hindrance everywhere among the Orthodox. Given the frustrations that Possevino experienced on his mission, it is scarcely surprising that the priest came to partake more and more of Batory's ambition, especially as the two men had developed a very high regard for one another. In addition, the execution of such a project demanded exactly the talents of enthusiastic visionary and practical organizer that characterized Possevino's temperament.

Upon his final departure from Moscow in March, 1582, Possevino escorted Iakov Molvianinov, Ivan's representative to the Holy See, to the Pope. The Muscovite envoy accomplished nothing at the Vatican because Ivan did not intend that he should; after the Truce of Iam Zapol'skii the Tsar had no further need of the Pope. Batory believed that in Possevino he had found a man better able to represent his interests in Rome and to assist him with his other projects than the representatives of the Catholic establishment in Poland. Possevino reciprocated the King's sentiments and assumed a position not unlike that of Batory's chief councillor and advisor. The two men cooperated in a number of undertakings, such as their attempt to recatholicize Livonia, and the establishment of a network of Jesuit Seminaries in the territories under Polish control. Unquestionably they also discussed in detail the King's plan to conquer Muscovy, which seemed to them even more feasible after the accession of Fedor on Ivan's death in 1584. At the time of his visit Possevino had learned that Fedor was not in full possession of his faculties and was supposed to be of a milder and more accommodating disposition than his father.

the Muscovite envoys adopted a hard line, stalled, and temporized, but when the people of Pskov suffered reverses, as, for example, when the Poles captured 300 of them making an ill-advised sortie in early January, 1582, they were more inclined to offer concessions. In the last analysis the Polish position was the stronger, and the terms of the truce reflected it.

The final commentary on Possevino's failure to have Ivan acknowledge the primacy of the Pope was the stubborn insistence of the Muscovite envoys to include the Grand Prince's titles, such as Tsar of Kazan' and Tsar of Astrakhan', in the treaty. The Poles refused to incorporate them into their version of it, but by tacit agreement of all parties the titles were written into the separate Muscovite version. This showed that the Muscovites were conscious of their expanding role in European affairs and were determined to assert and secure recognition of their new religious and political status. The reaction of the Poles, although theirs was the moment of victory, indicated that they too recognized the new presence, which they both feared and distrusted. Possevino did not fully comprehend all these nuances; his chief concern was to obtain credit for the role the Pope had played in the negotiations.

A question that naturally arises is the degree of impartiality displayed by Possevino as mediator. He was instinctively sympathetic to the Polish cause, but at the time when the negotiations took place he still thought it possible to achieve church union with the Muscovites, and this belief led him to treat their envoys carefully. The simultaneous existence of these two contrary tendencies ensured that Possevino would try his best to serve as an honest and impartial arbiter. It is a moot question as to which side had the best of it. On the whole, it would seem to be the Muscovites. Their country was prostrate, and even the men of Pskov, who strengthened the Tsar's hand at this crucial juncture, were moved to complain of Ivan's failure to relieve them.[7] Like another Russian leader some three hundred and fifty years later, Ivan was determined to obtain a "breathing-space" by accepting a disadvantageous peace, although all he had to cede was territory which he no longer had the power to retain.

Possevino's activity after the conclusion of his mission to Muscovy should be briefly considered. His experiences there convinced him that church union, as he and others envisaged it, was unattainable, and he modified his attitude accordingly. He began to lay greater stress upon the role of Lithuania as a bridge between Catholicism and Orthodoxy. Typically, he emphasized education as a proselytising force, advocated maximum utilization

This phase of Possevino's career constituted one of the first illustrations of a difficulty the Jesuits were to encounter in other parts of the world as well. The devotion and abilities displayed by members of the Order rendered their services extremely valuable to particular rulers, who would try to use the Jesuits in order to advance their own interests. However, the Order, as an arm of the Papacy and in its founder Loyola's conception of it, was international in scope and function; the surest and most certain way to compromise its effectiveness was to have its members become embroiled in the politics of a particular region. Sooner or later such activities would be bound to offend others, whose support was equally or more important to the maintenance of the Church's international position. Possevino's situation provided an excellent example. Batory was an inveterate enemy of the Habsburgs; while still Prince of Transylvania he had acquired his formidable military reputation by the operations he conducted against Austria. He strove to check Austrian influence wherever he could and to keep the Habsburgs out of Polish affairs. However, the Pope required no demonstration of the necessity of Habsburg support of the Counterreformation, and thus when the Emperor's councillors complained that Possevino in his unqualified support of Batory was acting in a way inimical to Habsburg interests, the Pope was obliged to take their allegations very seriously. Furthermore, some members of the Order, who had labored long and diligently in Poland, and were convinced they understood the situation there better than Possevino, a comparative newcomer, resented his swift rise to prominence, and believed that his aggressiveness and politically-oriented policies were neither benefiting nor advancing the cause of religion. This view was shared by the leaders of the existing Catholic hierarchy in Poland, whom Batory continued to ignore in his preference for Possevino. Both of these groups assailed Possevino, and although their attacks may have to some degree been motivated by jealousy, the rising chorus of complaints compelled the General of the Jesuit Order, Claude Acquaviva, early in 1585 to instruct Possevino to leave the Polish court and take up residence in the Order's Seminary at Braunsberg in Prussia, where he was henceforth to confine his activity exclusively to religious work. Possevino unhesitatingly obeyed the command of his superior, but he remained in contact with the King and continued to advise him in the formulation of his projects. It was unclear what would happen next.

Two months later Gregory XIII died, and was succeeded by Sixtus V, a Pope thoroughly imbued with the ideals of the Counterreformation and less hesitant than his predecessor. Sixtus was immediately attracted by Batory's scheme to conquer Muscovy, enforce church union, and attack the Turks, and at once made known his support of the project. Batory insisted that Possevino be summoned from Braunsberg to handle the negotiations in Rome, which would pertain chiefly to the amount of subsidy the Pope was prepared to make available to finance the King's undertaking. The Pope approved, and early in 1586, without waiting for permission from Acquaviva, Possevino left Braunsberg for Rome, where he found himself once more at the summit of affairs, dealing with issues that affected the destinies of Europe. During much of that year he participated in secret conferences on Batory's project. The decision that emanated from the Papal chancery was a more hesitant one than Batory either expected or desired. The Pope was to approach Tsar Fedor's government with a request for its cooperation in the common enterprise against the Turks, but this cooperation was to assume a strange form. Tsar Fedor would be asked to cede territory to the Polish king, who would then proceed to utilize the additional resources it provided for his campaign. It is difficult to discern the rationale behind this move. Perhaps it represented a compromise between those of the Pope's advisors who supported a militant policy towards Muscovy and those who favored a conciliatory position. The minutes of these meetings have never been made public, but it is reasonable to assume that Possevino supported the aggressive stance which Batory himself favored, and was disappointed with the outcome. This may be why he expressed misgivings when he was once more chosen envoy to proceed to the Muscovite court and present this novel proposal to the new Tsar, although, true to his vow, he at once set out on his mission. On the way word came to him that King Stefan Batory had suddenly died in December, 1586. Even the most sanguine advocate of intervention was forced to realize that the King's plan to conquer Muscovy had died with him.

The issue at once became who was to succeed Batory on the Polish throne. The Habsburgs offered a candidate whom the Pope was inclined to support. Possevino remained out of favor at the Imperial court; thus, the Pope lost no time in endorsing a second command from the General of the Order for Possevino to desist entirely from the conduct of affairs. This time the order was final. Possevino returned to Italy, where he devoted his powerful intellect and inexhaustible energy to spiritual and literary pursuits.[8] He undertook no further major diplomatic missions and died in retirement at Ferrara in 1611.

A word should be said concerning the language and style of the *Moscovia*. Possevino wrote a good clear Latin prose which, like many of its Renaissance counterparts, displayed greater affinity with Classical Latin than with the Latin in common use during the Middle Ages. As the *Note on the Text* indicates, editions of the *Moscovia* are not numerous and do not contain sufficient variations to warrant collation. The present translation has made every effort to reproduce the style of the original. If at times it appears arid, pedestrian or obscure, this is no more than a reflection of comparable tendencies in Possevino. The man behind the offical mask is hard to discern, and unguarded revelations are rare. This is the way Possevino wished it, and for the most part he has succeeded in achieving his purpose. The numerous quotations from the Bible found in the work are given in the King James version.

1.   To this day the only full-scale biography of Possevino remains the uncritical paean of praise composed by J. Dorigny, *La Vie du Père Antoine Possevin de la Compagnie de Jésus*, Paris, 1712. A succinct factual outline of Possevino's career can be found in the entry by J. Ledit in the *Dictionnaire de Théologie Catholique* 12-2, Paris, 1933, Cols. 2647-2657.

2.   A sprightly account of Possevino's mission is found in the study by A. Arndt, S. J., "Ein päpstliches Schiedsgericht im 16 Jahrhundert," *Stimmen aus Maria-Laach* 31 (1886), pp. 480-503. The scholar who made the most comprehensive and thorough investigation of Possevino's activity in Poland and Muscovy was the Russian-born Jesuit, Paul Pierling. Among Pierling's numerous studies may be cited, *Un nonce du Pape en Moscovie: préliminaires de la Trêve de 1582*, Paris, 1884, and Volume II of his *magnum opus*, *La Russie et le Saint-Siège*, Paris, 1897. Information on the Russian side is supplied by N. P. Likhachev, "Delo o priezde v Moskvu Antoniia Possevina," *Letopis' Zaniatii Arkheograficheskoi Komissii* 11, SPb., 1903. A modern attempt to relate Possevino's activity in Muscovy to trends of the times was made by Hans Wolter, S. J., "Antonio Possevino (1533-1611), Theologie und Politik im Spannungsfeld zwischen Rom und Moskau," *Scholastik* 31 3 (1956), pp. 321-350. The ablest and most comprehensive recent account of Possevino's mission, in which the author emphasizes the religious aspects of it, is S. Polčin, S. J., "Un tentative d'Union au XVIe siècle: La Mission réligieuse du Père Antoine Possevin S. J. en Moscovie (1581-1582)," *Orientalia Christiana Analecta* 150 (1957). The study by Walter Delius, *Antonio Possevino SJ und Ivan Groznyj, Ein Beitrag zur Geschichte der Kirchlichen Union und der Gegenreformation des 16 Jahrhunderts*, Stuttgart, 1962, has been deservedly subjected to scathing criticism by Günther Stökl, "Posseviniana," *Jahrbücher für Geschichte Osteuropas* 11 (1963), pp. 223-236. Recently Andreas Kappeler has made extensive use of Possevino in his excellent study of Western European writers on Muscovy, *Ivan Groznyj im Spiegel der ausländischen Druckschriften seiner Zeit: Ein Beitrag zur Geschichte des westlichen Russlandbildes*, Bern & Frankfurt a/M., 1972.

3.   G. Hofman, S. J., "Briefwechsel zwischen Gabriel Severos und Anton Possevino S. J.," *Orientalia Christiana Periodica* 15 3-4 (1949), pp. 416-434.

4.   "Ratio amanter agendi cum Graecis, Rutenis, seu Moscis, et aliis, qui ritus Graecorum sequuntur," *Bibliotheca Sacra*, Vol. I, Book VI, Köln, 1607, pp. 245-246.

5.   Polčin, *op. cit.*, p. 75.

6.   Possevino himself lets Ivan say it: "multa nobis scripta tradis, Antoni," HRM *Supp.*, p. 109.

7.   A. N. Nasonov, ed., *Pskovskie Letopisi*, Vol. II, Moscow, 1955, p. 263: "The Grand Prince, Tsar Ivan, had at that time assembled 300,000 [men]at Staritsa, but at the behest of his Boyars he did not send [them to relieve]Pskov, nor did he come himself, because he was overwhelmed with terror."

8.   Carlos Sommervogel, S. J., ed., *Bibliothèque de la Compagnie de Jésus*, Part I, Bibliography, Vol. VI, Brussels-Paris, 1895, Cols. 1061-1093, is testimony to Possevino's indefatigable literary activity. The section on him includes 50 long entries. The *Apparatus Sacer* deserves special mention. Published in 1603, it is a compendium of the lives and views of more than 8,000 ancient and modern authors on ecclesiastical subjects. Possevino's bibliography shows that he was more of a polemicist, synthesizer and compiler than an original thinker.

A Note on the Text.

In his comprehensive study of the Counterreformation in Poland Father Stanisław Załęski commented[1] that few events in the history of sixteenth-century Europe have attracted as much attention or produced so voluminous a secondary literature as Possevino's mission to mediate between Poland and Muscovy. It is thus a matter of some surprise to discover that the text of the *Moscovia* has appeared in no more than four editions and has been anthologized only on rare occasions. Its history can be narrated with comparative brevity.

Three editions were published soon after Possevino completed his mission, and appeared almost simultaneously; in Vilna in 1586,[2] and in Köln[3] and Antwerp in 1587.[4] The Vilna and Antwerp editions are identical. In the Köln edition the first two chapters have been transposed -- the first treats Possevino's hopes for promoting the Catholic religion in Muscovy, and the second contains his general commentary on Muscovite affairs. The three disputations on religion follow, but in a somewhat abbreviated and more impersonal form. Next come the chapters on religious differences and Possevino's refutation of the "English Book." After this the author has inserted a section entitled *Questions and Answers on the Procession of the Holy Ghost, From the Father and From the Son, Taken from the Work of Gennadius Scholarius, Patriarch of Constantinople, Abbreviated and Rendered more Succinct for the Benefit and Improvement of the Muscovites,*[5] and a brief selection from the voluminous correspondence that passed among the principal figures who were parties to the Truce. The Köln edition concludes, as do the others, with the journal of the meetings held at Iam Zapol'skii. Another edition (virtually the same as the one of 1587) of the *Moscovia* appeared in Köln in 1595.[6] No further editions have been published since then.

Anthologies drawn from the writings of early Western visitors to Muscovy have appeared from time to time in later centuries, and on occasion Possevino's work has been selected for inclusion among them. An early example of this genre is *The State of Muscovy and its Cities.*[7] This book is divided into units under such headings as geography, the army, politics, *etc.* Chapter 6 is entitled *Antonio Possevino's Diatribe Against Muscovy* and consists of a reproduction of his Chapter on Muscovite affairs. The journal of the Iam Zapol'skii negotiations is found in another section. In 1861 A. de Starczewski included the bulk of the *Moscovia* in his comprehensive collection of the writings of Western visitors to Muscovy:[8] He used the Antwerp edition but did not print the chapters in the same way Possevino had originally ordered them.

Translations of the *Moscovia* are similarly uncommon. Possevino's nephew, Giovanni Battista Possevino, rendered the work into Italian and published it in Ferrara in 1592.[9] A second edition appeard in Mantua in 1596,[10] and a third was published there in 1611,[11] both without change. These translations contain no notes or discussion and only very rarely introduce alterations or amplifications into the original text. A Polish version[12] is so incomplete that it can scarcely be termed a translation at all. It is limited to the Iam Zapol'skii negotiations, and leaves more than half of the text in the original Latin. Recently Olsufieff[13] presented what appears to be an unacknowledged reprint of Giovanni Battista's translation, based on the Mantua editions, which is inferior to its original. The four-page preface is unenlightening, and the version, lacking either notes or commentary, contains numerous unexplained and arbitrary changes in the text.

A complete version of the *Moscovia* has yet to appear in Russia, although new research on Possevino is currently in progress there. In 1788 Novikov printed a neutral, factual paraphrase of Possevino's visit to Moscow, emphasizing the religious disputations, by an unknown author, which, he informed his readers, he had obtained from the private library of a certain Fedor Ivanovich Miller.[14] In 1846 Adelung published in St. Petersburg the substantial study in which he described and summarized the accounts of most Western visitors to Russia to the end of the eighteenth century, and a section in it is devoted to Possevino.[15] In 1864 Adelung's work was translated into Russian, where the unit on Possevino was reproduced without amplification or comment.[16] Notice should certainly be taken of Turgenev's comprehensive collection of documents,[17] which both parallel, supplement, and frequently overlap the material found in the *Moscovia*.

In his *History of the Russian State*[18] Karamzin often had occasion to utilize the *Moscovia* in his chapter on the final years of Ivan the Terrible's reign, where he sometimes paraphrased and in instances actually translated portions of Possevino's work, and the distinguished historian Kliuchevskii used the information supplied by foreign visitors to reconstruct a broad composite picture of life in Muscovy during the sixteenth and seventeenth centuries in which the name of Possevino figured prominently.[19] However, all of these studies are old; the Soviet mediaevalist Ia.S. Lur'e has urgently called for a modern critical Russian edition of the *Moscovia*.[20]

1. S. Załęski, *Jezuici w Polsce*, Vol. I, Pt. I, Lwów, 1900, p. 311.

2. *Antonii Possevini ex Societate Jesu Moscovia, s. de rebus Moscoviticis et acta in conuentu legatorum regis Poloniae et Magni Ducis Moscouiae anno 1581, Vilnae, apud Ioannem Velicensem*, 1586.

3. *Antonii Possevini, Societatis Jesu, Moscovia, et alia Opera, de statu hujus seculi, adversus Catholicae Ecclesiae hostes. Nunc primum in unum volumen collecta, atque ab ipsomet auctore emendata et aucta. (Coloniae)*, 1587.

4. *Antonii Possevino Societatis Jesu Moscovia. Eiusdem novissima descriptio, ex officina Christophori Plantini, Architypographi Regij. Antverpiae*, 1587. The present translation has been made from the Antwerp edition.

5. It was not known during his lifetime that this, as well as the other dogmatic treatises which Possevino so frequently quotes throughout the *Moscovia*, attributing them to Gennadius, were not written by him, but by John Plousiadenos, later Joseph, Bishop of Methone (d. *ca.* 1500), a Greek of Cretan origin who remained an unflagging champion of the Church Union proclaimed at the Council of Florence during his entire ecclesiastical career.

6. *Antonii Possevini, Societatis Jesu, Moscovia et alia Opera, quibus nunc recens, propter materiae similitudinem, et regionum quarum historias explicant, vicinitatem, adjuncta sunt, Martini Broniovii de Biezdzfedea, bis in Tartariam nomine Stephani Primi Poloniae Regis Legati, Tartariae Descriptio, antehac numquam in lucem edita, cum tabula geographica ejusdem Chersonesus Tauricae: Transylvaniae, ac Moldaviae, Aliarumque vicinarum regionum succincta descriptio Georgii a Reichersdorff Transylvani, cum tabulis geographicis tam Moldaviae, quam Transylvaniae. Item, Georgii Werneri de Admirandis Hungariae Aquis hypomnemation, addita tabella lacus mirabilis ad Cirknitz. (Coloniae)*, 1595.

7. *Respublica Moscoviae et Urbes. Accedunt quaedam latine numquam antehac edita. (Auctore Marco Zuero Boxhornio). Lugd. Batav.* 1633, pp. 195-260, and pp.. 365-518.

8. A. de Starczewski, ed., *Historiae Ruthenicae Scriptores Exteri Saeculi XVI*, Berlin & SPb., 1861, Vol. I, pp. 47-84, and pp. 275-330.

9. *La Moscovia del P. Antonio Possevino, tradotta di latino in volgare da Gio. Battista Possevino Sacerdote Montovano, Teologo di Monsig. Rev. Giovanni Fontana Vescovo di Ferrara. In Ferrara appresso Benedetto Mammarelli*, 1592.

10. *Commentarii di Moscovia, et della Pace sequita fra Lei, e'l Regno di Polonia. Colla restitutione della Livonia. Scritti in lingua latina da Antonio Possevino della Compagnia de Giesù. Et tradotti nell' Italiana da Gio. Battista Possevino. Aggiuntevi, oltre la correctione, varie cose, et Lettere di più eminenti Principi, et dell' Autore, pertinenti alla religione, et alla notitia di Gottia, di Suetia, di Liuonia et di Transylvania. Co'l sommario de' Capi delle materie, che vi si trattono. In Mantova, per Francesco Osanna, stampatore Ducale*, 1596.

11. *Commentarii della Moscovia et della Pace che per ordine della S. Sede Apostolica procurò Antonio Possevino Mantovano della Compagnia di Giesù tra Basilio Granduca di Moscovia, et Regno di Polonia colla restituzione intiera della Livonia, et di 33 fortezze di lei, scritti prima in latino dallo stesso P. Possevino, e più volte stampati in Lituania, Francia, Fiandra, Germania et in Italia, et tradotti nella lingua Italiana di Gio. Battista Possevino, suo nipote, Teologo et Arciprete di S. Leonardo in Mantova et hora ristampati coll' occasione delle nuove et segnalate vittorie avute quest' anno 1610 dal Sereniss. Sigismondo III Rè di Polonia et di Suezia nella Moscovia, ove si apre la porta alla Cattolica Religione verso il Settentrione e l'Oriente, aggiuntevi oltre le correzione, varie Lettere di più eminenti Principi, et dell' Autore a loro colla notizia di Gottia, Svezia, Finlandia, Livonia et della Transilvania, etc. In Mantova per Aurelio et Lodovico Osanna fratelli stampatori Ducali,* 1611.

12. "Dyaryusz negocyacyi o pokój między Moskwą a Polską w Kiwerowej Horce dnia 15 Stycznia 1582 roku, przez Antoniego Possewina spisany, a z dzieła jego *Moscovia et alia opera* w Kolonii roku 1587 drukowanego wyjęty," in E. Rykaczewski, ed., *Relacye Nuncyuszów Apostolskich i innych osób o Polsce od roku 1548 do 1690,* Berlin-Poznań, 1864, Vol. I, pp. 386-437.

13. Maria Olsufieff, ed., *Le Lettere di Ivan il Terribile, con i Commentarii della Moscovia di Antonio Possevino,* Florence, 1958.

14. N. Novikov, ed., *Drevniaia Rossiiskaia Vivliofika* 6 (1788), pp. 71-107.

15. F. Adelung, *Kritisch-literarische Übersicht der Reisenden in Russland bis 1700, deren Berichte bekannt sind,* Amsterdam, 1960 (reprint of the 1846 SPb. edition), Vol. I, pp. 321-349.

16. "Drevneishie puteshestviia inostrantsev po Rossii; Antonio Possevino 1581-1582," in the section *Materialy inostrannye* of *Chteniia v Imperatorskom obshchestve istorii i drevnostei rossiiskikh pri Moskovskom universitete* 2 (1863), pp. 204-221.

17. A. Turgenev, ed., *Historica Russiae Monumenta, ex archivis ac bibliothecis extraneis deprompta,* Vols. I & II, SPb., 1841, and the *Supplementum* to this work, SPb., 1848.

18. N. M. Karamzin, *Istoriia gosudarstva rossiiskago,* SPb., 1892, Vol. IX., Chapter 5, "Prodolzhenie tsarstvovaniia Ioanna Groznago," pp. 173-231.

19. V.O. Kliuchevskii, *Skazaniia inostrantsev o Moskovskom gosudarstve,* Petrograd, 1918, *passim.*

20. His remarks were made in an article, "Russko-angliiskie otnosheniia i mezhdunarodnaia politika vtoroi poloviny XVI v.", A. A. Zimin and V. T. Pashuto, edd., *Mezhdunarodnye Sviazi Rossii do XVII,* Moscow, 1961, p. 434, n. 48. In a summary of her Candidate dissertation published by Moscow State University in 1970, *Istoricheskie sochineniia Possevino o Rossii,* L. N. Godovikova discussed Possevino in a rather polemical way as an agent of the Vatican and declared her intention to publish critical editions and translations of all his work pertaining to Russia · and Livonia. However, only one short ancillary piece has appeared to date. Cf. Note 52 to Chapter I.

CHAPTER I

A COMMENTARY ON MUSCOVY PRESENTED BY ANTONIO POSSEVINO TO POPE GREGORY XIII.

With God's help I intend to set forth in this Commentary the present state of affairs in Muscovy. I shall speak of what we may expect from Ivan Vasil'evich, the present Prince, and of what opportunities the Holy See may have of entering into friendly relations with him, since this might lead either to the introduction of a purer form of worship into that huge land in the northeast, or to arousing the Christian Princes to make a treaty with him. What is to be desired above all is that a higher form of Christianity be established in his realm.

I did not venture to touch upon these matters in my second Commentary,[1] which I sent Your Beatitude from the Polish camp before Pskov as I was preparing for my previous journey to Muscovy. I had not then completed the negotiations with the Prince in which I was engaged, and I felt that I could accomplish more on my second journey in the calmer atmosphere prevailing after God's Goodness had brought about peace between the Prince and King Stefan. To this end I kept my eyes open during the course of the negotiations on which Your Beatitude had sent me, and while I was passing through the chief towns and fortresses in a territory of 240 miles under the Prince's jurisdiction. Furthermore, during my absence of five months from Muscovy I left two men with the Prince and they were able to make numerous observations. The method I have adopted is to compare my own impressions with what I had previously learned from various writers and envoys or heard on more than one occasion from the rulers of both Sweden and Poland[2] concerning the Prince. In this way I hope in Christ's name to expound everything as clearly as the charge given me by Your Beatitude requires.

How the Present Prince of Muscovy Came to the Throne; the Enlargement of his Realm, and Diverse Items.

Ivan Vasil'evich was born in 1528.[3] Since he is a man of rather impetuous spirit, intensely anxious to exalt his position, on coming to power he decided to avenge the harm Muscovy had suffered from the Tatars, and to conquer Livonia. King Stefan told me that when Ivan attacked Kazan' he had no difficulty taking the place because he used cannon against a people unfamiliar with weapons of this kind. Ivan next occupied Astrakhan', situated at the mouth of the river Volga, a fine Eastern market town on the Caspian Sea. Since Astrakhan' is the chief city of the Second Tatar Horde (*i.e.*, Kingdom), he has thus managed to extend his control to the borders of Circassia,[4] 300 miles beyond Astrakhan'. The Circassians inhabit the hills along the coast of the Caspian Sea; their realm used to stretch as far as Persia until last year, when Selim took the Iron Gate[5] and some other fortresses from the Circassian king. Contiguity and the common possession of the Greek rite have enabled the Prince of Muscovy to draw very close to the Circassians; he married the daughter of one of their chief men, although she later died.[6] They once asked Ivan to send men skilled in fortress construction to help them check the incursions of the Turks.[7] He did so, and from that time on cultivated them, so that in the absence of other neighboring princes they in effect came to look upon him as their protector. They are a simple folk, more given to religious observance than many of the other local tribes, or the Cossacks, who have by now practically become a single nation within the Muscovite Dominion. Another group is the Nogai Tatars,[8] who frequently raid Muscovite territory. They did so this year, and only substantial gifts could induce them to withdraw. The Crimean Tatars, who inhabit the Tauric Chersonese, are more powerful, since they are allies of the Turks. The Prince, who has sustained numerous defeats at their hands, feared that worse was to come as he was preoccupied with the war with Poland. He thus made peace with them, and when I was on the point of leaving Moscow he told me that he could not join King Stefan in a war against the Tatars because he was daily expecting the arrival of ambassadors from their Emperor, as well as his own envoys, to ratify the peace treaty both rulers had already signed.[9]

In turning to Livonian affairs we find that the fifty-year truce expired in 1550. Ivan's predecessors had agreed to it after the Muscovite army was totally destroyed near Pskov by Plettenberg, Master of the Livonian Order.[10] Various pretexts for its abrogation were alleged; as, for example, that the Livonians had failed to adhere to the terms of the agreement, or that the Lutherans had destroyed Orthodox churches where the Muscovites worshipped in Reval and Dorpat, and had displayed gross impiety towards Catholics. Ivan declared war, captured Dorpat and other strongholds, and conquered the greater part of Livonia, although his action caused great loss of life among the Livonians and sowed the seeds of a long war with Poland. I have discussed this entire matter in the Commentary on the Province that I recently sent Your Beatitude.[11]

2

All these actions, which for a time seemed to portend a felicitous outcome for the Muscovites, ultimately brought the greatest misfortunes upon them. They now had to station garrisons in a large number of fortresses scattered over a wide area, and they had to fight alone, without allies, in numerous places over a long period of time. The men on foreign field duty had left their wives behind in Muscovy without issue, and whenever one soldier died another had to take his place. This resulted in a drastic decline in the population. Within the army has been formed a corps, previously unknown in Muscovy, the members of which are called *Pyxidarii, Fistulati*, or commonly *Sclopetarii*.[12] They employ small arms, usually no more than bows and arrows. One soldier out of ten is chosen for this corps; they may serve as the Prince's bodyguard, go on campaigns, or be assigned garrison duty. In every instance they must leave their wives and children behind, and since some of them are bound to be killed, Muscovite homes are gradually becoming bereft of male inhabitants. It is also reported that the plague, heretofore unknown in Muscovy because of the intense cold, has been stalking this huge land and carrying off many of its inhabitants.[13] Thousands upon thousands, including members of the nobility, have been slain in the innumerable wars. The Tatars make incessant raids into Muscovy; in one of them, twelve years ago, the capital was burned to the ground.[14] King Stefan has won an unbroken string of victories during the past three years. Under the circumstances people have every right to assume that the Prince's resources are not so much reduced as almost totally exhausted. It is general knowledge that one can travel 300 miles in any direction in his kingdom without seeing a single person. Villages still stand, but no one lives in them. The fields are universally deserted, but the forest growth over them is fresh. This is proof that the population which previously inhabited the region was substantial.

The area north of the city of Moscow is still well inhabited, because the Tatar raids do not come that far and the climate is healthier. I learned this when I carefully questioned the Italians and Spaniards who, thanks to the intercession of Your Beatitude and the Catholic King,[15] were granted their freedom by the Grand Prince of Muscovy, and whom I brought back with me to Italy. After escaping from Turkish captivity across the Sea of Azov, they covered an enormous amount of territory, and for eighteen months they wandered all over the land before they finally made their way to Vologda. The distance between Kazan' and Astrakhan' is immense and the territory is very sparsely populated. Those who move about in it, or those who are sent there by the Prince often have to subsist for months at a time on the products of their hunting and fishing, for no other food whatsoever is available.

Prominent Cities and Peoples Belonging to the Grand Prince.

The cities northwest of the river Don which are considered great in terms of the size of their populations and their distinction are Moscow, Smolensk, Novgorod, Pskov and Tver'. Vologda is further north, while to the east lie Kazan' and Astrakhan', the area which Giovio[16] and others call Citracha. Iaroslavl', Aleksandrovskaia Sloboda and a few other places could be included in this group, although they would more properly be considered towns if they did not possess the substantial kind of fortresses that are built in this part of the world. As a matter of fact, I am astonished at the huge population estimates, --in the hundred thousands for ordinary people and the ten thousands for noblemen (who are called Boiars),--that have been given by some authors, and the same holds true for some other persons who did an official tour of duty and returned home. Among later writers who have discussed these matters only Alberto Campense[17] and Giovio are at all reliable. Your Beatitude gave me Campense's work to read before I left for Muscovy, and Giovio based his Commentary on what he was told by a certain Muscovite named Dmitrii, whom the father of the present Prince had sent to Pope Clement VII. My own opinion is that no one has fully understood the Prince's highly elaborate method of stationing large numbers of men on the battlements of fortresses and in other lofty places whenever he gives a state reception to ambassadors from other rulers. As so often happens, when discussing customs that differ greatly from their own, observers are inclined to give more credit to appearances than they should. However, those who wrote about early times may not have been so far wrong, for then, as we have noted, the Muscovites waged fewer wars, were less afflicted by disease, and did not sustain such severe losses of manpower. Since they required fewer men for garrison duty they did not leave their descendants so many homes without a head. There is no doubt that the Prince's capital, which, as I have said, is Moscow, now contains less than 30,000 inhabitants, including women and children.[18] Although Moscow appears large as one approaches it, when one draws closer (to say nothing of entering it) one notices that the houses themselves take up a great deal of space. This impression is strengthened by the great wide streets, the numerous large squares, and all the big churches, which seem to have been built more for show than worship, as most of them are closed during the bulk of the year. Moscow was a handsomer and more populous place during the earlier part of this Prince's reign, but in 1570[19] the Tatars destroyed it; many of its inhabitants perished in the fire, and the city was reduced to its present and smaller confines. Traces of the older and larger city

4

remain. It probably used to be eight or nine miles in circumference, whereas now it can scarcely be five. The people keep oxen, cows and other such animals in their homes with them, and lead them out to pasture every day. Most of the houses are enclosed by wattle fences; they are reminiscent of the homes of our peasants. There is, however, a degree of elegance in the two citaedels of Moscow, which are interconnected. One of them contains the Prince's palace and some fine brick churches (the other churches in the city are made of wood), while the other is filled with new shops, each trade with a street of its own. The shops are tiny; a single enterprise in Venice would do more business than a whole street in Moscow. Very few of the artisans live on the premises. They have homes in town, and show clearly how highly they value this privilege.

I should be inclined to estimate the number of inhabitants in Smolensk, Novgorod and Pskov as approximately the same: *i.e.*, in times of peace each one of them would contain 20,000 people at most. They allege that their populations are somewhat larger, but I would not put the numbers higher, for the reasons I have already given, and because the houses and buildings take up so much space. On the approach of envoys the Prince orders the peasants living in the villages and the countryside to come to town and create an appearance of large numbers, as I have already noted. The population of Tver' is much smaller today, although from a distance it gives the impression of a large and beautiful city. It is not surrounded by walls, and a considerable number of houses lie scattered around and about, because it has not seriously experienced war or enemy attack, which is also the reason why Vologda, Kazan', and above all the regions further north still have large populations. However this may be, and in spite of the fact that the territory belonging to the Grand Prince of Muscovy, which extends from Lithuania and Livonia as far as the Caspian Sea, and from the Lapps to the Cheremis, consists of more land than people, there is general agreement that the Prince can field forces of two or three hundred thousand cavalry, or an innumerable multitude of Tatars, whenever he wishes.

Fortifications and Defense Against Assault.

The fortresses and other means of defense the Muscovites possess today are quite different from those they had before, and not all their centers are protected in the same way. Some fortresses are built of brick and stone, like the two in Moscow, the ones in Novgorod, Pskov, Porkhov, Staritsa, and Aleksandrovskaia Sloboda, a partial construction at Iaroslavl', the one in Beloozero, and some others. Other places are fortified with ramparts held together by vines and tamped down till the earth within them becomes hard, as at Smolensk, and like the new wall put up around Moscow itself after the Tatar sack. The rest of the towns are protected by piles of treetrunks placed in squares, which are packed with earth or sand. They will not collapse under attack, but they are susceptible to fire and are often smeared with mud to guard against it. In general the experience of the past two centuries has failed to impress the Muscovites with the need for high towers and comparable fortifications.

Muscovy lacks the architectural tradition of this nature that prevails among us, although Vasilii, the father of the present Prince, did have the two citaedels of Moscow constructed by an architect from Milan and Italian workmen. A Latin inscription, preserved over the entrance beneath a pious ikon of the Virgin Mary, is a memorial to their work.[20] With its high walls and towers set in a circle the place conveys a majestic appearance. A similar fortification is found in Novgorod, but the citaedel contains scarcely any houses besides the church and the adjacent manse inhabited by the Archbishop and his clergy. This structure was built a long time ago in a kind of circle; last year another Italian architect[21] surrounded it with a rampart and included a nearby monastery within the new fortification. At appropriate positions on the rampart he placed platforms capable of sustaining the weight of heavy artillery to ward off enemy attacks.

Pskov's first line of fortifications consists of a stone wall with towers standing before a river bed; next a second wall approximately the shape of an oblong triangle runs through the center of town; three forts are located near it, one after the other, and the whole complex presents a formidable appearance. Such a system of fortifications encourages the besieged while causing besiegers great concern and anxiety, as we were made constantly aware when we were in the Polish camp. The Poles succeeded in knocking down battlements, but they failed to sap the underground foundations of the wall with their axes and mattocks to cause its collapse. As a result, even though they managed with great effort to scale the high wall, they had still to climb down, in constant danger of being dislodged by the Muscovites. Those who tried to jump found themselves cut off from the rest of the army by the city wall and perished to a man. Even if a charge was at first completely successful and the attackers got down from the walls they would eventually find themselves driven inside the wooden houses in which the city abounds; the Muscovites then set fire to them, and thus the enemy was bound to be destroyed, while the Muscovites withdrew to the safety of their enclosed turrets. Furthermore, within the walled turrets the Commander had ordered wooden platforms capable of sustaining the weight of heavy cannon placed in a circle, and the cannon kept up a continuous fire.

Similarly at Polotsk the Muscovites had built a large tower out of beams, from which they kept such a close watch on the enemy camp and all the rest of the terrain that it was virtually impossible for anyone to approach. However, the tower was struck so frequently by barrages from the Polish artillery that it actually appeared to be leaning over to one side and the fortress of Polotsk was finally captured by the valor of King Stefan and a bold assault by his troops. Porkhov has but one tower, located above the single entrance gate; hence, it is possible to set ladders and mount anywhere. In the absence of other towers from which to assail an approaching enemy the issue can only be settled by hand-to-hand combat at close quarters on the wall or by hurling down javelins and rocks. The fortifications of other towns are constructed in a similar manner. However, the ramparts of Smolensk abut on one side upon the waters of the river Dnepr and form protective layers three deep, and the fortress and the church are built high on a hill. This alone would render the task of any attacker extremely difficult, but, in addition the rampart itself is honeycombed with tiny apertures set very close to one another, which permits intensive small-arms fire to be directed against an enemy seeking to penetrate the defenses. Those observations should convey some idea of Muscovite fortifications.

Although the Muscovite soldiers do not oppose the Poles vigorously on the regular field of battle, they give an extraordinarily fine account of themselves when defending their fortresses and cities; even the women often perform military duties,--bringing water to put out fires, piling up stones and pushing them down from the walls, or hurling stakes which they hold in their hand for this purpose,--and their actions are of great help to their side and dangerous to the enemy. Whenever one soldier is killed in a barrage during an attack another takes his place, and so on down the line; in short, no one spares his energy or his life. They are inured to cold; often their only shelter against it, or rain, snow or wind is a heap of branches, or their cloaks hung up on stakes thrust into the ground. They can subsist on most meagre rations, content to drink a bitter and tasteless mixture of water and oat dust and to eat nothing but bread. The Polish King told me that he had found Muscovite soldiers in Livonian fortresses who had subsisted on such a diet for a long time. Most were dead, but those who had managed to survive, although scarcely breathing, were still fearful that their surrender would constitute a betrayal of their oath to serve their Prince to the death. This characteristic endows them with great strength; all concentrate simultaneously upon the same goal, and it often happens that the more robust of them are able to survive numerous engagements, or at least their stubborn endurance and dedication wear down an enemy. However, other writers have noted this on other occasions.

Other Resources of the Prince.

The Prince alone controls everything. Cities, towns, villages, houses, fields, estates, forests, lakes, rivers, rank and position: everything in this huge country bears witness to the enormous power and resources he possesses. It is believed that these were formerly even more substantial, when war did not hamper commerce, Livonia was prosperous, and navigation on the Baltic Sea was more extensive. When these favorable conditions ceased or diminished an inevitable decline in the general level of prosperity took place, but the ostentation of the Prince's court has remained unchanged and he is thought still to possess enormous treasure. He acquires as much of the gold coin and bullion brought into Muscovy as he can, and he scarcely ever allows the export of gold. The Prince rarely exports silver either, except to ransom prisoners or hire foreign mercenaries, things which he does only very sparingly. The Muscovites often use skins and hides instead of coins for money, and when they go on a journey they generally take their own food with them. They convert Thalers (a German currency) into *Dengas* and *Moskovkas*,[22] as their monetary units are called. At the present time the Muscovite coinage contains a higher percentage of adulterated silver than it did formerly because they have abandoned their previous caution and indiscriminately allow any artificer to strike coins. Any gifts of gold and silver brought back by envoys returning from a mission the Prince adds to his stocks of treasure; he takes all the silver money the envoys have received, and even confiscates any personal gifts that may have been made to them. It is general knowledge that his relative[23] seized all the works of art, bullion, gold and silver vessels, chalices and many other such objects in the cities and churches of Livonia he could, loaded them on wagons and carted them off. In this way the Prince acquired an enormous plunder, which, after the great Tatar invasion and the sack of Moscow, he distributed among the three fortresses of Moscow, Iaroslavl' and Beloozero.

The cities and districts of Muscovy are no longer ruled by the kind of petty princes we are accustomed to calling Dukes. Although the Muscovites use this title to enhance their own dignity, to curry favor with the Prince, or to designate an official position, they lack all the realities of power. A certain Tatar, who had proved his loyalty to the Prince during the capture of Kazan' and by accepting the schismatic Muscovite religion, relinquished some of his own land and was given the town of Kolomna and certain other territory, but virtually all the real power remained in the hands of the Prince, who even juggled the revenues just as he pleased. Lands and villages assigned to individuals cannot be bequeathed by them to their descendants without the Prince's approval, and the peasants pay a tithe to and perform labor for the Prince in addition to the services they render their masters. They use for their own sustenance or sell the small surplus they manage to produce. The result of this policy is that no one can really say what actually belongs to him, and every man, whether he wishes it or not, exists in a state of dependency upon the Prince. The more a person has, the more he recognizes this dependency; the richer he is, the more he is afraid, for the Prince often takes back everything he has given. Prudence and caution constrain men to hold their tongues, for any attempt at conspiracy is cut short by uprooting entire families or by exiling (not assigning) men to different outposts. When the Prince believes a conspiracy to exist he frequently orders the death of those he suspects, including their sons, daughters and peasants, even though the latter are entirely innocent. A nobleman of the Prince's court told me that he had acquired several estates, but for a number of years he was not allowed to thatch the wooden huts or even to repair them, because the peasants he needed for the work were so heavily burdened with the duties they had to perform for the Prince that they did not even have time to breathe.

Forty kindred families were among those forcibly removed from Livonia and put to work in the factories of Moscow on the Prince's orders; many others were sent to Kazan', and elsewhere, and all of them have to pay an annual tribute.[24] Manifesting their displeasure, they referred to the Pope in the most respectful terms and showed me every possible deference. They reminded me of how much Livonia had once contributed to the Apostolic See and recalled how peaceful it had been when that country, known as a bulwark of the Christian Commonwealth, had born the title of Province under its own legitimate Catholic rulers, particularly at the time when it was under the protection of the Pope. When the Pope's paternal rule was overthrown the Livonians became the prey of the Teutonic Knights when the latter were in revolt against the Church. With their country in danger of partition their appeals for aid to numerous quarters proved in vain, and they were finally brought under the yoke of heretics. Now they are living a most wretched life in Muscovy, if indeed an existence among heretics can be called living at all.

The best specimens from the huge amounts of valuable skins and fish that are taken from the forests, lakes and rivers are reserved for the Prince's own use as gifts or for sale. Some of the fish are dried and sent to be used as food for the garrisons. The consignments destined for the Prince are set aside and given preference over all the rest; no one may dispose of his own wares until the Prince's goods have been sold.

The Muscovites call their Scribes, or Secretaries, by the title of *D'iaki*[25], which is a corruption of the Greek word for Deacon, or Minister. These officials maintain very careful records and accounts at the Prince's palace, keep accurate records of all developments in each province, and send in reports to the Royal Treasurer.

Revenues are low. Ambassadors may bring any number of merchants with them, who ply their trade, pay no taxes, and receive maintenance at the Prince's expense. At one time fairs were frequently held in Astrakhan' which attracted traders from the Caspian Sea littoral and even from Persia, but now that the Tatars have been largely expelled from the region, and the war with Persia has been dragging on for some time,[26] these fairs are held but rarely. I heard nothing about gold and silver mines. A few iron mines exist, but the miners do not work efficiently, and they are not effectively utilized.

The deference universally accorded the Prince is something the mind can scarcely comprehend. Even if the Muscovites do not really believe it, they incessantly declare that they owe their lives, their health, and all their worldly possessions to him and convey the impression that they attribute everything to the Grace of God and the Mercy of the Great Tsar (the title they use to address the Prince, which means King, or Emperor). Even when beaten to the point of death they will sometimes say that the Prince has done them a favor by chastising them. One would assume that the Muscovites were a people born more to slavery than achievement were it not for the fact that most of them fully realize the nature of their servitude and know that if they should flee the country their children would be killed on the spot and all their property would be immediately confiscated. They have grown accustomed to this sort of life from childhood and it has become second nature, as it were, for them to praise the Prince extravagantly, to declare that they can only live and prosper when the Prince lives and prospers, and to denigrate everything else in comparison, although if those of better understanding did not fear informers and had an opportunity to visit foreign countries, they would have no difficulty discerning the resources and strength possessed by other peoples.

Every year a number of Dutch and English ships, laden with copper and other merchandise, sails the Upper Northern Ocean (which others call the Glacial Ocean, but they call the Harsh or Deadly Ocean) and puts into the harbor of St. Nicholas on or about St. Peter's Day [June 29]. These traders then convey their goods some 300 miles south to Vologda, a famous market-town of Muscovy. Other merchants regularly cross the Baltic Sea from Pomerania, Holland and England to Muscovy in order to buy wax, hides and skins.

The Councillors of the Prince.

The Prince has 12 Senators,[27] who hear cases and refer the more serious ones to him. They also receive petitions, and other requests, for these are never given to the Prince directly. They hold their office and powers at the Prince's pleasure, and at the time when I was in Muscovy their names were as follows: Ivan, son of Fedor (they put it Fedorovich)[28] and his two sons Fedor[29] and Simeon;[30] Nikita Romanov,[31] whose sister Anastasiia was once married to the Prince, as I wrote to Your Beatitude in my Second Commentary; Andrei Shchelkalov,[32] the Chancellor; his brother, Vasilii;[33] Bogdan (which means either "God has given" or "Given by God") Iakovlevich Bel'skii,[34] who has enjoyed

11

the highest favor with the Prince and used to sleep in the Prince's chamber; Bogdan's cousin Nevezhin,[35] Vasilii Ivanovich Zuzin,[36] who was born in Lithuania after his father, a Muscovite, had fled there, but who later returned to Muscovy on reaching maturity. Of the entire group Zuzin was the only person to know a little Latin, while Andrei Shchelkalov knew a little Polish. Three others were Ignatii Tatishchev,[37] Abain Voiekov,[38] and Mikhailo Andreevich Beznin.[39] The name of the Royal Treasurer, who is not numbered among the Councillors, is Petr Ivanovich Golovin.[40] The Chancellor is responsible for making the nobles their military assignments and for distributing the lands and estates allotted to them by the Prince in order to supply their needs. Under this system they are scarcely ever paid a salary, nor do they win exemption from service even after many years. The town and fortress commanders handle the rest of the administration. They know to which Senator they should direct letters destined for the Prince, and who is entitled to respond in his name. The Prince never signs his letters, either to them or to other rulers, with his own hand.

The Sons of the Grand Prince of Muscovy.

By his first wife, Anastasiia, the Grand Prince of Muscovy, Ivan Vasil'evich, had two sons, Ivan and Fedor. Both were alive when we came on our first mission, but the elder son, Ivan, had died before our second visit. He was 20 years old,[41] already capable of ruling, and popular with the Muscovites. It is said that the Prince had other sons by other women, but they subsequently died.[42] It will prove worthwhile to say something concerning young Ivan's death, both because the event itself was of consequence and because it had a good deal to do with causing the Prince to listen to what we had to say with more graciousness than he otherwise might have done. There is strong evidence that the Grand Prince of Muscovy slew his own son in the fortress called Aleksandrovskaia Sloboda. One of the interpreters[43] assigned to me had been in the young prince's service at the time. He was among those who looked into the cause of his death and gave me the more probable account of it. Decent women of means customarily wear three garments, which may be heavy or light depending upon the weather, and those who wear only one garment are not considered to be of good repute. Tsarevich Ivan's third wife was attired in only one garment because she was pregnant and not expecting anyone to approach her. It chanced that the Grand Prince came upon her resting on a bench. She immediately rose, but he flew into a rage, boxed her ears, and hit her with the staff he was carrying. The following night she was delivered of a stillborn child. Meanwhile the Tsarevich had rushed up to his father, but when he sought to prevent the Grand Prince's beating his wife he brought down his father's wrath upon himself, and was mortally wounded by a blow on the head near the temple from the same staff. Before this happened the son in a rage had taken his father very severely to task, saying: "You thrust my first wife into a nunnery for no good reason; you did the same thing to my second, and now you strike my third, causing the son in her womb to perish! "[44] After wounding his son the father later began to grieve and hastily summoned physicians from Moscow, together with Andrei Shchelkalov and Nikita Romanov, to make sure that every possible remedy was tried. However, the Tsarevich died five days later and was transported to Moscow amidst universal mourning.[45] His father followed the bier, and as the cortège approached the city he actually went on foot, while nobles dressed in mourning bore the coffin aloft on the tips of their fingers. They were still in mourning, deliberately making themselves look untidy, on our return. They had let their hair grow long, a sign of mourning, and were not wearing the little cap which is a mark of nobility. This affair was an amazing example of God's merciful providence and justice. When we had appeared before the Prince earlier the nobles had mocked us because we were wearing dark clothing (they are unused to this color, which has sad connotations for them) and appeared somewhat unkempt, but in mourning the Tsarevich they were obliged to dress in similar clothing and no longer dared to make allusions to our attire.

The Prince summoned his Senate and declared that his own sins had caused the Tsarevich's death. Since certain difficulties made it seem unlikely that the succession would fall to the rather unstable Fedor, the Prince urged his advisors to consider which great noble of the realm should succeed to the office of Prince. They replied that they wished no other than the surviving Fedor; it was enough for them, they said, that he was the Prince's son. They further exhorted the Prince to banish sorrow from his mind, and as for his hint that he might become a monk, they begged him to postpone such a decision, at least for a time, until affairs in Muscovy were in a better condition. In dealing with the Prince's idea that another should succeed to the throne the Boyars gave as their opinion that Ivan should be vigilant; if he detected anyone favoring another candidacy he should take prompt steps to remove that person and his supporters.

Each night grief (or madness) would drive the Prince from his bed, to scratch the walls of his chamber with his nails and utter piercing sighs. His attendants had the greatest difficulty making him go back to bed, although later, when he had regained control of his faculties and became master of himself once more, he would be quiet. Even then he could not stop pondering various problems, such as who would finally succeed to the throne if anything happened to Fedor. There was no other direct lineal descendant, and there had been no Master of the Stables, to whom, like the Count of the Stables, the succession should pass, for thirty years.[46]

After the death of the Tsarevich the Prince wept copiously, dressed in a most unbecoming way, and even went so far as to order the envoys he was sending to Your Beatitude to wear dark clothes, although, it is true, they were made of silk. His whole kingdom, but particularly the court, presented the same appearance and observed the same sad rituals. The Prince laid aside his diadem and all other bright adornment, even though he scarcely ever wears finery. He transmitted large sums of money to all the monasteries to pray for the salvation of his son's soul. He also sent two Muscovites to the Patriarchs and the monasteries of the East in the company of Acomatus, the Turkish ambassador, or Procurator, who had been waiting three years in Muscovy, because the movements of the Polish King's forces had rendered his return home unsafe. He gave them 10,000 rubles (a ruble is worth a little more than two crowns) for charity and prayers for his dead son.

Every three years the Prince sends money to the Patriarchs of the East because the Muscovites originally drew their understanding of the Greek faith they still observe from there, although they now differ from the Greeks in many respects.

How the Muscovites Receive and Negotiate with Embassies.

Herberstein's[47] observations on the ways in which the Muscovites receive envoys from foreign rulers are accurate, and these practices have been in effect for a long time. We were shown comparable attentions, but in addition we were received into the fortresses at Smolensk and Novgorod with the highest honors and a salute from the huge cannon, an action which, so they say, is done for very few envoys on their way to the Prince. The Bishop of Smolensk and the Archbishop of Novgorod had both been instructed to show us every courtesy and attention, of the sort the Muscovites are accustomed to display, as long as we remained in their cities. The Prince had also given orders that the churches should be filled with torches and other adornments while the service was performed, and

14

the bishops asked us to honor the service with our presence. Similarly in Moscow the Prince himself escorted us to the church, where he had commanded a place of the highest honor to be prepared for us to behold the service and the ceremonies. To render the occasion even more solemn and majestic he had assembled 5,000 men in the open street when he came out of his palace, attended by his Senators and Nobles and preceded by priests carrying an ikon of the Virgin Mary. However we had not the slightest intention of attending a service celebrated by their bishops (if bishops they can be called), or of entering the church with the Prince. Since we kept making our refusal openly in the presence of the Prince and his vast multitude, everyone was convinced that our last hour had come, although some began to doubt the inflated opinion of their own religion that they had always held. Among the reasons we advanced publicly to the Prince on that occasion, and later set forth in writing, the most telling was that I, a priest sent by Your Beatitude, could not appear in any way to sanction their rites or show honor and reverence to bishops unconsecrated by the Holy See, whose hands the Prince and everybody else would kiss with their heads bowed down to the ground. The Prince had summoned the Metropolitan and six other Bishops to be present at the event and dispute religious questions with me. After they were given the treatise which the Prince had publicly asked me to prepare on the differences between the Catholic faith and Muscovite beliefs, they all fell silent. One of them, the Archbishop of Rostov, indicated that he had accepted all of my views; whereupon he was stripped of his office and sent into exile.[48] It was thought that he lost his life; if so, he was more fortunate than the rest who survived.

On both our first and second visits the Prince entertained me and all my associates at three very elaborate banquets. No effort was spared to make them as opulent and elegant as possible. He also ordered the *Pristavs* (noblemen assigned to envoys; the term means something like "adjutant") to provide us with the most costly foods, and every day he sent us food from his own table. Two days before the day appointed for me to negotiate with the Prince and his Senators, and again on the morning before, he sent three men, different ones on each occasion, to announce that we would soon behold the serene eyes of the Great Emperor and should hold ourselves in readiness. On the morning itself, an hour later, the *Pristavs* told us that a company of nobles and some of the Prince's councillors were approaching our residence with some 100 knights to serve as escorts. The first three nobles, while still on horseback, extended their hands and greeted me in the name of the Prince. We set out between two lines of the royal Fusiliers, some

1500 in number, who were closely drawn up and disposed along both sides of our mile-long route. When we came inside the fortress, which was filled with men attired in expensive garments and wearing costly swords, I was asked to dismount. Next I was welcomed by other Senators standing at the foot of the staircase, and then escorted up into the presence of the Prince.

Asking me to be seated he spoke with me himself and then indicated that I could withdraw to a separate room to discuss matters with his Senators. We were sometimes closeted together for hours on end as we discussed all pertinent topics through our respective interpreters. Our talks were very thorough and often extremely fatiguing. Whenever I proposed a new item, as the nature of our task frequently made inevitable, not daring to respond on their own initiative all the councillors would immediately repair to the Prince, ask him what their reply should be, and bring back and present an accurate digest of his views. It is difficult for me to convey how extraordinarily careful they were to repeat word for word any proposal that I had made. On each occasion I was summoned, knights and Senators came to escort me in the same elaborate way, and whenever I appeared before the Prince, the Senators would read out his views, which were written out on long strips of parchment, and these strips were handed over to me after the Senators had taken turns reading from them. I never saw a more careful procedure than this one during the whole two months I was engaged in intense negotiations with the Prince, or during the five months more I spent travelling back and forth in negotiations with the King of Poland and his envoys and the Prince's representatives, for a total of seven months in all. Whenever the Senators came upon any historical evidence that might strengthen their position in regard to Lithuania, Poland, Livonia or their own country, they would conscientiously cull it from the archives. This practice subsequently proved extremely helpful to me when I sought to study and deal with this whole complex situation. However, these matters can be more clearly understood from the official documents I have sent Your Beatitude, and so this is enough on this topic.

I have not deemed it necessary to go into detail concerning all the attentions the Prince showed us, since I have touched upon them elsewhere. Couriers bearing safe-conducts were awaiting our arrival and as soon as the Prince learned that we had come he rushed guides, horses and supplies all the way to the frontier of his kingdom, where we had pitched our tents. He assigned 60 men to see to all our wants at our residence; as a matter of

16

fact we were not allowed to leave the premises or send anyone out except on matters of great necessity unless we were attended by them. He sent us some finely-equipped horses, and since it is the Prince's regular custom to make gifts of this sort to envoys, we felt bound to use them. When we went to the Polish camp, which was 600 miles away,[49] or when we wanted to leave his kingdom in safety he supplemented our escort with bands of Tatars or Muscovites.

One unpleasant thing was that the Prince's suspicious nature often made him refuse to allow doctors to attend us when we were ill. As I mentioned previously, I left two men[50] with the Prince, who were to look into matters while I returned to King Stefan. Whenever they saw an opportunity of inspiring true piety among the Muscovites they were to make every effort to do so. Before 100 of his nobles the Prince promised to treat my men as he would myself if I were present, but he did not allow them to go out even once. The men who went from Staritsa to Moscow were confined to a single narrow room, in which they had to keep the altar for worship and a table for reading and writing, and where they had to sleep. Guards were on duty at the gate at all times, three boyars and three peasants, whose names were Sunebul, Chufara, Rudear, Chufara, Miroslav, and Ruroiedav. After my men had spent four and a half months in this place they complained that the Prince had failed to keep his promise. An intelligent man told them that the Prince promised one thing to foreigners but gave quite different instructions to the *Pristavs*. He would say one thing but think another; many foreigners had been officially granted freedom of movement, but if they asked to return to their own country they were condemned and executed on the spot. This man went on to say that even those who had given a solemn oath to remain in Muscovy all the rest of their lives were not allowed to meet other foreigners or have any chance to talk to them if they did meet them. The Prince would execute anyone, whether Muscovite or foreigner, who did so or incurred even the slightest suspicion of doing so. This was why many who wished to visit my men did not dare do so. For example, a doctor, who earnestly desired to receive the Sacrament of Confession and be restored by the Most Holy Eucharist, asked permission to come to us. He failed to obtain it and the refusal was couched in threatening language: "How dare you, a foreigner, visit people like that? If you value your life, see that you do not make such a request again!" Some Muscovites deplored this virtual captivity, but they said that no hope of advancing the cause of true piety would exist until the Prince had adopted another mode of life.[51] To avoid arousing suspicion I sent the dispatches to my men from the Polish camp and elsewhere unsealed as part of the bundle destined for the Prince, although they contained matters of interest only to members of our Order. Even so the Prince would refuse to transmit them and had some of them translated from Latin to Russian. I assume he was attempting to discover hidden meanings; this is the mark of a keen but suspicious mind that fears when it has no cause for fear.

While we were preparing to leave Moscow for Livonia, at the conclusion of a public banquet the Prince extended his hand to me and all my associates, arose, and asked me to greet Your Holiness and the King of Poland. After I had returned to my residence he sent me a letter and some gifts. A part of the revenue realized from them has been allocated to maintaining German novices at Olomouc, Prague and elsewhere, while the rest has been used to bring an occasional Muscovite to our seminaries. I had twice refused these gifts, but the Senators warned me not to flout the traditional customs of the realm or spurn the Prince's generosity, for he had not refused the gifts sent by Your Beatitude, and he always allowed his envoys to accept gifts. I took their advice (which had also been tendered to me before this), expressed my thanks, and distributed the money among several members of the Court. At the same time I wished to avail myself of this opportunity to provide the Prince with a loftier and truer understanding of the purposes of our Order; thus, I had the Senators convey to him the following sentiments:

"Most merciful Great Lord, by the blood of Jesus Christ suffer me to beseech you for the third and final time not to take offense but not to ask me to accept these gifts which in your magnanimity you have ordered bestowed upon me. God knows that I do not scorn them out of contempt or through failure to recognize the noble generosity displayed by Your Serene Highness. But in the name of my calling to the spiritual life and by the vow of poverty that I have often uttered under God's compassion, grant me, by the vitals of the merciful Christ, this boon, which I should consider the greatest kindness you could show me. Remember what you said to me a few days ago. It matters not that you were speaking of other men, who are not bound by the conditions of my calling. You said that there can be nothing finer then to imitate the humility and poverty of Christ our Lord. Allow me to follow His example. You needed no garments or skins to secure peace; God's compassion saw to that, and God's favor is all you will need to bring to pass everything you desire. In me you have a person who will faithfully and carefully fulfil his every obligation. The subvention you have provided to send my comrade

Paolo[52] to the Pope, and the gifts you have sent His Holiness, are more than enough. I would certainly never have condoned accepting a subvention had not our journey been so protracted and our stay in the Polish camp and in your realm so long, and had we not feared to offend you and jeopardize the felicitous outcome. We are not going to use these costly skins ourselves, and we would gladly give up not merely them, but our very lives, in order to disseminate the Catholic faith, if God should consider us worthy of so glorious a sacrifice. This was the reason why I refused to allow merchants to accompany me, no matter how earnestly they entreated. I had no wish to have the unsavory activities in which such people may engage, or the altercations with your people into which they might enter, detract from the purpose of my mission. I have, thank God, ample resources to return to the Pope. If you wish to make me a valuable gift, continue to display towards me the kindness you have already shown, and whenever you proclaim yourself to be a sheep in Christ's flock, consider that you ought to follow the leadership of the Pope, the Visible Shepherd to whom Christ our Lord entrusted His flock for feeding.

"I should like you to know that in this century, when a new part of this earth was discovered, and Europe became rent with heresy, God summoned several thousand members of our Order to form a kind of army, composed of men free of all material considerations and personal concerns. In Jesus' name we have all sworn a solemn oath to bring Him and the spiritual treasures of His Church to the peoples of the Indies,[53] heretics, and those who are not fully joined to the body of the Church. In order to do this we have forsaken everything. The members of our Order have not held and do not hold any office unless it is without salary or a clear question of life and death might be involved. Some thirty years ago some of our members were raised to the rank of Patriarch and Bishop in India and Ethiopia,[54] but they spent their lives in unremitting toil, without thought of material reward, for the glory of Christ in these faroff lands. We have been sent here by the Holy Apostolic See for the same purpose. Perhaps one day we can return if we are needed. Please do not make us accept these gifts. They are not necessary."

My plea failed to induce the Prince to withdraw his gifts, but he imbibed a draught of the Truth, and a foundation was laid on which the glorious edifice we are all sure will be erected in Muscovy can rest when the right time comes. The Prince generously ordered us to be provided with guides and all the supplies we might need. We took leave of him and made our way through Russia[55] to Livonia to meet King Stefan of Poland.

19

Classes of Envoys the Prince of Muscovy Sends to Foreign Rulers. Their Mode of Travel. Events Involving the Prince's Envoys on Their Way to the Pope with Antonio Possevino.

The Prince of Muscovy employs Couriers, Messengers and Ambassadors (called Great) to negotiate with foreign rulers in times of both war and peace, and to handle commercial matters. Couriers, known as *Gontsy*, merely carry letters. Messengers, called *Poslantsy*, are minor envoys; they undertake small commissions as well as carry letters and are usually accompanied by a few associates. Great Ambassadors, usually sent out in groups of three assisted by a Secretary, are called *Velikie Posly*. The latter seldom go further than the Kingdom of Poland, because they are attended by a large unpaid retinue (a practice peculiar to Poles and Muscovites alike), and long journies beyond Poland require very considerable expenditures, for which the Prince makes almost no provision at all. The Polish King and the Prince of Muscovy, who support this practice, usually arrange to attach 100 or 200 people, including merchants, to their delegations. In fact the Muscovite envoys are themselves merchants and traffic in goods, most improperly, in view of the responsibilities they bear. Since they consider all gifts they receive as an increase in their compensation, whenever they fail to receive any, they demand and will even go so far as to extort them.

This was the case at Kiverova Gora, the hamlet near Iam Zapol'skii. The Muscovite envoys arrived with 300 people. They opened shops and between negotiating sessions found time to supervise closely all the trading and bartering that went on with the Poles. To reduce expenses they brought in supplies from Novgorod, some 200 miles away, which included food already cooked and preserved by the cold. This practice was of benefit to me and my associates because each of the four Muscovite envoys, on the Prince's orders, took turns sending food to us. We were in the hamlet in the dead of winter. There was an enormous amount of snow, in which we had to pitch our tents. We lit fires everywhere and never allowed them to go out in an attempt to stave off the appalling cold, while some of us took shelter in little wooden huts, which were filled with smoke and soot. On every side the fields had been devastated by the Polish soldiers and the only food we could find to buy was bread. The water was contaminated, and even when we used the fires to melt snow we could barely obtain enough water for the horses or to cook our food.

Whenever envoys from the Prince of Muscovy arriving at the court of a foreign ruler fail to receive free horses, lodging, food, escorts and gifts, they immediately fall to praising the liberality, generosity and resources of their Great Lord (as they usually refer to him) to the skies and calling their host miserly, no matter how eminent he may be. This was my experience with Shevrigin, the first Muscovite Messenger who came to Your Beatitude. After that I acquired more knowledge from my contacts with the others, and when the Prince decided to send a second delegation to Rome, I urged him not to send more than ten men. Prior to my return journey, which was to take me first to Orsha, then on to Livonia and Poland, and finally through Germany to Italy, three short trips I took convinced me that it would place an intolerable burden on local inhabitants to provide food for 100 or 200 men, but at the same time, unless all amenities were provided without cost, the immense effort, zeal, toil and expense which the Holy Apostolic See had lavished upon the Prince might prove to be of no avail.

Both delegations were headed by Princes,[56] with whom it was my task to mediate problems of the gravest moment and to discuss the question of amity among the Christian rulers. As interpreter for his delegation the Grand Prince had assigned a man who had abjured the Catholic faith and adopted the Muscovite schism, which, of course, he had done for reasons of security and gain. We rejected him at once, requested another, a Catholic Polish nobleman, and managed to obtain him.[57] We considered it extremely important to have someone in the delegation who on his return would be in a position to give the Prince a true account of affairs and reveal to him the humanity of the Catholic rulers, in case the other members of the group tried to cast aspersions on our work.

Shevrigin and particularly his associate, an Italian interpreter, a resident of Muscovy who had once been a Catholic, then became a Lutheran, and finally accepted the errors of the Muscovites, and who was murdered in Carinthia,[58] became involved in some highly unsavory incidents. These events occurred immediately after I had left the group to visit the Archduke Karl[59] and soon after they had left Italy, where they had been received with the highest honors and given splendid gifts. The members of the second delegation did not meet with violent death and never engaged in the sort of wrangling that can lead to a passage of arms, although such occurrences would inevitably have taken place if they had not been continuously restrained and held in check, sometimes by banter, or with hope of reward, and occasionally through fear. They were required on occasion to pay

21

for their lodging themselves and although this irritated them, the practice had the merit of forcing them to recognize the extent of the benefits they were receiving and to gauge more accurately the generosity shown them in Italy and the Papal States, where the quality of their welcome had far exceeded what they had any right to expect. During the course of our journey I had an opportunity to take a more effective measure of the character of the Muscovites accompanying me, and I came to know them even better when I afterwards took them to Poland on the instructions of Your Beatitude.

When we entered Poland on our first journey from Muscovy the envoys expressed surprise that the King had not adhered to the custom of supplying horses and food. They were told that they could expect no more than a civil greeting from the King, who had no intention of initiating a custom of receiving delegations in transit from the Prince of Muscovy to other rulers. At our request, however, he did receive them at Riga in a reasonably friendly manner. There we learned that the Muscovites had destroyed many buildings in Livonia, which had been erected at great expense by the Archbishop of Riga and by various Masters of the Teutonic Order. They were falling down, filled with dirt, and their windows were broken, exposing the interior to the elements. The envoys scorned them and preferred to live in little wooden huts full of smoke which they threw up themselves. The scene reminded me of the Goths squatting in the Colosseum, amid the triumphal arches, after their sack of Eternal Rome, and I was no longer surprised at what lurked in the hearts of a race that is unable to endure the splendor and majesty of other peoples. They were not even impressed by the elaborate retinue of the Emperor, who was then proceeding to the Imperial Diet at Augsburg, nor could they be aroused to give genuine praise to the splendid cities and the throngs of distinguished citizens they saw.

This is the way things went in Bohemia and Germany, where His Caesaric Majesty ordered all the envoys' expenses defrayed and gave them several silver vessels. On reaching Italy and entering Venetian territory all the cities received us in a truly magnificent manner. At Verona the envoys were invited to inspect the fortresses, near which numerous bodies of soldiers stood ready to escort them inside with every mark of distinction. The people of Vicenza did everything in their power to make the envoys welcome; they displayed that loftiness of spirit they possess and the generosity for which the city is deservedly famous. It was the same at Padua. Then we arrived in Venice, where the Most Serene

22

Republic received us with every mark of distinction. The Muscovites were unprepared for the degree of freedom they enjoyed in Venice, accustomed as they are to referring everything to their Prince. They objected to being lodged in a very comfortable Dominican monastery; it required a great deal of care and patience to keep them under control, and finally the men assigned by the Senate to look after the envoys earnestly requested us to remain with the Muscovites constantly. In the midst of all this and while I was pressing them to depart, suddenly the Greeks, who had settled in Venice many years ago, secretly began asking the Muscovites to attend their church and celebrate the service and the other observances according to the Greek rite. The young noblemen whom the Senate had assigned to show the Muscovites the city failed to realize the seriousness of the situation and had allowed the place where they lodged to be very elaborately decked out. The following day the Greek schismatics entertained the Muscovite schismatics. The minute I got wind of these developments, I rushed to the monastery and there I found the Muscovites and the Venetians about to set out for the church in company with the Greeks. I addressed the Muscovites: "Iakov Molvianinov (the chief envoy's name), you were entrusted to my care by your Prince, and you are expected to conduct yourself as I tell you. I am taking you to the Pope, not to the Greeks. You must return to your lodging." He obeyed, but the Greeks took great exception to my action; some of them actually thought I had insulted the Republic, and said that an official order had been issued to escort the Muscovites to the Greek church. My answer to the Greeks was: "When you have agreed to restore communion with the Catholic church you can come and negotiate with me and I shall be glad to entertain your requests." Next, however, other persons took up the affair; I was unable to win them over, and had to appear before the Senate. That body heard both sides of the case and adroitly calmed down the Greeks, who were ready to file a complaint. The whole matter was unfortunate; it afforded many people an opportunity to observe the suppleness of the Greeks with their schismatic views at close quarters, and those of greater perception well understood the dangerous possibilities, for the Greek colony in Venice contains numerous spies, who would lose no opportunity to report everything to the Perfidious Ones.[60] The Muscovites were given heavy gold necklaces by the Republic, but they said to their interpreter: "Go to your Chief and tell him he has to send us some silks and other valuables from his treasury." The interpreter, an astute man, managed to avoid fulfilling their request.

Leaving Venice we passed through Ferrara and reached Bologna, where, acting on the instructions of Your Beatitude, the Most Illustrious Legate, Cardinal Cesis, manifested the fullest and most generous tokens of his paternal affection. Stores were closed and the envoys were received with honor greater than that shown to ordinary dignitaries. The other Most Illustrious Legates, Vercelli in Reggio Emilia and Colonna in Piacenza, made similar arrangements: they dispatched bands of soldiers outside town to meet us, and city officials stood at the gate. With a salute from the cannon and a blast of trumpets we were escorted most honorably to the Governor's Residence, where entertainment and the most exquisite repasts awaited us. Since the Muscovites showed no restraint in demanding things, our noble hosts were advised not to give them everything they asked for; this was done to make the Muscovites behave within the bounds of propriety. While we were staying with the Governor of Arimini, the Muscovites removed the holy images and set up tiny ikons of their own, painted in the Muscovite manner. We took them down and had the others put up again to avoid giving offense to Catholics, and after that the envoys behaved in a more circumspect manner. Then we came to Loreto, where the glorious shrine of the Virgin Mary is located, a place that attracts enormous crowds of people. Because of the miracles associated with it the shrine is always full of pilgrims, who feast their eyes and nurture their souls with perpetual prayers.

We were received, modestly at my request, in some more towns, and finally crossed the Tiber near Borghetto, where we were welcomed and most warmly greeted by the Chamberlains of Your Beatitude. After another day's journey we at last entered Rome. Led by the Marquis de Cesis, the nobility of Rome came out to meet us. Accompanied by an enormous throng and greeted by rounds fired from all the cannon of the Castello Sant' Angelo the Muscovites were most honorably conducted to the palace of Cardinal Colonna, who was away at the time. The envoys were well entertained in the palace, and members of Your Beatitude's own staff saw to all their wants and served as guards at the gates. Every day until Your Beatitude returned from Frascati the Muscovites were conducted about the city in carriages to see its outstanding features. They were struck with the care, concern and affection for the sick and the expenditures made upon them, and with the dispensaries and private rooms available to them. They especially admired the Hospital of the Holy Ghost, as well as the other major hospitals. However, what made the most powerful impression on their mind was the ubiquitous piety, which affected the envoys themselves.

When they toured the Colleges and Seminaries in which the different peoples study they began to grasp the extent to which the Roman religion predominates throughout the world and to realize that they were not the only Christians, as they are so fond of saying. They kept a careful daily journal and made notes of what they saw to report to their Prince, a practice they had also followed when, during their journey, they had inspected the Colleges of our Order in Lithuania, Poland, Moravia, Bohemia, Germany and Italy. They were astounded to find an English Seminary in Rome because they had heard that England was totally lost to heresy. They were amazed when they beheld the modest demeanor of the students, and they piously venerated and kissed the relics of the Martyrs preserved in the English church, an act they performed frequently in other churches as well, both in Rome and elsewhere. Certain young Roman noblemen took them to the Palazzo del Compidoglio, where they entertained them lavishly in the Roman way and asked them carefully to examine fragments of ancient marbles and ridiculous replicas of pagan gods, as though this were a matter of the greatest importance, but they showed their contempt for all this, as indeed they ought. As all good Christians should, the Muscovites showed the strongest dislike for any kind of lewdness, including images, even sacred ones, suggestively painted, or nude statues, or other contrivances of the Devil, no matter whether they found them in their lodgings or in the homes and gardens of individuals, where apparently they came upon more representations of Cupid and Venus than of Christ and the Virgin Mary. When they saw the churches of Rome and the Shrine of St. Peter they openly admitted that these were by far superior to their own wood and stone churches, the only ones they had ever seen before. They thought these churches surpassed all others in the world in beauty and the excellence of their workmanship.

It was a matter of considerable difficulty to induce the envoys to kiss the cross on the feet of Your Holiness when they came to greet Your Beatitude, and it was even more difficult to have them do so on their departure. My own opinion is that they were hoping to obtain more gifts, particularly money, although all of them had received heavy gold necklaces and some cloth of gold, and the two chief envoys had been given clothing made of pure silk, while the rest had received two garments made from a combination of cloth and silk. They were quick enough to do obeisance whenever they heard any remark they thought touched upon the interests of their Grand Prince, for the Muscovites throw themselves at the feet of their Bishops and strike their foreheads on the ground, and in behaving thus they show them a respect which the early Christians reserved solely for

25

the Apostles. The envoys were annoyed that only my travelling companions and myself were there to accompany them from Rome, because the Muscovite custom is to have a large retinue escort foreign envoys some four or five miles out of town, a practice I twice encountered when I was leaving Muscovy.

Their return trip was characterized by the same sort of experiences as their original journey. They removed their necklaces, which they had been wearing en route, the very beautiful cross adorned with Greek letters Your Beatitude had given them, and the gold ikon of St. Mark the Evangelist, which was a gift from the Venetians. If each member of the group had been alone and had not been afraid he might be denounced to the Prince, the envoys would have adapted themselves quite easily to every situation. They had grown somewhat more restrained, perhaps as a result of their contact with more civilized peoples, or perhaps because they had to make the rest of their journey outside Italy at their own expense. We finally brought them to the Polish King in Warsaw, and on that portion of the journey, to avoid quarrels we took particular care not to lodge in the same premises with them. The King bestowed gifts upon them in regal fashion, and they took a letter from me to the Prince, in which I had given him a digest of all that had occurred, and a beautiful ikon of the Savior, a gift to the Prince from Your Beatitude, etched in bronze, with Greek letters, and flecked with ivory and silver. In this way I sent them on to Muscovy in a reasonably good frame of mind. I have chosen to dwell upon these matters at some length so as to forewarn and prepare anyone who might some day receive a similar commission. Such a person will need to muster all the patience and sagacity he possesses, but these are qualities he can obtain from God through prayer.

The Character of the Prince and the Schism.

There is general agreement that the peoples of the northern expanse, especially those who have not been freed from savagery by the influence of the true religion, possess highly suspicious temperaments because they know that they are lacking in natural ability. They strive to acquire by deceit and violence (and, in the case of the Muscovites, by stubbornness as well) what they cannot obtain through zeal or compromise. These traits are clearly discernible in Scythians and Tatars, and since many Muscovites originally came from among these peoples, or assume that they did so, it is not surprising that they have not yet succeeded in ridding themselves of these characteristics, which religion has tamed and refined in others. Their ruler, who enjoys unrestricted power over his people, and who practises a kind of Christianity, perhaps not surprisingly considers himself to be the mightiest potentate of all, because he knows nothing of the resources possessed by other rulers and is constantly surrounded by the praise and adulation of his subjects. These three circumstances render the Muscovites astonishingly prone to exalting their Grand Princes, a tendency that has been particularly marked since the Princes began to strive to free their people from the Tatars, to whom the Muscovites once were subject. This is especially true of the present Prince, for although he has occasionally indicated his awareness that another power might possess resources greater than his own, he is absolutely convinced that no one can be more learned or possess a truer religion than he. Whenever I mentioned the names of leading and powerful Christian rulers he would ask who they were. He could not endure comparisons, for he considered praise of another's resources a derogation of his own. This attitude has led the Grand Princes of Muscovy to refer to themselves in their speeches, their rescripts, and on their coinage as Lords of All Russia, even though much of what they call Russia is in the hands of the Polish King. In addition to the list of titles he desires to use, such as Tsar (King) of Kazan' and Astrakhan', the present Prince, Ivan Vasil'evich, when writing to the Turks has on occasion ordered himself called Emperor of Germany as well. When coveting Livonia and casting an eye on Prussia Ivan claimed that he was descended from a brother of Augustus Caesar called Prus,[61] and his specious offers of friendship to Charles V, his brother Ferdinand and the latter's son Maximilian revealed the plots he was maturing against Germany and the countries further West.[62] His hopes in this direction were fostered by the dissension among the Christian princes, the various accursed heresies, his success in Livonia, his previous conquests of Kazan' and Astrakhan', and his conviction, derived from what is better termed a schism than a religion, that God had chosen him to serve as the Light destined to illuminate the whole world.[63] Those seeking the aid and support of the Prince to bring about the collapse of the Polish Kingdom had sent an increasing number of delegations to him.[64] When I was at the Prince's court the fortunes of Muscovy were at a very low ebb; the Prince frequently mentioned these delegations and became cheerful at the recollection. The Prince had been greatly encouraged in his design by receiving a letter from a prominent ruler who recommended spreading the Lutheran heresy in his own kingdom.[65] This led the Prince to assume that all Catholics (whom he calls "Romans") had lapsed into heresy, which would make them easier to overcome. Finally, he expected that indiscriminate cruelty would help shorten the time needed to accomplish his design; the terrorism he had employed in Lithuania and Livonia had convinced him that he could crush all opposition and that similar methods would serve him equally well when conquering other countries.

Let us turn to the Schism. It is simply unbelievable how tenaciously the Prince clings to it. He prefers the things of this world to life everlasting, for he is constantly engaged in broadening the gulf instead of narrowing it. The Muscovites have undergone experiences comparable to others who break with their past in the belief they can improve conditions, but who do not end up where they had intended, the situation in which the innovators of this century obviously find themselves. The Muscovites adopted their Schism from the Greeks, who were themselves schismatics, but they subsequently became separated from the Greeks as well. They make all kinds of foolish and inept statements because they are ignorant and without learning, a subject I have treated in my Second Commentary. The only person who can readily understand the Muscovite schism is someone who has seen the stubbornness of the Greeks, remembers the Donatists,[66] who sundered themselves from the Church and never returned to it, ponders the nature of the Ethiopians, who acknowledge the Pope but have never sent an embassy to the Apostolic See,[67] or has considered the Hussites, who have often talked about union but have refused to return to the Church.[68] The Prince's stubborn attitude is reinforced by his firmly fixed views, which lead him to assume that the Schism will endure untroubled forever. The Muscovites have been exposed to the Schism since earliest childhood, and with their wholly untutored minds they are sunken in everlasting obsequiousness and servitude to a Prince who washes his hands in a silver basin after any foreign envoys he has received have withdrawn, thus implying he has been defiled and that all other Christians are unclean. When I objected to this practice (a fuller description of my protest is found in my previous communications) he tried to justify his actions, but he did not wash his hands. He will not allow Armenians to enter his churches, for he says that they profess the Nestorian heresy.[69] He allows Greeks to enter, but the doors are barred to Lutherans and other heretics, and he has had the churches they built destroyed.

The Prospects for Fulfillment of the Prince's Promises To Propagate the Most Holy Name and Faith of Christ in Asia and Elsewhere.

The purpose of this chapter will be to discuss more fully whether we can expect the Prince to spread the Word of Christ if we assume that what he wrote in his letters to Your Beatitude and the other princes is of specious intent. We know why he made the promises he did, but we also can see how greatly the Christian Commonwealth would benefit if the Muscovites were to adopt the Catholic faith, or at least, when the situation is in better order, obtain another and a gentler Prince, for many are now virtually certain that the present one does not have long to live.

I remember that before I went to Muscovy a certain N.[70] replied at length to numerous questions I put to him on such topics as these. The Prince's dominions are located at a very considerable distance from the sworn enemies of our faith. To the south stretches a vast tract of land where the soil is barren, no trees grow, and one can often proceed for more than 20 days at a time without finding water. All these factors would create enormous difficulties for any army. South of that lies the Tauric Chersonese, the home of the Crimean Tatars, mortal enemies of the Muscovites, where the Turks maintain a good number of well-equipped fortresses. In response to a further inquiry my informant stated that the Muscovite possessions touched on the Caspian Sea and afforded access to it; in spite of the enormous size of the intervening territory ships have no difficulty navigating the entire length of the river Volga during certain months of the year. When I asked whether the Muscovites could sail down the river Don, which rises in Muscovy and empties into the Sea of Azov, N. replied that they could, but pointed out that the fortress of Azov, situated at the mouth of the Don, belongs to the Turkish Sultan. In connection with the Crimean Tatars, he observed that since the Prince had added Kazan' and Astrakhan' to his empire he could probably take the Crimea as well, giving this further reason for his conclusion: when the Muscovites conquered the Tatars they moved up heavy cannon and ordered thick perforated stakes fastened to the front of their vehicles, through which the fusiliers could see to discharge missiles lethal to the enemy with no danger to themselves. It is a simple matter to surround and crush an enemy with new weapons like these, and this is particularly true in the case of the Tatar Hordes, because each group of them constitutes a distinct entity: when one unit is overcome, it becomes that much easier to reduce the remainder. After the adjacent land of Kazan' was conquered and fell under Muscovite control it was inevitable that the same thing would happen to Astrakhan', as its people were in no position to summon immediate support from any source. The Prince has found it easier to keep both conquered peoples under control by building and manning fortresses to watch over these territories. I asked how the Muscovites had managed to inflict a severe defeat on the Turks a few years ago, when the Sultan ordered the diversion of the river Don into the Volga. N. replied that the defeat in question had not been inflicted by the Muscovites, but by the Crimean Tatars, even though they were allies of the Turks. Angered at certain measures taken by the Turks which they felt portended heavier servitude for themselves, the Tatars, when serving as guides to the Turkish forces, led them through huge forests and places where they could not obtain supplies, so that almost all the Turkish soldiers perished from hunger and exhaustion.

When I inquired whether the boundary of Muscovy lay far from the Persian kingdom my informant told me that a substantial amount of territory intervenes between the two countries. Muscovy does not border upon Persia; between the two are found the Georgians and Circassians, known as "Five Mountain Men," whose language is entirely different from any other. It takes eight days to traverse the length of their land, and the people are ruled by seven Chiefs, or Prefects, something along the lines of Switzerland. Depending upon time and circumstance these peoples receive regular subsidies, sometimes from Muscovy, sometimes from Turkey, and occasionally from Persia. Nowadays the journey to Persia through Muscovy takes longer, because the Turks have captured the Iron Gate, which used to serve as the crossing point. N. said that he was sure of his information because he had had staying with him a brave and loyal Circassian soldier, whose uncle had been in Persia and fought in the war there. The uncle, who had just come from that area, had related all these facts to him. N. added that the Khan, the ruler of the Tatars in Asia, was much like these people; he had at one time been attracted to our faith, and to this day he still preserves much of the Christian ritual.

I heard from a prominent man that Muhammed, one of the Councillors of Suleiman, the father of the present Sultan of Turkey,[71] had once said that the King of Poland was undertaking a difficult task in attacking Muscovy, because the Sultan and the Prince of Muscovy were the only rulers in the world who kept their peoples under strict control, and this made them exceedingly powerful. This example illustrates the high opinion of the Prince entertained by the Turks, who probably still remember the defeats they once suffered at the hands of the Muscovites; that is, if one can credit the reports which Herberstein and others have drawn from the Muscovite Chronicles. The Turks are also of the opinion that the Greeks greatly fear the enormous power of the Prince even though he is so far away, for since they believe that he shares the same religion they would otherwise not try to avoid his domination but would seek to draw closer to him. There can be no doubt that once the immediate issues involving the King of Poland are settled, the Prince will take up affairs in this part of the world, for through his Senators he inquired of me whether he could send his troops through territories under the King's jurisdiction and build fortresses wherever he went, if he joined his forces to those of the King. His discussion made it clear that he was more concerned with the part of Russia under the King's control than he was with the Crimea, and was obviously afraid that the Poles might cut his troops off from their home bases. If the Prince had sent his forces against another area besides Livonia and Lithuania, the performance of his armies could have been gauged more accurately.

However all this may be, one thing is absolutely certain: the road to Asia through Muscovy is far less costly and dangerous than through any other part of the world, and this road leads to the propagation of faith in Christ Our Lord, which must always be the avowed goal of every devout person. As Your Holiness wrote to the Prince, it is absolutely essential that he join himself to us by the bond of religion, for failing this, the ties that link the rest of the human race can all too easily be sundered. However, to bring this about is not the work of a single day or the task of a single delegation. To build the Ark that saved the few who renewed the whole world required 100 years of devoted and uninterrupted toil. Perhaps not quite so much time will be needed in Livonia, for King Stefan of Poland is already engaged in establishing Colleges and Seminaries to train Catholic priests there and on the borders of Muscovy, and is making this one of his cardinal objectives in all the territories under his control, as well as in those he has recently acquired by war. Under God's tutelage the members of our Order are accomplishing miracles among the simple folk of this region, and many Muscovites are entrusting their sons to priests sent by the Apostolic See. All this makes me hope that they themselves will soon learn of the goodness of God, Who can instantly enrich the poor man and Whose way of making the lion to lie down with the lamb is well known. A prolonged and sustained effort must be undertaken to induce the Prince to enter into friendly relations with the rest of the Christian rulers, and if those responsible for the execution of this policy are inspired solely by the glory of God there is no telling what benefits this course of action may produce, although Satan is certain to employ all the wiles he can to prevent its accomplishment.

Here is a suggestion as to the correct way to deal with schismatics and heretics: once they conceive that religion is to be the sole object of discussion, on the instructions of their pastors they will either refuse to participate, reject all overtures, or profess unwillingness further to explore the topic. On the other hand, Catholic princes who have political issues to discuss with the Holy See know that it is incumbent upon Your Beatitude to advance the cause of peace, because they understand that peace is the proper provenance

31

of him who is the Shepherd, the Vicar of Christ, and the Holy Father. If a comparable approach is adopted at these other discussions the result will be that all princes, Catholic, heretical and schismatic alike, will be glad to listen, and will seek to discover solutions to their own and others' problems in the meetings. Many difficulties that have heretofore seemed insuperable will prove more tractable, and the restored self-confidence on the part of the rulers cannot fail to instil a greater degree of piety and religious feeling in their breasts.

In such circumstances the rulers will either be too embarrassed to refuse to engage in these activities, or else be stimulated to greater efforts to carry out the behests of the Apostolic See, particularly since they know that Scythians, the peoples of the Indies, and other savage races are now placing themselves under its banner, while the Enemy of the human race is doing everything in his power to help heretics destroy the authority of the Church established by Christ. Those who undertake such highly important work in the future must consider it their sacred duty to persevere in their task; they must create opportunities for future contacts, and on their departure they must, as the saying goes, make sure they are leaving the Royal Gate open, through which they can return. If these prescriptions are followed, wonders will eventually happen; Your Beatitude will once more have peace, God will demonstrate His love and wisdom, and, as has already been our experience, unparalleled new opportunities for helping these peoples will appear. If with a clear conscience and without detriment to our salvation we can develop basic human relationships with other peoples, even those who have not yet become Christians, I am convinced that some day such a policy will allow us to spread the Christian religion further throughout the realms of these peoples than anyone has ever been able to do. Only those who have reflected deeply on the patient martyrdom endured by the Roman Popes who held the Keys at the time of the frightful persecutions that occurred during the first 300 years of the Church's existence, who advanced the cause of Christianity with their own blood, and who, if I may express myself thus, intrepidly piloted the Ship of Faith, freighted with a host of barbarous races, to the Harbor, which is Christ Our Lord, are the ones who have the right to decide what should be done to instil greater awareness of the Truth in the minds of rulers.

Rules to be Observed by Envoys Sent to Muscovy by the Holy See and Other Catholic Rulers.

Those chosen for this mission must bear three cardinal points in mind when preparing for it: they should be genuinely dedicated to the glory of God; they should arrive at a favorable time, and they should be fully briefed. The personal characteristics each envoy should possess are a sturdy virtue, a knowledge of things Greek, and an elegant and dignified appearance. It is very important that no delegation sent to the Muscovites provide the slightest grounds for arousing justifiable suspicions on their part or on the part of the Poles and Lithuanians. For example, at the Diet of Ratisbon Cardinal Morone proposed in the name of Your Beatitude to send a Papal envoy to Muscovy in the company of the Prince's envoys, who were present on the occasion, and the Emperor Maximilian agreed. However, while the envoys were preparing to depart, a distinguished German theologian, who had some knowledge of the Muscovite language, received a letter from Your Beatitude naming him Papal envoy to the Prince's court. He died a few days after receiving it, and Your Beatitude made arrangements for another delegation and sent Alessandro Canobio, now Bishop of Forlì, from Rome for that purpose. However, his opponents succeeded in blocking his passage through Lithuania and he had to return to Vilna and ultimately to Rome without accomplishing his mission. On a previous occasion, when Vincenzo del Portico, who later became Archbishop of Ragusa, was serving as the Apostolic Legate to King Sigismund of Poland, he was selected by Pope Pius V of sacred memory to visit Muscovy, but when Pius subsequently learned of the cruelty displayed by the Prince he abandoned his plan. When Your Beatitude was seized with the desire to assist the northern peoples, the Bishop of Bertinoro, then Papal Nuncio at the court of King Stefan, asked me in Your name to ascertain whether a letter could be sent to Muscovy through John III, King of Sweden, at whose court I was then serving on Your Beatitude's instructions. When I took the matter up with him, the King said that it could not be done until the following year. There was no use trying to force the issue prematurely and God Himself gave increase to this humble beginning and smiled upon the quality of patience that usually brings serious negotiations to fruition: it was only a very few months later that Shevrigin, the Messenger of the Grand Prince, came from Muscovy to ask Your Beatitude to send a representative to mediate a peace between his Prince and the King of Poland.[72] This was clearly a most opportune moment and the mission was authorized. Two elements, however, were still lacking: adequate knowledge of the issues involved, and the person of the representative. As far as my selection as Envoy is concerned, there can be no doubt that God in His boundless love had decided to realize the desires He had implanted in the heart of Your Beatitude. We now see why those things came to pass and the reason for our journeys: God will not forsake His cause and will provide further opportunities to pass the torch on to abler hands, and those who truly long for the glory of Christ will succeed in bringing the Catholic religion to both the Russia controlled by the King of Poland and the Russia controlled by the Grand Prince of Muscovy.

Personnel to Accompany the Envoy.

The delegation should not be large, as this causes excessive expense to no purpose and attracts more attention, which in turn affords greater opportunity for hostile persons to impose obstacles in the way of its success. It is a good idea not to stop long at the courts of other rulers or even to pay them a visit, unless it is unavoidable. A too numerous personnel merely increases the danger of displays of arrogance and the substitution of shadow for substance. Any irregularities in the official conduct or public behavior of the members of the delegation provide opportunities for malicious individuals to subvert an excellent undertaking by making insidious representations designed to arouse the hostility of the very rulers to whom the delegation has been sent. In the manual he composed for Pope Clement VII, Alberto Campense wrote that the initial complement of a delegation of this sort should not exceed five persons, excluding drivers and interpreters. I agree that no more than five, or even less, should start out from Rome, but when they arrive in Poland, or Vilna, they may have to add a few local persons, because the inhabitants of the area are better able to endure the rigors of the climate, stand the hard work involved, and are well acquainted with the road. Furthermore, they are young, do not require large salaries, and can perform their fair share of the necessary tasks.

It is better to have two interpreters, in case one should be taken ill, or die, as happened to one of mine. The delegation must never rely on the Prince's interpreters; this can cause all kinds of problems. If the two countries are at peace with one another, the interpreters will carefully set down the memoranda, decrees and proposals put forth by both sides, compare each other's versions, and choose and preserve the truer and more faithful one. If, however, a state of war exists between the King of Poland and the Prince of Muscovy at the time when these rulers are involved in negotiations, there is need most carefully to scrutinize the religious views, human qualities, and even the credibility of the Muscovite interpreters. By credibility I mean the degree to which an envoy can trust them; when I say religious views, I mean that the Prince should not place excessive trust in them: if they are subjects of the Polish King their loyalties are divided, and if they profess the Muscovite Schism there is a real danger they will refuse to reveal things they think should be suppressed; thus, they may even fail to give an accurate translation of the substance of a discussion. I speak from experience.

It is the custom both in Lithuania and Muscovy for all those who travel to engage in trade; thus, particular care must be taken to see that interpreters do not become too involved in such activity, as their desire for gain might affect their capacity to perform their proper duties. It does not take a person of great discernment to appreciate the evil and disgrace that may arise from this situation, especially when the affairs of God are the subject of discussion. A Croatian or Bohemian interpreter will not immediately possess complete mastery of the Muscovite language, but the longer he works at it the more expert he will become. This was the case with the Croatian who was one of our interpreters, and of the two others who knew Czech. These men were unquestionably more acceptable to the Muscovites, due to the inveterate suspicion they harbor of the Poles. It is hard to trust Muscovite interpreters (unless they happen to be Catholic), particularly if they have to translate anything concerning religion into their own language; if they translate it at all, they dare not give an accurate version because of their fear of the Prince. If sufficient Muscovites cannot be found, the next place to seek interpreters is the part of Russia under the control of the King of Poland, where the Colleges of our Order in Vilna, Polotsk and Dorpat can render assistance in locating trustworthy Catholic interpreters, because many men of exemplary piety are engaged in study in them. Apart from the question of from which people interpreters and other members of the delegation are to be chosen, it is important for them to be men of mature years. This will enhance the envoy's authority and diminish the possibility that his associates might compromise him by making slanderous statements or displaying incompetence. This is always important, but it is absolutely essential when delegations are engaged in such delicate negotiations as these.

In addition to the interpreters, the priest of the delegation should be Croatian, Bohemian, Muscovite or Polish, and if he knows the Muscovite language he can serve as an interpreter as well. If men from these countries are unavailable, the priest chosen should at least inspire respect by his deeds rather than be just a talker. He should know his duties, see to it that all members of the delegation partake regularly of the Holy Eucharist, and use the time travelling for special instruction on how best to champion the Catholic religion before the Muscovites, while increasing the general level of all the group's knowledge in this area. More on this topic can be learned from my Second Commentary, and from the document I submitted to the Prince at his request, which contains an analysis of the differences between the Catholic faith and the Schism of the Muscovites and the Greeks. The envoy and the priest should take other books on this subject with them, read them on the journey, and leave them, either in Muscovy or at the border, on their departure.

Here are the Books an Envoy Should Take with Him.[73]

The short Treatise by St. Thomas Aquinas against the Errors of the Greeks. The pamphlet and certain Epistles of Pope Leo IX on the subject, later published in Köln.

St. Anselm's Epistle against the Greeks on the Procession of the Holy Ghost, which is found among the minor writings of this author.

The Replies of Pope Nicholas I to the Objections of the Greeks.

The Reply of Humbert, Archbishop of Sicily and Abbot of Silva Candida, later Cardinal and Legate of Leo IX to Constantinople, to Niceta Pettorato concerning Unleavened Bread and other matters.

The Proceedings of the Council of Florence, and the Defence of Them composed by Giovanni Turrecremata.

The writings of Gennadius Scholarius, Patriarch of Constantinople, on the Profession of the Holy Ghost, the Sacrifice in either Unleavened or Leavened Bread, Purgatory, the Powers of the Saints, and the Primacy of the Pope.[74]

At the end of the last century Sakran of the Chapter of Kraków[75] wrote learnedly and carefully against the errors of the Muscovites. People in the present century too have discussed these matters: *i.e.*, Sander on the Monarchy of the Church,[76] and the sixth and seventh chapters in the second book of Francesco Turriano's treatise against Andrea Freiubio. Another book by Turriano, in which he defends the Papal Epistles against the compilers of the Magdeburg Centuries, and a third, in which he comments on the Apostolic Constitutions of St. Clement, will also prove to be of great assistance to anyone who takes the trouble to peruse them carefully.[77] It would be helpful if several copies of the book on the Schism composed by Piotr Skarga (like Turriano, a member of our Order) in Polish could be introduced into Muscovy.[78]

There is no doubt that Stapleton's treatise *On the Church*,[79] Sokołowski's *Eastern Critique*,[80] and above all, the *Books of Controversies* by Robert Bellarmine, which were designed to refute schismatics, will all be very useful.[81]

The material on the Muscovite religion found in the works of Johann Faber,[82] Bishop of Vienna, Alberto Campense, Herberstein and Guagnini[83] is not particularly useful for refuting or converting the Muscovites. Perhaps this is because their understanding of the situation was different from the way things actually are, or because they were not sufficiently motivated in their writing to produce an antidote to the poison they set before their readers. I am sending a copy of the various additions the heretics have made to the German editions of Herberstein's books. These do not refute the schism; they confound the truth of faith, and I have exposed and refuted all of them elsewhere.

The priest should be accompanied by a doctor. If he knows the Old Slavonic,[84] Muscovite or Czech languages, so much the better, but the envoy and the members of his delegation need a doctor in any event, in case of illness. The strange food, the intoxicating beverages which people incessantly drink, the different climate, so unlike ours, and the fatigue of the journey are enough to exhaust even the strongest of men, and nowhere in that enormous expanse of Muscovite territory can one receive medical attention except at the court of the Grand Prince himself, and he, as I have said, will not permit his doctors to visit even those who are dying, or if he is moved to allow a single visit, he will scarcely ever permit a second. The doctor should carry with him the medicines he knows he will need, although they can be purchased along the way or in Vilna. If he is a capable and pious man, a display of his skill on the journey will do much to advance God's cause, for such activity on his part will provide an excellent opportunity to talk of eternal salvation with the heretics and schismatics.

The delegation should not admit merchants, who occasionally try to join it along the way, both to avoid the difficulties I have already mentioned and to prove to the Muscovites that the mission does not covet their goods but is directed towards their persons. God will be more disposed to grant the noble aims of the envoy if this practice is followed, as it will serve to prevent the quarrels and even murders that frequently occur. I scarcely need to add that men of this sort are almost never Catholics, or honorable in their dealings with others. The King can easily furnish a safe escort from among the people inhabiting the territory along the Polish-Muscovite border, and the Colleges of our Order, to which I alluded earlier, will cooperate by hiring trustworthy men. If the way lies through Livonia, it is better to wait in either Dorpat or Neuhaus, the last fortress there, until *Pristavs* arrive with safe-conducts from Novgorod and Pskov, as they are needed to make the road safe from the Cossacks. If the delegation takes the other route through Smolensk, the one envoys usually take, it should wait at Orsha until informed by the Voievoda of Smolensk that the Muscovites have arrived at the border, in order to avoid spending time in the dense thick forests, where it will be exposed to Cossack raids. This is an extremely dangerous experience, and one that happened to us.

The Kind of Letters and Gifts the Pope Should Send to the Prince.

The form of address Your Beatitude employed in your last letter to the Prince was fitting and should be used again. Your letter bore a gold seal, as the Venetians' letter did, but I am not certain whether this is always necessary. We should take advantage of the letters the Prince has sent to Your Beatitude and the other rulers to initiate further correspondence, or to send a delegation if the opportunity presents itself. A letter should not call an envoy "My Beloved Son," unless this is his official title, nor call him "Great" or "Distinguished," as they call their envoys, because Muscovite Couriers and Messengers, who almost never attain the rank of Ambassador, enjoy these epithets.

Gifts sent to the Grand Prince of Muscovy must be worthy of a powerful ruler; some must be sent in the name of the Apostolic See or the ruler to whom the envoy is accredited, while others should be bestowed in the name of the envoy himself. If this protocol is not observed, the Prince feels, as other Eastern rulers have felt from time immemorial, that he has been affronted. As I have indicated, the Prince often makes presents of greater value to the envoy when he is preparing to depart. In our case, following Your Beatitude's instructions we took a very valuable cross made of crystal, which had the Crucifix and the Passion of Christ cunningly embossed upon it and contained a sliver from the True Cross, and a goblet of the same material, of exquisite workmanship and chased with gold, a Rosary, or Crown as we call it, of precious stones and gold, a most beautifully bound Greek edition of the Proceedings of the Council of Florence, and some other pious objects of value, and all of these gifts found favor with the Prince. The Muscovites esteem and are delighted to receive gifts of this nature, or large silver vases encrusted with gold, of the kind which in Germany require more work than materials, silken garments skilfully inwoven with cloth-of-gold, or pious ikons in the Greek style, adorned with precious stones and large pearls, that veil the human form and possess a Greek inscription to show what figure the ikon represents.

The Clothing an Envoy and his Associates Should Wear, and Other Related Matters. How They Should Conduct Themselves in Certain Situations.

When the envoy is in holy orders, the less elegant and refined his clothing, the greater the honor in which he is held. The Muscovites choose their bishops from among the monks. They never eat meat, observe chastity, preserve an appearance of poverty, and, as a mark of their calling, wear robes stretching almost to their ankles. When they see a foreign cleric dressed in finery, instead of humble pious garb, they consider this to be further proof of the correctness of their schismatic views. They tried to have us wear our square hats instead of our skullcaps or other small headgear. The Muscovites somehow equate these large hats, if worn when there is no need for protection from rain, cold or sun, with the secular life, and their very appearance seems to make them think that men who wear such headgear cannot be clerics. The Muscovites are greatly offended by the short clothing worn by Italians, French, Spaniards and Germans, believing that they reveal parts of the body which should rather be concealed. Following the custom universal in the East, for the sake of propriety the Muscovites wear robes two and often three folds thick down to their feet, and these garments have long sleeves, to prevent even their hands from showing when they use them.

Anyone going to Muscovy should take clothing more ample than that which the Poles and Greeks are accustomed to wearing. Such clothing is cheaper, easier to carry, more comfortable, and, I might add, can serve as bedding. After entering Poland the only beds and mattresses an envoy can find at inns are the ones he brings with him; thus, he will badly need a bed, and one which, when unrolled, can be completely encased in leather or cotton. He requires such a device to prevent soot falling down from the roof of his chamber on his face when he is asleep, as happens in Muscovy and Lithuania, and to protect him from the flies, which bite fiercely and, unlike elsewhere, are active at night, working their way through the linen to cause intense discomfort. The envoy also needs to have a tent which he can pitch in a field, when no lodging is available, and plain black curtains to divide a room into sections. This is absolutely necessary, especially in winter and particularly in Poland and Lithuania, where the envoy and his entire staff are frequently obliged to pass the night all together with the draught animals in one room in order to keep warm. Such experiences are more conducive to modesty than I can easily express in words. The cloth and silk needed to make the delegate's official clothing are easier to carry and less liable to spoilage if they are transported unprocessed as far as Lithuania, where local tailors can convert them to the finished product.

Every single Muscovite wears a cross on his breast. Care should be taken by people wearing crosses suspended from their necks not to let them down below the chest towards the stomach, as the Muscovites are incensed when they see the Most Holy Sign of the Cross hanging down towards the private parts. They consider it scandalous for Rosaries with crosses attached to them to hang from a girdle, since they believe this is an indecent place for crosses to hang. They also consider it a disgrace to confuse holy ikons with profane things or articles of clothing. Crosses and similar objects defiled with spit must be wiped clean. They do not like anyone to stamp on the ground, or bare his chest, or to proceed in a disorderly or unusual manner, particularly if he is going to the Prince.

A Warning Against Taking Letters from Other Rulers to the Grand Prince of Muscovy.

Other rulers may request to have letters conveyed to the Prince which have been composed by heretics or schismatics, as nowadays there are many such people serving as scribes. The envoy should exercise great care to ensure that these communications are temperate, and worthy of the office of the recipient. Sometimes they allude to the Pope in most disrespectful terms, or fail to stress the issues of major concern to the cause of the Christian Commonwealth, or the need to introduce the true form of the worship of Christ's Name into Muscovy. During the course of the peace negotiations, as well as on other occasions, I have personally suffered at the hands of these individuals, and it will be a very long time before I avail myself of their services again. A ruler must himself approve an outline in Latin of the letter he proposes to send, which then must be transcribed by a loyal Catholic, and officially recorded in essentially the same words by a secretary acting under the ruler's specific instructions.

Gifts an Envoy Should Make to the *Pristavs* on Taking Leave of the Prince.

Some *Pristavs* (though not all) are quite demanding. Little more than a day or so after first acquaintance they have the interpreter inform the envoy that they possess ways of letting the Prince know what gifts they have received. When they behave well it is a good plan to encourage them, but when they are difficult it does no harm to imply that no one can expect to receive gifts until the Prince has been offered his, or else simply to tell them that they are free to report that they did not receive any gifts. No matter how greatly people of this type are attracted by hope of gain, they must conceal the fact, and they are bound to hold a higher opinion of a person whom they fear than of one who immediately concedes all of their demands. However, at departure time it is desirable to distribute 25 or 30 (or perhaps more) gold pieces among the *Pristavs*, and a like amount to the retainers who have performed service or brought gifts from the Prince. To prevent cavilling, on crossing the Muscovite border the envoy might distribute or hand out little gold rings, or Muscovite-style crosses, or a sum of money, to the remaining members of the escort.

How an Envoy can Best Conduct Himself Throughout his Entire Length of Service on the Delegation.

The envoy should in general manifest a most sanguine attitude. He will not fail to reap a rich harvest from his labors if during the entire course of the mission he consistently displays the essential qualities of modesty, courtesy and sobriety, while conducting himself like a true Christian cleric. In what does not pertain to Catholic worship he should be all things to all people, fasting when others fast, abstaining from meat on the Sabbath like the Greeks and Muscovites, joining the latter in abstinence from meat on Wednesdays, expressing favor and approbation of individual displays of piety, and worshipping the ikons of their Saints whose veneration is permitted by our Church. These were the instructions given me by Your Beatitude, as conveyed by the Most Illustrious Cardinal di Como. The envoy must refuse to go to the baths or participate in other similar activities. In negotiations he must be devoted to seeking the glory of God, and his desire to redeem souls from Schism must be genuine. He should pray to God often, and invoke the actual saints, our Intercessors before Christ, whom the Muscovites also venerate. The envoy needs chapters from the writings of devotional books, preferably in the Muscovite language, which discuss the essentials of the Catholic faith, virtue, and the avoidance of sin, and he must possess an abiding belief that no man can be so utterly depraved as to choose to immerse himself in sin and despise the Blood of Christ that flows within him. At the same time he must never abandon the glories of our religion nor forget the interests of the Holy Apostolic See and of the Catholic rulers, for no advantage he could ever obtain would compensate for that.

The actual journey is not as difficult as it might at first sight appear. During the course of it the envoy can place devotional books in inns and distribute other holy objects in many other places. He does not have to cross great rivers and oceans or high mountains, such as are often encountered in our other Provinces. The same vehicle that takes him from Rome can carry him right to the palace of the Prince, although it is true that a man accustomed to comfort, who does not have his mind fixed solely on the glory of God, the salvation of souls, and the general good might well be somewhat alarmed at the substantial differences in custom and climate he will experience on this journey.

A Facsimile of the Subscription to the Letter Sent by the Pope, Our Most Holy Lord, to the Grand Prince of Muscovy.

To Ivan Vasil'evich, Lord of Russia, Grand Prince of Muscovy, Novgorod, Smolensk, and Vladimir; Lord of Kazan' and Astrakhan'; Great and Most Esteemed Ruler of many other Provinces.

CHAPTER II

The Second Commentary on Muscovite Affairs by Antonio Possevino, S. J., Containing Special Reference to the Religious Situation in Muscovy, and Composed During the Author's First Mission to the Grand Prince of Muscovy on the Instructions of Pope Gregory XIII.[1]

This Commentary Discusses Plans to Advance the Catholic Religion both in Muscovy and in the Russia Under the Control of His Serene Highness, the King of Poland, as well as the Difficulties Involved in This Undertaking and the Hopes We Have of it.

Here follows a list of the cities and bishoprics of Muscovy, their Location, and their Distance from the City of Moscow, which is the Home of the Prince.

Moscow is a city and the Metropolitanate, where the Metropolitan resides, and it contains the Palace of the Grand Prince. Situated on the river Moscow, it is 300 miles from the Grand Duchy of Smolensk and Lithuania.

Krutitsa is a suburb of Moscow.

Rostov, lying to the north near the lake in which the river Kotorosel' rises, is 100 miles from Moscow.

Novgorod the Great, to the West near Lake Il'men', is more than 300 miles from Moscow; Pskov is 100 miles beyond Novgorod.

Riazan', facing East in the land between the Oka and Don rivers, is 100 miles from Moscow.

Kolomna, lying to the southeast, on the road from Moscow to Riazan', is 54 miles from Moscow.

Kazan', the former capital of the Tatar Horde conquered by the present Prince, Ivan Vasil'evich, is located to the East on the bank of the river Volga, 180 miles from Moscow.

Vologda, lying to the northeast on the road that passes through Iaroslavl', is 240 miles from Moscow.

Tver' is intersected by the river Volga, 100 miles west of Moscow.

Smolensk is situated on the river Dnepr near the border of Lithuania, some 270 miles from Moscow.

Suzdal' is located between Rostov and Vladimir, 130 miles from Moscow.

The territory controlled by the Grand Prince of Muscovy stretches far and wide to the north and the east but it contains no more than eleven bishoprics. The chief one is Moscow, which is administered by the Metropolitan, who outranks all his fellows. Archbishops administer the two cities of Rostov and Novgorod the Great, and bishops administer the remaining towns, Krutitsa, Riazan', Kolomna, Suzdal', Kazan', Vologda, Tver', and Smolensk. In the past the Metropolitans of Muscovy used to be confirmed by the Patriarch of Constantinople, but this practice has been entirely abandoned by the present Prince, who has either killed or consigned to monasteries several metropolitans who held office during his reign.[2] There is a theory that no further requests for confirmation were made after Vasilii, the father of the present Prince, arrested a Greek priest who had been recalled by the Patriarch of Constantinople. This priest had ascertained that the Muscovites differed, not only from the Latins, but even from the Greeks in articles of faith and ritual, and had sharply taxed Vasilii with his findings. In spite of a stern demand from the Turkish Sultan himself, he was never released, and it is said that he eventually died in prison.[3]

Today the Metropolitan is chosen by the Prince alone, and then consecrated by two or three bishops. He is reputed to have an annual income of some 18,000 Thalers, which amounts to approximately 13,000 gold pieces. However, from time to time the Prince demands a tribute, or a subsidy, as it is called, from the Metropolitan and all the other bishops, even the poorer ones, and thus they are unwilling to make major expenditures without his knowledge and permission. Although the Patriarch of Constantinople is no longer asked to confirm the Metropolitan of Moscow, I discovered that the Prince allocates the Patriarch 500 gold pieces a year for charitable purposes.

All bishops are chosen from the monastic ranks, on the assumption that monks lead more unblemished lives. They have no wives, never eat meat (this includes the Metropolitan), nor wear rings on their fingers. They are held in universal veneration for the holiness of their lives. Unlike Catholics, bishops do not visit or inspect their dioceses, perhaps because such action would arouse suspicion in the mind of the Prince, although they do have diocesan representatives, called Archimandrites and Igumens (Abbots and Priors). Furthermore, each year in certain towns they appoint some members of the population to serve as a kind of external vicars to scrutinize the lives of the *Popy* (their word for priests) and others, and they can impose a fine upon a priest who commits a crime. Their bishops are called *Vladiki*, from the Muscovite word *Wlodar*, which means *steward*, or *bailiff*.[4] Like their Greek counterparts, parish priests and other *Popy* may marry a wife who is a virgin, before they take holy orders. If the wife dies and the priest then chooses to adopt the monastic life, he can continue to perform his duties, but if he marries again he may no longer serve as a priest or even be considered as one; some in this situation work as custodians and the like in the churches. This means that a man can be a priest only as long as his original wife is alive, but he ceases to be one the minute she dies. Their priests and their monks, all of whom seem to wear the same attire and to belong to the same Order, are abysmally ignorant: when we asked them who founded their order, most replied that they did not know, and only a few hazarded a guess that it was St. Basil. Their monasteries contain living quarters, or individual cells, but they are maintained and kept very differently from ours.

The extent of the errors in which all the Muscovites are entangled can be understood from the fact that more than 500 years ago, when Vladimir was Prince of Muscovy, his people received the Christian faith from schismatic heretics. Steeped in these beliefs, and convinced that they are especially favored, the Muscovites can easily credit all the scurrilities about Latins uttered by the Greeks, who are jealous of Rome's glory and piety. They have been inured to this from earliest childhood; they read false Chronicles and have no scholars sufficiently competent to efface such calumnies from their Annals. As a result they possess an abiding horror of Catholics. The most terrible imprecation they can utter is: "May I see you a member of the Latin faith!" Whenever they see one of the simpler folk worshipping the same holy ikon that Catholics venerate they say: "Do not worship it; it is not of our faith."

46

To do his duty, or else to spy on us, the Prince assigned noblemen to see to our needs. They usually ate with us, but they refused to rise when we said Grace and gave thanks to God, or to venerate our images and show them respect, or to perform any kind of similar observances, although, it is true, they did not worship their own ikons either. We had an experience of the way the Prince behaves after he has spoken with foreign envoys. As they are withdrawing he always washes his hands in a silver bowl placed openly on a bench in general view, as though he were performing a rite of expiation. No other action contributes as much to hardening the schismatic view of and the distaste for our form of Christianity held by the Muscovite leaders and other nobles, who are usually present in large numbers. Although I knew that eventually the minds of the Muscovites would inevitably mature sufficiently to understand the nature of true piety, nevertheless I was extremely offended by the Prince's action. I hope the time will soon come when the other Christian rulers will take the Prince to task for this or inform him that they will send no more envoys to him until he desists from this disgusting practice of washing himself. The situation is complicated by the fact that each generation of Muscovites is accustomed from childhood to think and speak so highly of the Prince that its members often answer a question by saying: "Only God and Our Great Lord (*i.e.,* the Prince) know this. Our Great Lord knows everything. He can solve all our problems and difficulties with a single word. There is no religion whose ritual and dogma he does not know. All that we have during our entire life we possess through the Mercy of our Great Lord."

The Prince takes the greatest pains to encourage this view. He wishes to be considered High Priest as well as Emperor, and in the splendor of his attire, his courtiers, and his other appurtenances he rivals the Pope and surpasses other kings. He has borrowed these trappings from the Greek Patriarchs and Emperors and it could be said that he has transferred to his own person the honor that it is proper to pay to God alone. When seated on his throne he wears a tiara stiff with pearls and precious stones, and keeps several others by him, changing them to emphasize his wealth, a practice he claims to have inherited from the Byzantine Emperors. In his left hand he carries a crook or staff with large crystal balls, like knobs, attached to it. He is dressed in long robes, such as the Popes are accustomed to wearing when they solemnly proceed to Mass, and he wears rings set with huge stones on all his fingers. There is an ikon of the Savior to his right, and one of the Virgin Mary above his throne. Both wear white cloaks, and standing as they do on each side of the Prince with wings attached to their shoulders they look

47

like royal bodyguards. The benches in the interior and anterior chambers are packed with men clad in ankle-length gold costumes, which the Prince gives them to wear to receive envoys if they have none of their own, who look like Deacons attending priests to service. They never say a word and hang upon the ruler's every expression and gesture. The Prince's son, dressed in long and very expensive robes, sits to his father's left on a lower throne; he too has a tiara, though a smaller one, which lies on a bench. On sitting down to table both the father and son make numerous Signs of the Cross before beginning to eat and drink. They attend church several times a day and always remain standing during the service except at parts of the homily or a reading from the Life of one of their Saints. They strike their foreheads on the ground in religious zeal, and are careful to observe the fasts; in short, as I have said, they sedulously inculcate an image of piety into the minds of their subjects. The Prince has a personal Confessor who goes everywhere with him when he leaves Moscow. The Prince confesses his sins to him every year, but he can no longer receive the Eucharist because, in accordance with their laws, it is forbidden for anyone who has had more than three wives to have communion with the body of Christ Our Lord.

The Prince's two surviving sons are by his first wife, Anastasiia, who died some time ago. He subsequently took six other virgins as wives (or whatever one wants to call them), and shut a number of them up in nunneries for various reasons (where some are said to be still alive), while his seventh wife, Mariia, the daughter of Fedor Nagoi, with whom the Prince contracted his special kind of marriage last year, still resides with him.[5] His elder son, Ivan, cannot be more than twenty, but he has already had three wives, the first two of whom were thrust into nunneries on the father's order and over the son's objections.[6] Fedor, the Prince's second son by his first wife, is still alive; he is said to be an ingenuous young man, who does not loathe Catholics. He is big for his age and has a beard, which the elder son, Ivan, does not, but he is not allowed to be seen by foreign envoys sent to the Grand Prince. The wife (if she can be called that) of Ivan, the elder son, is called Helen, the daughter of Ivan Sheremetev, a Muscovite nobleman, while Fedor is married to Irene, the daughter of Fedor Godunov.

The Prince formally declares himself to be the residuary legatee of all the land in his country and everything upon it. He assigns goods and estates to whomever he wishes and confiscates them from whomever he desires whenever he pleases. The result of such a policy is that his subjects dare not abandon the Schism and no one receives any salary for fighting in the wars. The Muscovites are so dependent upon the Prince's favor that they hasten to go wherever he sends them; this they do not so much for themselves as for their children, because if the children behave well and their parents render good service the Prince may allow them to inherit all or a part of their estates. This is the way in which the Prince seeks to maintain uniformity in the possessions, persons, minds, and even thoughts of his subjects. Since he tries to find out everything his subjects do, very few of them dare to say anything, and they speak only to curry favor or avoid punishment. His subjects are not allowed to associate with foreigners unless the Prince has been informed and given his personal permission. Traders from other countries frequently visit Muscovy, but Muscovites go to other countries only on official business. They cannot even own ships, for fear that they would use them to escape or to form too close ties with foreigners, which is considered an embarrassment for the Prince. He does not even allow the representatives he occasionally sends to the Christian rulers to talk to the envoys whom these rulers in turn send to him. For example, Istoma Shevrigin was not permitted to talk to us even though on the instructions of Your Beatitude we conducted him through Italy in a most friendly and honorable manner.[7] Perhaps, however, this is less surprising when one realizes that even most important envoys, who are provided with splendid accommodations in Moscow, are assigned to a building surrounded with very high stakes, from which they cannot see other houses, speak to anyone, or even go out to water their horses, as our drivers found out. Not even a doctor can come in to attend a sick person without the Prince's permission, and there are only two doctors in the whole of the Prince's Kingdom, an Italian and a Belgian.

The Muscovites have no colleges or academies. They have only a handful of schools, where boys are taught to read and write from the Gospels, the Acts of the Apostles, their native Chronicles, certain homilies, particularly those of St. John Chrysostom, and the careers and lives of the Saints, including those whom they consider Saints. Anyone who appears trying to aim higher in his studies or to acquire other skills falls under suspicion and runs into difficulties. The Grand Princes seem not so much to be attempting to prevent the growth of heresies that might arise from such a source as to cut short the career of any individuals who might be regarded as more learned or wiser than the Prince himself. This preoccupation with preeminence is one of the reasons why the secretaries (or Scribes, as they call those who serve in the bureaux) and even the Chancellor in charge of them will scarcely ever write or reply to envoys from foreign rulers until the Grand Prince himself has recited a tedious and unnecessary list of his titles and repeated the agenda. The Senators take down his statements on pieces of paper, which they then distribute among themselves, and each takes his turn in reading out from them to the messengers and envoys what the Prince has just finished saying. This once happened to me; they took four whole hours to go through what they could have said in less than an hour. Before any recitation takes place all rise on hearing the Prince's name, and someone announces: "Envoy or Messenger So-and-So, the Great Lord of all Russia orders the following information to be given to you...," but no single individual reads the statement all the way through; he is duly superseded by another, who takes up reading what follows next in the same piece of paper.

There is an extraordinary degree of religiosity (if I may be permitted the term) in the way all rise at a banquet whenever the Prince drinks someone's health or sends someone food from his table. They consider it their chief duty constantly to venerate the Prince in every way and, as it were, to deliver up and consign their very lives as a sacrifice to him. If someone has committed, or is even thought to have committed, a serious crime, no matter how powerful he may be, all that is needed is an order, or even a hint, from the Prince to have him put to death, usually by drowning or beating. It is not regarded a disgrace for those who have received a beating to thank the Prince for it.

In addition to all these substantial difficulties that already stand in the way of negotiating affairs and advancing the cause of religion, when the Prince's envoys go to Vilna or other parts of the Kingdom of Poland, as they often do to treat for peace or arrange a truce, they discover that the country abounds in heretical sects, so much so that the Muscovites will say: "They strongly deny in the evening what they believed that morning." They are quite convinced that all Poles, including King Stefan himself, are Catholics in name only, a notion of which we did our best to disabuse them and their Senators. The German Lutherans, Calvinists, and othere heretics from England, who regularly trade in Muscovy, for some time had two churches there. They told the people, who know absolutely nothing of such matters, that these were Catholic churches, and they boasted of their devotion to the Roman religion. Great is the cunning of Satan, who employed this ruse in his attempt to win influence for these people by having them pretend that they were Catholics and to have Catholics blamed for their quarrelsome and wicked ways, all of which was designed to prevent us from throwing open the door to the faith. However, the mighty judgments and dooms of God in His multiform wisdom cast light upon that which is hidden and eventually turn the darts of malice upon the accursed brood of heretics who seek to discharge them at others. Two years ago the Prince, who may have ascertained the truth of the matter, or perhaps was afraid that his subjects might become intoxicated with this brew and import all kinds of sects into his kingdom, ordered the destruction of the two churches he had allowed. Now the heretics carry on their worship secretly in private rooms.[8] It is essential for us to root out from the minds of the Prince and his Senators the idea that we are the same as Lutherans and other heretics. When we requested a place for priests who were to come from Italy, at first the Prince stated categorically that he would not grant them freedom of assembly. Later, however, he declared that he would permit them to practise their faith in a private home and allow Catholics to be buried with their own rites as the Germans do in the cemetery assigned to them. By negotiating these matters we managed to obtain the Prince's pledge that Catholic priests and traders, as well as Envoys and Messengers from the Apostolic See, may worship freely, so that presumably those who come to Muscovy in the future will no longer be obliged to procure new letters of transit or safe-conducts. Pope Clement VII negotiated these matters with Vasilii, the father of the present Prince, but was unable to bring the issue to a successful conclusion. The Prince promised to grant transit rights and furnish guides through his realm to those whom the Pope may decide to send to Asia whenever he thinks there is need to go there in order to advance the cause of the faith.

Mass and the other Divine Offices are all recited in the Russian or, better, the Muscovite language, which is virtually the same as the one spoken by the Russians who are subject to the Polish King. The Muscovites copy all their books by hand, as they have no printing-presses, with the single exception of the Prince, who has installed one in the town of Aleksandrovskaia Sloboda, 60 miles, or 90 *Versts* (in their language), from Moscow. We shall append to this narrative, as best we can recall at this time, a list of the books the Muscovites usually read and their abler monks study, together with their Calendar, in which one can locate which Saints' Days they celebrate, as well as the days on which they honor other persons, whose sanctity has not yet been recognized by the Latins and the Greeks.[9]

In his *Muscovite Commentary* Giovio stated that writings by the four Doctors of the Latin Church, and of other Fathers, are well known among the Muscovites and have been translated into their language, which he thought was Croatian, but I have been unable to confirm this, although I have made careful inquiry. It is highly unlikely that even the names of those men can have penetrated to that region because, with the exception of St. Ambrose, they are not listed in the Calendar, which records such Roman Popes as Sylvester, Gregory the Great, and others, and the courtiers who attend the Prince do not yet appear to have heard of them. The Muscovites owe the very slight knowledge of the Croatian language they possess to the fact that it displays affinities with Polish, Russian, and other similar languages. I sent a Croatian priest to Moscow and he at once acquired a good knowledge of the Muscovite language, whereas the Muscovites appear to experience considerable difficulty in mastering the Croatian language.

Since the only language the Muscovites know is their own, it is useless to give the Prince the Proceedings of the Council of Florence in Greek, as I did, in the name of Your Beatitude and in the presence of a multitude of his nobles, at the fortress of Staritsa on the river Volga. The Prince has no one in his service who understands that language, with the exception of a few Greeks who, so we are told, came from Byzantium last year at the Prince's request to train a Muscovite interpreter. I think they taught their student the corrupt jargon the Greeks speak nowadays instead of Ancient Greek or the language in which the Early Fathers wrote their books and the Synods were published. This is the reason why we could not use the Act of Union, known as the Bull or Diploma promulgated by Pope Eugene IV, prepared for us from an authentic copy by Most Illustrious Cardinal Santori, even though it was supposed to be in Latin, Greek and Muscovite versions. The Muscovites could not even read, much less understand, the translation of the Diploma because, as the associates I had brought with me from the Russia controlled by the Kingdom of Poland and Austria observed, the translation had been made into a mixture of Bosnian and Croatian. We asked them to attempt a translation of the Diploma and the Profession of the Faith of Pope Pius IV into the contemporary Muscovite idiom, for we believed that once these translations had been scrutinized by experts in the Polish camp, to which I was then hastening, they could quickly be published in Vilna and serve, with God's help, to benefit the peoples of both the Russia under the control of the Polish Kingdom and the Grand Duchy of Muscovy.

The Muscovites possess only a handful of people who know Latin. Besides the physicians I mentioned earlier, there cannot be more than three others, who all are Poles: Jakób Zaberowicz, Jan Buków, and Krzystof Kajew. The first two came many years ago from the Polish town of Września; three years ago the third man was on his way to his Lord, Bogdan Alexander,[10] the Voievoda of Wallachia, who he thought was still alive, when he was captured by the Prince. Although he was reputedly fluent in Latin he was never allowed to meet with us the whole time we were in Muscovy. This lack of assistance made it enormously difficult for us to translate the material the Prince requested from us, and the gist of our discussions with the Senators, prior to official distribution. The Muscovites often translated our words ineptly and inaccurately, and they were particularly anxious to omit any statements they feared might offend the Prince or bring down his wrath on their heads; it was primarily our attempts to negotiate on religion that fell into this category. I also think that they very probably made mistakes in rendering some of the letters from other rulers because they were written in the Russian language current in Lithuania, which contains constructions different from those in use in Muscovy. However, God in His goodness overcame this difficulty. The Muscovites had previously refused to place any trust in our interpreters, but their work finally won general acceptance. They translated everything we said word for word, wrote it down, and gave their versions to the Prince and his Senators, who thus were in a position to make us a fuller response, both orally at our sessions, and in writing. I shall send an example of a Muscovite translation done by our interpreters, together with the Latin original, which can be brought to the attention of any persons who may in the future undertake similar negotiations with this Prince, or with his son.[11]

The ordinary Muscovites scarcely ever stop working, except on the Day of the Annunciation of the Virgin Mary [March 25]. They work on Christmas Day and all other holidays, even Easter, since they are convinced that it is exclusively the nobles' prerogative to go so often to service and to church. The common folk are happy in their simplicity; they make innumerable Signs of the Cross and devoutly worship their holy ikons. They portray their ikons in a most modest manner; although they represent the human form, they detest revealing any portion of the body. They are extraordinarily zealous in observing fasts, when they abstain from meat and milk products, but they rarely go to church. The wives and daughters of the nobility likewise very seldom go to church, except to receive the Eucharist, which they usually do at Easter. There are no preachers; the people merely listen while the *Popy* read from the Lives of the Saints I mentioned, or of those individuals whom they venerate as saints, and selections from certain homilies, particularly those of St. John Chrysostom, as I likewise indicated. They remain standing to pray, but from time to time they strike the ground with their forehead, which is also their custom on occasion when greeting members of the nobility or asking for alms. They baptize infants with three total immersions after placing four lighted candles at the four points on the font and then extinguishing them. The only cures for the sick they know are drinking mulled wine or water into which relics of saints have been dipped, sprinkling holy water, or making vows, which they usually offer to the Virgin Mary and those individuals whom they consider saints. When a sick man recovers his health he dedicates silver ikons just as it used to be done in the days of the Early Church, save that they err in venerating certain individuals as saints. The dying receive the Eucharist in darkness and are given Extreme Unction while they confess their sins to a priest, something they do once a year or oftener when in health. The clergy and laity accompany a funeral procession holding small lighted candles in their hands and do not carry a cross in front of it. A holy ikon is fastened to the chest of the deceased, who is completely swathed in a shroud except for his face. They chant only the *Trisagion*: "Holy, Holy, Holy, God Brave and Immortal." When a body is consigned to its resting place they say: "O Lord, remember the soul of this person," utter some similar words from the Greek Liturgies or St. Dionysius the Areopagite, and kiss the corpse. If it is a nobleman who has died, the Metropolitan and any other Bishop who is in the town accompany the procession to the burial place.

They hold St. Nicholas, Bishop of Myra,[12] in the highest veneration. We saw a statue of him. It was not a painting, but an entire figure, and this ikon, or statue, had been devotedly erected in a place near Novgorod the Great, where monks came to meet us and tendered, in accordance with their custom, holy water and a cross in one patin and bread and salt in the other. They call St. Nicholas *Chudotvorets*, in Greek, *Thaumaturgos* (one who performs miracles), but only those who are too ignorant to understand the truth honor him as highly as Christ Our Lord or consider him the greatest of the saints. They have what they call an "oblique" or "curved" week of six days, known as *Niedziela Wsiereiedna*, which they use to denote the full week of Christmas.[13] They eat meat and rejoice from Christmas Day to Epiphany, the eight days after Easter, certain other days before the Fast which they say is in honor of St. Peter, and the day preceding the Great Quadragesima.

They have no Vigils, as Catholics do. When a Feast Day or the anniversary of some other holiday falls on Easter, they do not transfer it to another day. Twice a year, once on Epiphany and again before the Assumption of the Virgin Mary, the Metropolitan blesses the waters of the river Moscow while other priests bless the waters of other rivers. At this ceremony large numbers of men and women totally immerse themselves three times. They also perform a kind of baptism of their horses and ikons; the ceremony is called *Khreshchenie* in their language, which means baptism. This ritual or custom is not universally mandatory, but many engage in it out of piety. Sick people, who think this ceremony will help them recover their health, have a hole cut in the thick ice, and are lowered through it into the water below; they often perish from the experience. When I was in White Russia, I was told that at Dorogobuzh, in the land known as Red Russia, which is also, like White Russia, under the control of the Polish King, there is a well of salt water, which the priests, with solemn prayers, employ to sprinkle the people after giving them their blessing. The ranks of their priests include *Protopopy*, a kind of Archpriests or Archdeacons, who are objects of higher esteem, as is also the case with us.

The observations we made ourselves and the things we learned from the Muscovites on our journey clearly demonstrate how beneficial it would have been for the worship of God and the cause of the Church if the Muscovites, whose land comprehends both Europe and Asia, had originally received the true Orthodox faith, or at least were to adopt it now. If this had happened the Catholic rulers adjacent to the Muscovites could have ensured among their people (especially in prior times) the same steadfastness in the Catholic faith that the Muscovites display in their Schism. With God's help, when I return from the King of Poland to the Grand Prince of Muscovy I shall describe the further rituals, and the errors followed by the Muscovites, and also include an appropriate refutation of them.

Difficulties Involved in, and Plans and Hopes for Advancing the Catholic Religion in Muscovy.

My remarks up to now have indicated how very difficult it will be to introduce the Catholic faith into Muscovy, and the difficulties will become even more apparent when I briefly touch upon some further considerations that require attention. In the first place most of the people are unaware that a schism exists, for no one has ever shown them how the rituals they practise and the beliefs they hold are foreign to the true faith. The door still remains firmly closed to the Gospel and the preaching of the Truth, but a Catholic priest come among them might also experience some hesitation as to whether he should instil a doubt concerning the schism into the minds of a people who are quite primitive, and even perhaps saved by their very simplicity.

Anyone who ventures to cast aspersions on Muscovite ritual and beliefs is very severely punished. No opportunity at all exists for preaching, the chief means by which God in His wisdom has regularly chosen to propagate the Gospel, and, in addition, as I have already pointed out, most Muscovites do not attend church. Anyone who attempted to preach might well incur real danger, and if he failed to prove effective it could cause even greater difficulties. The Prince and his courtiers, who hold all the power, have been continually exposed to many tales about Roman Catholics told by traders, almost all of whom are heretics. They take the worst possible view of what they are told, because they have never heard of our virtually inexhaustible numbers, our enormous works of piety, our unanimous agreement in matters of faith, and the majestic worship of God that exists among us. The abominable blasphemies uttered by the heretics (a characteristic they possess) lead the Muscovites, when comparing our archpriests and priests with their own bishops and monks, to assume that the latter are holier men, more sincere in their devotion, and more steadfast in their faith. Since the schism retains the shadow of piety and actually a good deal of the substance, in the treacherous times in which we live it naturally lends itself to such deceptions at the hands of heretics. The whole problem is further complicated by the fact that the schism lacks a ministerial head and therefore has no leader from whom it can derive spiritual strength and direction. The schism is scarcely receptive to rational persuasion and seldom retains for long any perceptions which the power of Truth may have constrained it to admit. This situation might make one think that the labor and effort expended upon a people who have much in common with Scythians and Tatars will serve no purpose and tie down men who could more profitably be used elsewhere. In the days of St. Augustine, the Church learned how stubborn and utterly unyielding the Donatists could be, although they were only slightly (if "slightly" is the proper word to describe a major cleavage) sundered from the Vicar of Christ. The Greeks too, from whom the Muscovites derived the schism, have experienced the great goodness, generosity and honesty of the Apostolic See, and on fourteen occasions have publicly professed their union with us, but they still continue to draw back from the consequences of their action. Such behavior shows what one can expect from an inherently bad seed.

By the time the Grand Prince had learned from his envoys who had come to Vilna to treat for peace that I had arrived at the court of the Polish King from Your Beatitude, he had already sent a letter to the King by Krzystof Dzierzek stating that at the Council of Florence the Muscovites had already joined the Catholic Church in the same faith, and he would allow Catholics to practise their religion in Muscovy. There is every reason to believe that he fully intended to do so at the time he wrote the letter. However, he subsequently conquered almost all of Livonia, drove out the Catholics to a man, forcibly introduced the Muscovite form of worship, and following the example set by his grandfather in Novgorod, and his father as well, took vigorous measures to establish it everywhere in the region. When I was engaged in protracted discussions with his Councillors he had various documents and treaties brought out from remote archives in order to buttress his position and oppose the stance taken by the Polish King. He was anxious to have these documents brought to the Pope's attention, as those he had chosen were designed to illustrate the fact that unbroken friendship had existed between his father Vasilii and the Popes, Emperors and other rulers since the days of Popes Leo X and Clement VII, as well as between Your Beatitude and himself. They also alluded to the need for extending the boundaries of his realm and of the schism, the power of his arms, and the preparations he must undertake in order to achieve his goals. It was the sort of performance the Turks used to give in years past, when they employed the skills of unscrupulous persons to solicit or profess friendship with Christians while they drove on into the heart of Europe.

The Prince seeks no Royal or Imperial titles from any source: he appropriates them to himself. He has managed to persuade certain prominent rulers to address him as Brother of the Emperor, and Tsar (*i.e.,* King, or Emperor) of Kazan' and Astrakhan' in their letters. He was annoyed at not having been given these titles in the letter from Your Beatitude and displeased that the only salutation your letter contained was a list of some of the territories he possesses. Perhaps Your Beatitude will consider this matter carefully in the event that the hope of winning this Prince and the huge realm he controls to the better cause ever leads to further efforts and does not wear out all our pens! He should not be addressed as "Lord of All Russia," only "of Russia," nor as "Heir of Livonia" or anything like that, as the use of such titles might well prejudice the claims of another.

57

A palpably ridiculous circumstance, but one which would nevertheless make it extremely difficult to detach the Muscovites from the schism, is their triumphant conviction that the bodies of certain Schismatics are preserved intact and frequently perform miracles; they steadfastly assert that these relics restore sight to the blind and cure the sick. In view of their belief it is obviously very risky for anyone to deprecate the sanctity of these corpses or to inquire in a sceptical way whether these people really were saints and martyrs. They include Boris and Gleb,[14] the Metropolitans Peter and Aleksei,[15] whose bodies are supposed to be preserved in Moscow, and a certain monk, Sergei,[16] who died nineteen years ago and is preserved in the Holy Trinity Monastery, 40 miles from the capital. It is claimed that there are some 200 monks in this monastery, which is quite wealthy and the leading one in all Muscovy. As we were setting out for Pskov on September 15, the Prince left the fortress of Staritsa three days later and travelled to his palace in Aleksandrovskaia Sloboda in order to celebrate Sergei's anniversary.

We must be fully aware that the Muscovites would intensely resist abandoning their Mass, exchanging it for the Latin Mass, or allowing us to use the Greek Mass. A temporary concession might be made to them in this, but careful attention would have to be paid to ensure that the translations that have been made from God's Old Testament and the Gospels are correct; this is something that has apparently never been done, even by the Greeks. It is not easy to do, for up to now I have not come across anyone who knows the Muscovite language, understands how to accomodate its idiosyncrasies to the Latin or Greek texts, and at the same time possesses a thorough grounding in theology.[17] I have heard that a few bishops among the Russians subject to the Polish King have occasionally celebrated the Mass in Greek. However, scarcely any of them understand the language, and thus we could not expect much from these bishops in the event of their joining the Catholic church, for even if they knew both languages they are entirely ignorant of theology. Your Beatitude will have to decide whether to entrust so vital an undertaking to a small handful of people like these.

Sources of Hope.

The one thing that allows us to hope for the better is He to Whom nothing is impossible, and Who always bestows so much on those genuinely seeking the Kingdom of God. In just a few years in this century alone He has cast down idols in the far distant Indies, the East, the West and the South, raised the Cross Triumphant everywhere, and caused the most diverse peoples to say the Mass in Latin. One quarter of the world remains, however, located to the north and east, where the Gospel must be truly proclaimed, in which God in His Wisdom has shown that a mighty haven for the true Orthodox faith can be built, if the task is undertaken (if I may say so) by high-principled and dedicated men, who utilize the techniques which have brought so many other realms beneath the yoke of Christ. It is God Who decided to open the way into Muscovy now, at a time when Your Beatitude holds the Keys of the Church, and workers are assembled to establish institutions to cultivate the vines. God's Inspiration willed that after the Council of Trent all should see that our Seminaries constitute a unique device for propagating the Gospel, and King Stefan of Poland has opened the door to Muscovy for Catholics with his armies. Out of esteem for Your Beatitude he allowed me to go to Muscovy in safety while a war was raging, which no one has ever been allowed to do before even in peacetime, because he wisely discerned that my journey would not prove deleterious either to his interests or to the Polish Republic.

We should also note that the Grand Prince himself received us in a splendid manner. He provided us with everything we needed, and even amid the distractions of war, gave us to understand that he might well be more conciliatory in the other matters of concern to us than the reports of his temperament had led us to believe. It is virtually inconceivable that the humblest of mortals, such as I, could at any other time have had the opportunity of conversing freely with the Prince or of so soon learning so much about all the inner workings of his court, unless the Divine Providence had decided that the time had come to undertake this mission and would, in effect, preside over the negotiations. For example, I found a splendid opportunity to suggest to the Prince that he should reflect whether God might have justly placed the immense burdens of the present war upon his shoulders because he had failed to reply to the Vicar of Christ on the question of religion and had procrastinated and dissimulated instead. He was plainly very upset by my remarks, but then he adopted a more reasonable frame of mind and, because I pressed for an answer, stated that he would not fail to give me one concerning this question on my return. The Prince is also reputed to have made other statements from which we might infer that he will grant us permission to worship and, once peace is attained, even to build a church, but time alone will tell whether he meant it or merely said so because the pressures of the war still made him need the Pope's good offices. Even if our sole accomplishment were the concessions the Prince granted to Catholic traders and priests, the initiation of peace negotiations with the kings of Poland and Sweden, and God's

59

indication that He wishes the Christian rulers (if they are genuinely concerned with the public good rather than personal advantage) to become more closely united, such developments should not by any means be considered contemptible, especially by those who know that whole buildings are not built in a day, and that in advancing the faith God is disposed to manifest His power only to the shepherds of His flock who have labored long and diligently. Now that we have embarked upon these tasks, no opportunity must be overlooked to treat of religion or to enter into religious discussions with the Prince's Councillors and Courtiers. We can reach some of them through preaching, or simply by setting them a good example, and we should strive to train others. In addition, we must learn the Muscovite language, and compose and publish pamphlets in the Muscovite vernacular, written in Muscovite characters. If the Prince restores Livonia, Polotsk and Dorpat may be in our hands, where we would have safe places in which to train Muscovites for our work. Such planning invariably facilitates smooth and effective management of the affairs of God.

We must again refer to the schism and the temperament of the Greeks, because the Russians, or Muscovites, closely imitate the example set by them. The Greeks would not have so often returned to the vomit (if my coarseness may be excused) if pamphlets concerning the Council of Florence had been repeatedly distributed, immediately after the Council ended, to inform the peoples in the common language of the East about its decisions, and if schools had immediately been set up to teach the truth as soon as the participants in the Council returned to Greece. Had this been done, Mark of Ephesus alone could not have overturned God's firm establishment. If the same methods had also been employed at the time to convert the Muscovites as well, the Church would now have a fertile field in which to reap the harvest. This is no consolation however, if I may say so, because none of these steps was taken.

After Pope Eugene IV had shown the way, Innocent III, Gregory X, Alexander VI, Leo X and Clement VII should have seriously put their hand to the task; they should not have been satisfied merely to convoke synods or send one man on a mission with a letter. They ought to have employed all the means that have always been available to the Legates and Apostles of Christ, and to have seen to it that the part of Russia belonging to the Kingdom of Poland was saturated with the Catholic faith. This could easily have been achieved, for the Polish Kings would have conferred Privileges on Greek bishops only on condition that they accept the Council of Florence. Had this been done, we would have constructed a most powerful engine which could (in military parlance) advance and take the Muscovite schism. However, the approach involving this part of Russia, although it is nearer and is already one of our Provinces, was overlooked; instead it was decided to put the cart before the horse and attempt to initiate activity in Muscovy itself, where the outcome is more uncertain. God, Who arranges everything in its proper order, and Who spent three years instructing the Apostles and Disciples before He carried out the conversion of the world, has rightly refused to permit us to advance either undertaking, to say nothing of a successful outcome, because the example which Christ gave to us has not been fully followed.

The fact that the Muscovites have much in common with Scythians and Tatars should in no way diminish the enthusiasm of Christ's devoted toilers for the undertaking; the Lord has need of the Muscovites, whom He has created in His Own likeness and image, and He wishes them to be saved. The Apostolic See is charged with the task of teaching all peoples, just as the Apostles were. God wonderfully assists the Holy See to fulfill its Apostolic duty by sending workers, who labor, not for themselves or mere mortal concerns, but for the sake of Christ, to snatch souls from the pit of error. To return to the Muscovites, certain qualities still possessed by that people may be compared with the attributes which the Catholic Church has valued since earliest times, such as simplicity, abstinence, obedience, and ignorance or avoidance of blasphemy, and this circumstance affords real hope that someday the Muscovites may become zealous champions of true piety and the Catholic religion. A merit of the Heavenly Grace is that sooner or later it will temper the savage habits of debased natures: Christ came to heal the sick, not the well.

Anyone who thinks that if he were sent to Muscovy his efforts and energies would be expended in vain and that he would be laboring among people who would not appreciate his skills should reflect on the achievements of Andrew of Oviedo[18] of our Order over the past 30 years. A man of outstanding capacity, he was sent to Ethiopia with some of his associates, and although he did not accomplish as complete a conversion of the ruler of that country as he had hoped, with his labors he sowed seeds which God, Who is all truth, will someday bring to fruition. Even if he had accomplished nothing at all, his experiences were valuable and the example of his endurance has blazed a trail for others to follow. If poverty had not prevented him from devising ways to send students from Ethiopia to Rome he would soon have reaped a rich harvest. Perhaps in your generosity Your Beatitude will water the seeds which this devoted man culled from schism; Abyssinian merchants and pilgrims come every year from Ethiopia to Jerusalem.

It is highly important to obtain from God the living stone on which Scythians, Tatars and the people of the remotest East, who have strayed from the Lord, may be builded up [cf. I Peter 2:4]. It is burdensome for students to complete the philosophical and then the theological curricula and to study languages they will probably never use. They would never regret spending two years in mastering more useful languages, which would allow them to read the writings and come to know the minds of living men. Our objective cannot be achieved among the Muscovites until the knowledge derived from our teaching, the example of our unsullied lives, and the use of the Holy Sacraments have nullified the malicious charges made by heretics and eradicated the inveterate hostility that exists towards Catholics. These measure can succeed only if they are supplemented by the devoted service of men, the sole aim of whose calling is the salvation of souls, who are familiar with the example of Francis Xavier, S.J.,[19] of blessed memory. He voluntarily became the slave of an Indian, as this was the only way by which a foreigner could reach Japan and China in order to bring the Light of the Gospel there, just as the Apostle Paul was a prisoner in Rome when he preached the Gospel, and the Popes of those early centuries were captives or in hiding, when they brought the Word both to Rome and to the whole world.

We can discern the marvelous working of the Divine Providence in that the Grand Prince of Muscovy chose this particular moment to seek the friendship of the Pope and the other Christian rulers, even though he did so for his own benefit and to advance the Schism. God's wisdom transcends the cunning of men and has permitted this temporary triumph of the flesh over the spirit in order to encompass the ultimate victory of the latter.

I hope that someday the Church will say: "Great is the Mercy of the Lord, Who by His Spirit, unique and multiplex, is able of these stones to raise up children unto Abraham" [cf. Matt. 3:9, and Luke 3:8]. We should win no advantage if our motives for propagating the Catholic faith were the same as those animating the Grand Prince in advancing the schism, because we should be ignoring the behests of God, Who would arise to condemn us, especially as this undertaking makes the breast of a true Christian swell, and constitutes a sacrifice for a sweetsmelling savor most pleasing to God [cf. Ephesians 5:2].

A Plan to Promote the Catholic Religion in Muscovy.

Clearly one essential task is to establish a Seminary, as this action will prove to the world the paternal solicitude Your Beatitude feels for the Muscovites. We must also furnish the workers to erect this most holy edifice, because God never brings such labors to fulfilment without them. To build the Seminary in Rome would bring glory to the Apostolic See and enhance its reputation among all peoples, especially the Muscovites, and it would doubtless help them as much as the operation of their College has benefited the Greeks. On the other hand one has to take into consideration the long and expensive journey, and the arrogance which men from these northern countries invariably acquire as the result of their experiences in Rome, since they assume that what is freely given to them out of love belongs to them by right. However, a select number of them might be placed on a kind of probation, like the poor, and be exposed for a period of time to serious learning at home, and after that a few of those could be sent to Rome. This plan is sounder, because it would not be worth the effort and expense to send people who had to master Italian before they could start learning their Latin and Greek. This is a most time-consuming procedure, as we found out in the case of the young Muscovite whom I brought to Your Beatitude with some Russians three years ago on my return to Rome from Sweden.

Your Beatitude has permitted our Order to establish a College and a Chapter in Vilna, the metropolitan city of Lithuania, and it contains a substantial number of novices. The College attracts some Russians, but if they are poor (as most of them are) they follow a course of study designed to equip them to make a living, and if they have means, their studies are directed to fields other than theology and missionary work. Furthermore, the Grand Prince has never yet allowed any Muscovite to go abroad to study, and he would unquestionably be even less inclined to permit it if he thought that his people were going to study among the Lithuanians, with whom he is usually at war, or at least on bad terms. If I were asked where it would be easiest to locate the Seminary, taking into consideration the interests of both branches of the Russian-speaking people I would say that it should be in Vilna, or, failing that, in Polotsk, in order to serve the Russians in the Kingdom of Poland and those who have been prisoners in Muscovy as a result of this three-year war. Those who come out from Muscovy could be sent to the Pontifical Seminaries in Olomouc or Prague, where they could more easily learn the necessary doctrine because the Czech language has some affinity with the Muscovite. Once this system became operational it would seem highly desirable to charge a trustworthy and discreet worker with the task of occasionally visiting these Muscovite students, as well as those from other Northern countries, such as the Swedes, Danes, etc., and arrange for them to transmit as best they can epistles and books to their peoples. When the students have received sufficient instruction they should be sent forth to various regions, like into the vineyards [Cf. Matt. 20:1], and from all the Northern and Eastern countries secure others to take their places. These tasks can easily be accomplished provided that the rulers, kings and bishops continue to supply premises and food, but if they should fail in their duty, it would be difficult for the Seminaries to become self-supporting. Their Rectors have enough to do with seeing that the rules are obeyed and the program of studies is carried out, because at the outset of their careers students are not usually filled with zeal for the conversion of souls and are singularly lacking in the discipline required for the achievement of this goal.

The negotiations I began in Your Beatitude's name with the Most Serene Republic of Venice are assuming increasing urgency. It is essential that we dispatch a few upstanding merchants, even if they have no official standing, in order to take advantage of the opportunity the Prince has just afforded for Catholic priests to enter Muscovy. To promote the greater glory of God, we should realize that in addition to the dispatch of capable and discerning men, it will prove important, and thus is certainly worth the effort, to attempt a definition of the place of the Prince of Muscovy among the Christian rulers. Negotiations can be carried on with the present Prince, or with his more gentle son, or, perhaps, even with his future Catholic successor. To this end I have insisted that the Prince answer the friendly communications he has received from these rulers, and shall include his replies with the letter I send them in Your Beatitude's name along with the safe-conduct guaranteeing our people entrance and exit privileges for Muscovy, as soon as I reach the Polish camp.

Those who are to organize the commercial aspect of affairs must understand that the long journey and the purchase and sale of goods will require a substantial financial outlay, but if they come and inspect the merchandise available in Muscovy and buy skins, wax, honey, hides and other similar items, they will make large profits. It will not prove expensive to take the overland route through Poland, and an Enabling Document, which can easily be obtained from the Polish King once peace has been made between the two rulers, will ensure a safe and comfortable transit. Silks and other Eastern clothing accessories presently brought to or manufactured in Venice could be shipped to Muscovy; a single vehicle can carry a great deal of merchandise through Poland direct to Muscovy without payment of the heavy taxes that are exacted in Italy. If the Republic should hesitate to embark on this project for any reason, then, like a father speaking to devoted sons, Your Beatitude might perhaps consider it desirable to inform the Venetians and their Representative concerning the nature of my negotiations with the Prince. In this way the glorious Republic will more clearly understand that the effort it must make for the Cause will actually redound to its own advantage, and once it realizes this, the Republic will be bound to act. In view of my splendid reception in Venice I felt certain that on my return I might possibly persuade the Venetians to start this trade and perhaps do something else as well, but my need to return to negotiate the other issues I had raised with the Prince rendered it impossible. If it is pleasing to God's Will, I hope that men whom the Holy See considers more skilful instruments of the Lord will very soon have a better opportunity to bring this task to accomplishment.

For the moment I entreat Your Beatitude to search carefully in Rome and elsewhere for some wise and devout merchants, and two priests, who can embark on this journey immediately. I have obtained a second Enabling Letter from the Grand Prince in which, out of regard for Your Beatitude, he agrees to allow whomever you choose to travel in safety to Muscovy and to remain there. Since the Prince has granted this concession to Your Beatitude, it seems only fair that he should receive a comparable letter in return, granting Muscovite envoys and others free passage to Italy. To show your great paternal love I urge Your Beatitude to request such a letter to be written, and have it ready for consignment to the man I shall send from the Polish King's camp, who will in turn deliver it to me. The Muscovites are greatly impressed by outward show; such a letter will afford us a splendid opportunity for a return visit, to discuss goals that God Himself ardently desires – above all, the salvation of the Muscovites.

In religious matters Muscovy has been accustomed to defer to some extent to the Russia under the control of the Polish King. Not long ago Muscovite bishops used to be confirmed by the Metropolitan of the Russian rite residing in Kiev, which is located in the King's Russia; thus, to convert Muscovy it would help enormously if the bishops, or *Vladiki,* in the King's Russia were joined to the Catholic church. There is reason to believe that we might advance the cause if Your Beatitude were to write friendly Epistles to these *Vladiki*, eight in number, whose names are obtainable from the Metropolitan of Vilna. These Epistles should not be sent in the name of a particular individual but rather delivered by a Churchman; this device will allow the person best qualified for the task to undertake negotiations with them. Your Beatitude could invite these bishops to recognize the Truth, and tell them of all the benefits the Apostolic See and the Father and Shepherd of the Church Universal could confer upon them if they were his sons. One of two things would happen: either the bishops, after reading your exposition and the religious books I shall arrange to have published in Vilna in the Russian language, would come to a better understanding of the whole issue, or the pastoral care displayed by Your Beatitude would win approval in the sight of God and thus lead the Russian Magnates, some of whom have already been converted to the Catholic faith, to welcome with open arms the true religion represented by the Holy See. As we passed through the King's Russia on our way to Muscovy, certain noblemen, who had abandoned their schismatic beliefs, told us in all sincerity that the conversion of the Muscovites would be assured if the common people only had a chance to hear what they (the nobles) had learned from us. The Schism is fostered by its leaders, such as the Ostrogski and Słucki[20] families, who maintain schools and printing-presses. The city of Lwów contains, besides the Catholic archbishop and the Russian *Vladiki*, an Armenian bishop and his congregation. If they, with God's help, should by any chance adopt the Catholic faith it would spread as far as Armenia!

To recapitulate, when in Muscovy members of our Order and other priests should observe the fasts, of which the Muscovites have many, and should also abstain from some foods or fast entirely on those days which the Muscovites celebrate in honor of the men whom they regard as saints, even though these saints are Schismatics, as I have already pointed out. Out of the affection you bear for your children and workers Your Beatitude will soon be pleased to determine and rule what reply should be given to the following questions: what obeisances should be made before the Muscovite ikons, worthy of worship though they are, in view of the fact that the Muscovites refuse to venerate our images; what deference an Envoy from the Holy See should show to the Metropolitan and the *Vladiki*, and what should be done about the common people, in awareness of the danger that ultimately they might conceivably be damned if they acquired any doubts concerning the Schism.

CHAPTER III

The First Public Discussion on the Catholic Religion Between Antonio Possevino S.J., and Ivan Vasil'evich, the Grand Prince of Muscovy, Held in the Latter's Palace in the Presence of his Senators and 100 Other Nobles, on February 21, 1582.[1]

When on one occasion the Senators of the Grand Prince replied to me concerning the various issues I had raised with them three days earlier, they stated that the Prince was not in the habit of negotiating privately on important subjects, such as religion. Acting on the Pope's instructions I had myself placed this topic before the Prince at Staritsa the preceding summer, and I raised it again when I came to Moscow. They stated that the Prince was concerned for fear that a discussion of religion might cause friction between myself and him which could adversely affect the peace just concluded with King Stefan or give offense to me. I replied that the last thing I desired was to engage in strife with so mighty a Prince; I merely wished to put forward a proposal designed exclusively to achieve closer relations between the Grand Prince and the other Christian rulers. I had never intended to exclude the Senators from the discussion if the Prince had decided their presence was desirable. My remarks were related to the Prince, who invited me to a place where he and his Senators, and 100 other nobles and prominent courtiers, were assembled.

The Prince arose and repeated the very same words the Senators had uttered to me a little earlier. Then he said: "You see that I am now fifty years old and have not much longer to live. I have been brought up in the true Christian religion, and I cannot change. The Day of Judgment is approaching, when God will decide whether our faith or the Latin faith is the repository of truth. I am fully aware that Pope Gregory XIII sent you to champion the cause of the Roman faith, and you may say what you wish."

I said: "Your Most Serene Highness, of all the great kindnesses you have shown me, the greatest is that you are allowing me to speak to you today on this most vital question. I want you to know that under no circumstances is the Pope asking you to make changes in the most ancient Greek religion as taught by the Fathers and in the lawful Synods. He is simply urging you to acknowledge its pristine form, embrace it fully, and preserve it intact in your kingdom. If you do so there will no longer be an Eastern and a Western Church; we shall all be as one in Christ, and we of the West shall no longer shun your churches, your rites, and your priests, who will then canonically assist at the Divine Mysteries of the true faith.

"Please do not feel surprise at His Holiness' present proposal to you; he is spurred on by Christ, Who has entrusted him with the care of the Christian Church. His Holiness is highly attracted by the suggestion contained in your letter that he arrange for a treaty among the Christian rulers. He is also impressed with the letter you wrote to King Stefan, in which you said that the Emperor of Constantinople and the whole of the East acknowledged the unity of the faith at the Council of Florence, at which Isidor, the Metropolitan of Muscovy,[2] was present, as you yourself pointed out. You added that Catholics and people of the Roman faith generally would be free to live and practise their religion in Muscovy. Since you wrote as you did under no compulsion, the Pope cannot be blamed for assuming that so mighty a Prince as yourself sincerely meant what he wrote, and that you have been moved to bear witness to the truth by Him, Whose hands hold the hearts of kings and without Whose approval not even a leaf moves on the tree.

"The Faith constitutes the strongest bulwark and the firmest bond Christian rulers can build and forge to resist the onslaughts of the Perfidious Ones and the pagans, but they must all be at one within it, and this principle must underlie any treaty, for otherwise the remaining edifice cannot be erected on a sure foundation or else will soon collapse due to its initial inadequacy. That is why it is essential to undertake preliminary negotiations for the treaty. I would ask you to reflect on the following proposition: at the Council of Florence it was generally agreed that all Christian rulers, including the Eastern ones, had at one time possessed a perfect Christian faith; thus, if your faith now differs from theirs, it inevitably follows that such a discrepancy proves the existence of the most sinister kind of error in either your or their form of the faith. But since, as you yourself noted, so distinguished a ruler as Emperor John VIII Paleologus and others, including (to repeat) your own Metropolitan and the rest of the Eastern delegates, came to the sober conclusion that the Roman Church is the sole repository of the true faith which all Greece and Asia preserved intact in ancient times, you have no choice but to follow the same road as they. If you think that the decisions taken at the Council of Florence do not pertain to you, you should summon Greek interpreters and obtain direct from Byzantium the books of the Greek Fathers, composed in the authors' own hand if you do not trust our Greek editions, and I shall accept your assurance that you are citing from the same works by the same authors. I should be most happy to provide you with the chief citations from the Fathers found in the Greek edition of the Proceedings of the Council of Florence, which the Pope sent with me as a gift to you, if you wish me to do so. Heaven will rejoice; you will have every reason to expect that your titles and distinctions will enjoy greater prestige than they have heretofore, and you will soon be called the Emperor of the East, if you advance the cause of the Orthodox Catholic faith there, a task in which you will receive strong support from the Christian rulers, who will help you in a variety of ways."

To these observations the Prince replied: "I did not refer to the faith in the letter I sent to the Pope and I am not anxious to discuss it now, for fear that I might touch upon matters that could give offense to you, Antonio, and because my duty is to attend to temporal affairs, for which I have received the blessing of my Metropolitan, not spiritual ones. I do not believe in the Greeks; I believe in Christ. As for any Empire of the East, it is for the Lord of His Own volition to assign realms to whomever He chooses. I said nothing at all about the Council of Florence or Isidor, the Metropolitan of Muscovy, and I never implied that religious unity was mandatory before all the Christian rulers could proceed against the enemies of Christ's name. I again promise that I shall honor the pledge my Senators made to you today; namely, that Catholic priests may freely accompany traders and envoys entering Muscovy, and that they may stay here and administer the Sacraments to Catholics, but I refuse to allow you to hold public meetings or build churches open to Muscovites. I have confirmed this pledge with my Great Seal and shall have it conveyed to you before you leave."

I had earlier sought in vain to obtain this charter at Staritsa. I asked the Prince: "Would you be good enough to express your general views on the possibility of negotiating the whole question of religion? Nothing you say will offend me. I think your statement that you do not believe in the Greeks but believe in Christ is excellent. I shall be glad to cite testimony from the Greek Fathers and bring the weight of their authority to prove to you that the Roman Popes have always taught the most true and the most Orthodox faith, through which we believe in Christ and by which we set our course."

The Prince replied: "We received our Christian faith from the early Church at the time when Andrew, the brother of the Apostle Peter, visited these lands on his way to Rome.[3] Vladimir was converted to the faith, and Christianity spread far and wide among us. We received the Christian faith here in Muscovy at the same time you received it in Italy, and we have preserved it intact, whereas within the Roman Faith there are seventy faiths. You yourself are witness, Antonio, for you told me about this at Staritsa."

69

I grasped the purport of the Prince's words, for at appropriate junctures I had on more than one occasion pointed out, to the Senators and others, that the Christian faith had existed in Italy for some 1200 years before the Muscovites had heard the name of Christ. To avoid giving the impression I knew the Prince was not speaking the truth I made a few remarks about St. Andrew, and then said: "The abiding and unchanging faith that has always existed in Rome is the one which Peter and Paul originally preached and the one for the sake of which the Popes who succeeded Peter shed their blood for 300 years. Later Popes, although they have lived in more peaceful times, have preserved the vessel of faith undamaged and intact in the face of many a storm. Rome has no seventy faiths, as you allege, but only one, and Rome has hurled anathema against the seventy and even more heresies spawned by Luther. You suffer these heresies to persist in the small part of Livonia remaining to you, as I wrote to you at Staritsa, but the Church pursues them with unrelenting mien, just as it always did the heresies of Africa and the East."

"Antonio," said the Prince, "I like your statement that the Popes shed blood for the Christian faith. For the Savior has said: 'And fear not them which kill the body, but are not able to kill the soul' " [Matt. 10:28].

I replied: "Our devotion to God has brought us to Muscovy. Out to the Indies and all over the world the Pope has sent other men who, in the name of Christ, are ready to endure anything in order to make the truth of Him known and to plant the Cross Triumphant as far and as widely as possible."

Ignoring these remarks the Prince said: "It is written: 'Go ye therefore, and teach all nations, baptizing them in the name of the Father, and of the Son, and of the Holy Ghost' [Matt. 18:19]. When all the Apostles did this, no man was greater than any other man, and they produced Bishops, Archbishops, Metropolitans and many others. It is from these men that the religious leaders of our country are descended."

I said: "You have cited the Word of God from Scripture, which we too unquestioningly believe. At the same time we also believe that Christ, Who sent all the Apostles forth into the world, as the need to promulgate the faith everywhere required, gave all of them equal authority, but different degrees of power. As He never did with the rest of the Apostles, to Peter alone he entrusted the Keys of the Kingdom of Heaven, the strengthening of the brethren, and the care and feeding of the sheep. If we grant that the bishops who are descended from the other Apostles retain their authority, we must also agree that the See of Peter retains much greater authority. The Gates of Hell shall not prevail against it [Matt. 16:18], and it will last to the consummation of the ages, as God, Who is all truth and cannot lie, has borne the irrevocable witness of His promise. This cannot be said of the other Apostolic Sees, for in many of their dioceses the succession and the faith have either altered or perished."

The Prince answered: "We acknowledge Peter as a Saint, as well as a number of the Popes, such as Clement, Sylvester, Agatho, Vigilius, Leo, Gregory[4] and others, but the Popes who followed them were also in a sense the Successors of Peter. They led evil lives: can they enjoy like authority on Peter's throne?"

"A man as wise as you are, Prince," I said, "will readily understand, if you are willing to recognize the truth, that all the Popes down to the present time have administered the Church with the same authority as Peter administered it, and have invariably followed the writings, decretals, and teachings of those Popes of early times of whom you approve, as well as, and above all, the exposition of Scripture. I shall not spend much time on the question of whether they led upright or wicked lives. The power of the Sacraments and the administration of the Church conferred upon the Popes do not depend upon the lives they lead, but upon the inflexible precept of Christ. People who are denied communion with the body of Christ have a way of talking too boldy and publicly about things they have never seen, and they do not understand what they are affirming or denying.

71

They are not always right, and they act thus to prevent the rest of the world from scrutinizing their own lives more closely. Most Serene Prince, I ask you of your magnanimity to answer me. Are you, who have succeeeded Vladimir 500 years later, the legitimate heir of his empire, and his successor?"

When the Prince nodded his assent, I continued, "if anyone tried to impugn your authority, or that of your ancestors, or erred through human weakness, would not everyone think such a person should deservedly be reproved, to say nothing of punished?"

The Prince was more aroused by this question than he had been by anything that had gone before, because certain Englishmen, most abandoned heretics, and a Dutch doctor, an Anabaptist, had recently been inveighing against the Pope to the Prince. Half rising from his seat the Prince declared: "I would have you know that the Roman Pope is no shepherd." I was highly offended at this insult, all the more so because such a remark, uttered in the presence of so large an assembly of nobles, effectively slammed the door on any serious discussion of the faith. I told my young interpreter, who, though in most respects a loyal Catholic, was hesitating because he feared for his life, to ask: "Then why did you send to the Pope concerning your problems? You and your predecessors have always called him Shepherd of the Church."

The Prince flew into a rage and stood right up from his throne. Everyone was sure that he would strike and kill me, as he had others, including even his own son, with the iron-tipped staff he carries the way the Pope does his pastoral rod. "There are peasants outside," he cried, "who would show you what it means to talk to me like a peasant!"

I heard these words impassively and then said: "Most Serene Prince, I know that I am speaking with a wise and good ruler. As far as I am concerned, you know the loyalty and devotion that I displayed at the peace negotiations, and the Pope himself has a great paternal love for you. I hope you will not be angry at any statements I make, because they are the words of Christ that I am uttering, and you yourself gave me permission to speak freely of those things." In this way I managed to sooth the Prince, to the amazement of the Senators and the rest of the nobles.

When the Prince had once more resumed his seat, his speech was more moderate, but he kept on asking the same four questions, which these heretics had been drumming into

72

him. The essence of them was: "Why is the Pope carried in a chair?" "Why does he wear a cross on his feet?" "Why does he shave his beard?" "Why does he pretend to be God?" In the ensuing confusion it was some time before I was able to reply. All were on their feet, for these extraneous issues and false calumnies, combined with their natural fear of the Prince's power, had roused the nobles to such a pitch that a few were openly saying I should be drowned on the spot. Finally I was able to say: "Sometimes carrying the Pope in a chair has nothing to do with pride; it is to enable him to bless the people, not in his own name, but in the name of the Holy Trinity, when the crowds are very dense, as on the important holy days. The Pope often goes about with others in a most humble way, and in his devotion frequently visits holy places on foot. As for the cross on his feet, you, Prince, are surely aware that in ancient times people threw themselves at the feet of the Apostles. The same thing happens over and over again to the Successors of St. Peter. To make sure no one thinks that this obeisance is made merely to them, the Popes have placed crosses on their feet. By kissing these crosses the faithful acknowledge and worship the mystery of the Cross of Christ, and in this way the Popes demonstrate that all the wealth and power they have comes from the merits and passion of Christ."

The Prince said: "It is a disgrace to wear a cross on one's feet. Our people consider it base if a cross hangs below the breast towards the stomach. I have seen some of your companions, Antonio; they let their crosses hang down from their necks to a little below their chests."

I replied: "Christ was crucified in His whole body, and thus it is our whole bodies which must be nailed to the Cross together with Christ. We commit no sin if we wear a cross on any part of our body as a token of our piety, and the question of whether we are truly pious is decided by God in His wisdom on the basis of our sincerity and the purity of our conscience, not on who or what we are in this world. As for kissing feet, the Pope washes and kisses the feet of poor people. Surely there is no one who can think, when he kisses the Pope's feet, that he is honoring God. Other members of the Church of God, but above all the Prophet Isaiah, 700 years before the founding of Christ's church, predicted the inevitable coming of this observance. Here is what the Prophet said: 'Thus saith the Lord GOD, Behold I will lift up mine hand to the Gentiles, and set up my standard to the people: and they shall bring thy sons in *their* arms, and thy daughters

73

shall be carried upon *their* shoulders. And kings shall be thy nursing fathers, and their queens thy nursing mothers: they shall bow down to thee with *their* face toward the earth, and lick up the dust of thy feet' [Isaiah, 49:22-23]. O Prince, the Lord God took the honor away from the Gentile kings and bestowed it upon His servants, and He adorned them with the Light, the Rock, the Fundaments, and the titles appertaining to Himself. How could He fail to fulfill His promise? Would the people not kiss, would they not lick the feet of those whom, as Scripture says, Christ placed in charge of His Church for all time, to confound the Devil? Your people prostrate themselves before your bishops, who have not been confirmed, and reverently sprinkle their eyes and their faces with dirty water, in which these bishops wash themselves in church. You are sufficiently intelligent to know that any honor shown to your legates, viceroys, or governors by the people or even by your great lords is in reality being paid to you. You have received your power from God. Will he whom God has instructed to confer honor on you and your people take away that honor in the name of God?"

The Prince said: "As a Christian Prince, we always go forth with all our courtiers to greet our Metropolitan and kiss his hand, when he comes to us, but we do not pretend that he is God."

I replied: "It is your intention to honor God, not your subject, when you acknowledge the latter's spiritual authority. Far greater honor ought to be paid to the man to whom God entrusted the administration of the Church Universal than to any Metropolitan, even one canonically elected and lawfully confirmed. The Pope does not pretend to be God; he omits many titles he has the right to assume, and calls himself the Servant of the Servants of God. His influence extends to all the nations of the world, as your courier Shevrigin saw, and he constantly sends workers everywhere to preach the name of God and of Christ, His Son. This none of the Patriarchs of the East has ever done or could ever do.

"The Pope most certainly does not shave; in fact he possesses a full and ample beard, but even if he did shave, he would be doing no wrong; Saints and early Popes, as can be seen from their portraits preserved to this day on old coins, were allowed to shave, for just and pious reasons, to accomodate to changing styles. Another example is the Apostolic Constitutions drawn up by St. Clement.[5] They forbid lay persons to shave off

74

their beards, but this is designed to emphasize a husband's supremacy over his wife and prevent people from imitating the Turks, who shave in order to arouse impure and lustful desires. On the other hand, priests are permitted to do so in order to avoid any appearance of ostentation when they reverently celebrate the   mysteries of the Body and Blood of Christ."

To eliminate any surviving traces of animosity in the heart of the Prince, after making these remarks I indicated that I wished to kiss his hand. Graciously extending it, the Prince said: "I offer you my hand and embrace you." He stood up, and to the great astonishment of all present clasped me twice in full embrace. On withdrawing he observed that he had been unwilling to discuss religion because he was afraid that some unpleasantness might arise, and dismissed me in a friendly manner. At lunchtime he sent three noblemen to us with food and drink, and an hour later sent another courtier with an assortment of drinks. Everyone was astounded at these repeated signs of the Prince's favor, since he was not at all accustomed to behaving in this way to envoys and messengers from even the mightiest rulers, and a short time before they had believed my life to be in actual danger. The following night the Prince asked me to write down and send him the passage from Isaiah I had quoted. I complied with his request the next day, and included an exposition from the Fathers, and five chapters from the treatise of Gennadius, Patriarch of Constantinople, on the Primacy of the Pope. I had arranged to have this material translated into the Muscovite language during the journey for this express purpose, and in the hope that someday the whole of Gennadius' treatise might be published in that language.

The Second Discussion Between Antonio Possevino and the Grand Prince of Muscovy and His Senators, Held on February 23.

I was summoned that day, and when I arrived I found the Prince surrounded by an enormous company in a room larger than the one he had occupied previously. In spite of the signal tokens of the Prince's favor (which were not well received in certain quarters)[6], many feared that my associates and I were in very great danger, particularly as I had been given to understand that the Prince intended publicly to show me a book, which, however, he did not do after all. I advised my associates to make a full confession, expiated them with the Sacraments, and fortified them with relics of the Saints, in case the

Muscovites should harm them. However, whether the Divine Wisdom had rendered the Prince's disposition milder or had simply postponed the time when worthier servants of God will endure martyrdom in Muscovy for the sake of Christ, the fact is that when the Prince caught sight of me he not only followed his regular practice of asking visitors to sit on a bench covered with tapestry near himself in the center of the assembly of nobles, but beckoning to all his Senators he said in a loud voice: "Antonio, if I said anything yesterday concerning the Pope that displeased you, I ask your pardon, and please do not tell His Holiness. We wish to enter into a state of amity, brotherhood and unity with him and the other Christian rulers, even though differences in the matter of faith may exist between us. To this end we shall send with you an envoy to the Pope, and in our name our Senators will make reply to the other issues you have recently placed before us."

I thanked the Prince, commended his graciousness, and said that I would prove myself to be as dependable in other matters as I had been in arranging peace with King Stefan. Then later in the morning the Senators and I withdrew to the regular conference chamber, where I spent several hours listening to them and negotiating issues of the highest importance. These included a description of the transit route to the lands belonging to the King of Persia, the problem of the Tatars, the treaty with the Christian Rulers, the need to negotiate peace with John III, the King of Sweden, and to investigate the reasons why the Prince had once offended this King's envoys,[7] and, above all, the question of the Catholic and Muscovite religions. On this issue in the Prince's name the Senators asked me to be good enough to set forth in writing the difference between the two religions, because there was no one in Muscovy able to read the Greek in which the Proceedings of the Council of Florence were written. I promised to do so, produced the complete Latin text of Gennadius' treatise I had brought with me, and gave it to the Senators to convey to the Prince. I had already given him a Greek version of this treatise, but now the Prince could have interpreters translate the chapter headings, which outline the differences, from Latin into the Muscovite language.

The Third Discussion Concerning Religion Between Antonio Possevino and the Grand Prince of Muscovy, Held in the Presence of the Same Nobles and Senators. The Subsequent Events of that Holy Day, March 4, the First Day of Quadragesima, When, as it is Written in the Gospel, 'Then was Jesus led up...into the wilderness to be tempted of the devil' [Matt. 4:1].

76

On each occasion when I went to the Prince, large numbers of nobles riding in carriages, or on horseback, were assigned to escort me. In addition, the Prince's bodyguards stood in enormously long lines, each man touching the next, and with iron cannon set among them, along both sides of the street in the second citaedel where my residence was located, while some 1500 of them lined the street in the first citaedel, where the Prince had his Palace. Commoners packed the stairs, courtyard, window-sills and galleries as tightly as the nobles and other dignitaries filled the Prince's interior and anterior chambers. On the first of the month the Prince had issued special orders that on the fourth an even greater crowd should assemble outside in the first citaedel; it was estimated that at least 5,000 people were present there. The doors of the Church of the Virgin Mary, whose seven gables are covered with gold sheeting, and of the Church of St. John were thrown open, so that an unprecedented sight greeted me as I was crossing the square: priests dressed in sacred (if they can be called sacred) vestments formed a crown in the center of the church and were duly chanting Muscovite prayers. During that week the Prince had remained sequestered in his chambers, observing stricter fasts and praying more intensely, because unlike ourselves (who begin it on Wednesday), but like the Greeks, the Muscovites begin Quadragesima on Monday, and have been abstaining from meat, though not from eggs and milk products, since Septuagesima. Amid this great pomp and ceremony I was escorted into the presence of the Prince, who directed me to be seated close to his throne, and then said: "Antonio, my Senators have told me that you are anxious to visit our churches, and in this matter I have wished to show my favor towards you (a phrase the Prince is fond of using). I have ordered my nobles to take you to them, where you will see how reverently we adore the Most Holy Trinity, honor the Virgin Mary, and invoke the Saints. You will also perceive the exemplary piety we manifest before the holy ikons, and you will behold the ikon of the Virgin Mary which was made by St. Luke.[8] But you will not see either my Metropolitan or myself carried in a chair."

I was taken by surprise at the Prince's remarks, for only a few days earlier, when the Prince had asked me about visiting churches, I had told my interpreter to make an unqualified refusal. I replied: "We approve and praise services rightly and piously performed in order to honor God, but I want you to know that I never asked anyone for permission to visit your churches, witness a service, or hear the prayers of your priests. I know how your priests celebrate the service, and we cannot be present when they officiate until there is agreement between us concerning the faith, and your Metropolitan has been confirmed by the man who holds the See of him to whom the Lord said, "Strengthen thy brethren" [Luke 22:32]. I have already told you that the Pope is carried in a chair to enable him to bless the people, and also it seems desirable to indicate in this way that the great authority possessed by the Apostolic See was conferred upon it by Christ Our Lord. The honor your people pay to your bishops (if bishops indeed they be) is much greater than this. These bishops wash their hands in water, and then they sprinkle the people's eyes and others parts of their bodies with this same water, and the people very often bow low before your bishops and strike the ground with their foreheads." When the Prince had grasped the purport of my remarks, he said: "The Mystery of the water symbolizes Christ's Resurrection."

I replied: "To avoid annoyance from having me labor these matters, Your Majesty should peruse the memorandum I have composed at your request on the difference between the Catholic and the Greek faith, as it will supply you, if you wish, with answers to a host of questions like this." The Prince accepted the memorandum and ordered me escorted to the Church of the Virgin Mary. As I was leaving the chamber the Prince called to me: "Antonio, see that you do not take any Lutherans into the church with you!" I said: "Prince, until they come to their senses we do not admit Lutherans, or have any converse with them whatsoever."

As we made our way out the nobles tried to direct my associates and me to the right side of the Church of the Virgin Mary to await the arrival of the Prince. I was unprepared for any such action and had not in fact expected it, since I had been careful to inform the Prince that I had no intention of attending service or public prayers. When I realized what was happening I gradually but firmly began to withdraw with all my associates, in spite of the determined protests of the nobles, who said that I had been behaving correctly to their Prince in all other matters, but by this action I was offering him a mortal insult. My action astonished the large crowd and astounded the rest of the nobles, who were sure that something terrible would befall me. Suddenly the Senators, who had accompanied the Prince to the street, learned of the development. They came up to me (by this time I had withdrawn a fair distance from the church), asked what I was doing, and took my answer back to the Prince, who was in a procession led by priests bearing an ikon of the Virgin Mary.

The Prince halted with all his courtiers in the center of the street, rubbed his head with his hand as though at a loss what to do, and finally sent some Senators to me to say that he had come down to the street because he wished to show his favor to me, but since I did not choose to accept his favor, I was entirely free to return to the regular council chamber in the palace, where the Senators would shortly join me to continue the discussions already under way. The Prince then continued his course to the church, and the Metropolitan and other bishops and priests came out to greet him and escort him within the premises, where they gave him a cross to kiss. From the nobles I learned later that inside the church a platform had been built and a chair placed on top of it to enable me to watch all the proceedings, and plans had been made to direct remarks concerning the faith to me. I managed to weather the storm and avoid kissing the Metropolitan's hand, which the Prince had been extremely anxious for me to do. When I reached the council chamber I drew from my breast my cross covered with relics, and with all my 15 associates genuflected and forcefully intoned the hymn, *Te Deum Laudamus*. When the nobles in attendance asked me what this meant, we told them that my associates and I were giving thanks to God because we had firmly and publicly defended the true Christian faith. The nobles were amazingly affected; they fell silent and actually turned pale. From earliest childhood the Muscovites have absorbed the belief that they are the only true Christians, and they consider all others, including Catholics, to be unclean people and aberrant heretics.

This whole affair caused the Prince considerable embarrassment. He had plotted to make the Pope's emissary perform an act of submission to the Metropolitan and use it as a device to implant the Schism more firmly than ever in his people by pretending that the Pope had learned the truth and sent an envoy to acknowledge it. The Bishop, or *Vladika*, of Smolensk and the Archbishop of Novgorod the Great had both vainly attempted the same kind of manoeuver before. We met cunning with cunning, and we can only hope that the public witness of our action will long remain in the memories of the Muscovites: in the presence of their Prince they saw that truly Orthodox Catholics deem the faith they consider unique unworthy of having a devout person behold its ceremonies.

After this episode the Senators came to me, and I stated my reasons why the Prince, if he genuinely desired to show his favor to me, as they claimed, should not have sought before everyone to denigrate the Pope, Christ's Own Legate, nor have thought that the Pope's envoy was inferior to a Metropolitan, especially as the individual who occupied that office was an usurper. His predecessor, still called Metropolitan, was still alive immured in a monastery.[9] Another man, who had preceded him and who had had the temerity openly to censure the Prince's conduct, had been executed together with all his associates. Not a single one of these persons had been confirmed by the Vicar of Christ. I took advantage of this opportunity to discourse at length on the true Catholic faith, and the Senators listened quietly and attentively. They promised to report all I had said to the Prince, and did so that same day. Then, referring to a written memorandum, they replied to the other issues I had raised with the Prince a few days earlier.

CHAPTER IV

The Chief Points on which the Greeks and the Muscovites Differ from the Latins in the Faith After the Greeks Seceded from the Catholic Church. A Document Presented by Antonio Possevino, S. J., to Ivan Vasil'evich, Grand Prince of Muscovy, Before a Large Assembly of Nobles, in the City of Moscow, on March 3, 1582, Containing a Brief, Clear and Firm Refutation of the Errors of the Greeks and the Muscovites.

Your Highness, two days ago in your name your Senators conveyed a request for me to set forth in writing the difference that exists between the Roman Catholic and the Muscovite faiths. Such an undertaking would require more time than the small amount I have available, because I am under orders to proceed to Livonia to meet with His Highness, the King of Poland, and from there to go to Pope Gregory XIII in company with your Representative,[1] for purposes of which you are already aware. You can consult the work of Gennadius, the Patriarch of Constantinople (a copy of which I gave to your Senators to convey to you), who attended the holy Council of Florence, in order to learn what the chief differences are, and thus I shall content myself with a brief analysis of the main issues, with special reference to the time at which the Greeks cut themselves off from the Roman Catholic Church, since it was from them the Muscovites received their version of the Christian faith, which is neither pure nor correct. Such a presentation will prove of considerable assistance in arriving at a clearer understanding of the entire situation.

When the Faith in the East was more honest and straightforward, the Greeks believed that Christ Our Lord had conferred the Primacy of the Visible Church Militant upon the Apostle Peter and his Successors. Expressing their approval of this in the Councils, they acknowledged the essential authority of the Successors of Peter, to whom the words of Christ refer when He said: "Peter, strengthen thy brethren" [Luke 22:32]. Whenever the Patriarchs and other bishops of the East were persecuted by heretics, or even by the Emperors, they found refuge and protection at the See of the Roman Pope. This was the experience of Sts. John Chrysostom, Athanasius, and many others. From every part of the world bishops regularly corresponded with the Roman See on questions of faith and other highly important matters, and at the bidding of the Pope they convoked councils or asked confirmation for these councils once they were convoked. The Pope conferred on the Archbishop of Thessaloniki (which is a city in Greece) the power to adjudicate cases and resolve any disagreements that might break out in the East, and he used the Pope's authority to confirm bishops nominated in the dioceses, for otherwise their nominations would be invalid. Pope Leo I, who lived many centuries ago and is respected by your Muscovites, bears witness that the Pope conferred such powers upon the Archbishop of Thessaloniki.[2]

When Constantine the Great transferred the seat of his Empire to Byzantium he was inspired by God to place Rome under the control of the Vicars of Christ. The Greeks thus should have had even more reason to uphold and venerate the See of Peter, but instead the presence of the terrestrial emperor made them so arrogant that they came to believe that the authority of the Church at Constantinople derived from the Emperor rather than from the institutions of Christ, which had rendered the See of Peter preeminent above all others. In 381 A.D. they tried to make the Bishop of Constantinople, who prior to that time had not even been a Patriarch, superior to the three Eastern Patriarchs and second only to the Roman Pope, as the Fifth Canon of the First Council of Constantinople proves.[3] Not content with such effrontery, in 451 they tried to make the Bishop of Constantinople the equal of the Roman Pope, as the 16th. Canon of the Council of Chalcedon indicates.[4] Their presumption knew no bounds, for approximately 600 years after the birth of Christ they actually dared to call the Bishop of Constantinople *Oecumenicus* -- Bishop of the Whole World, or Universal Bishop. The Sainted Pope, Gregory I, wrote numerous letters to John, Bishop of Constantinople, the Emperor Maurice, the Empress Constantia, and the Eastern Patriarchs, in which he stated unequivocally that such an action constituted blasphemy against the institutions of Christ Our Lord.[5] But insolence always feeds upon itself, and finally in 1054 A.D. its heresy and sin caused the East to lose the Light of Truth.[6] The Greeks declared the Bishop of Constantinople the equal of the Successors of Peter, went so far as to trump up false calumnies against the Latins and to hurl anathemas against them, and actually dared to drive them out of their churches in Byzantium.

Such behavior as this readily demonstrates to you that since the pontificate of Gregory I, a most holy man, the Greeks have tried to confound and destroy the Succession established by Christ, not because of any sins committed by the Popes, as some Greeks deceitfully allege, but because pride and falsehood have blinded them. Thanks be to God, it is they themselves who have been utterly confounded and destroyed: they have become slaves of the Turks, while their books and the remains of their Holy Fathers have been removed to the custody of the One True Roman Catholic Church. Their authority is so bankrupt that they have never been able to convoke a single Council, whereas the Apostolic See has mustered more than ten General Councils since the Seventh one took place. During this time the Greeks have admitted their errors on fourteen occasions, but, as James the Apostle said: "like unto a man beholding his natural face in a glass and beholding his blemishes he goeth his way" [cf. James 1: 23-24], they have returned to their vomit.

At last God, the Just Judge, decided to take an axe and chop down this barren fig tree to the roots, and ordered convocation of the Council of Florence. The Emperor of Constantinople and the others from the East who attended it acknowledged the truth, pledged friendship with the Apostolic See, and abjured their errors, after a public reading from the Greek Fathers, whose works they had brought with them from Asia and Greece. Gennadius, who later became Patriarch, refuted the most flagrant of these errors in his disquisition on the Primacy of Peter, and I have arranged for his observations to be translated into the Muscovite language and given to you. However, many of the Greeks subsequently turned their back on the light they had seen, and thus God brought it to pass that they lost the Greek Empire of Constantinople, their Orthodox faith, and all their glory. Since they preferred darkness to light, they were consigned to interior and exterior darkness. Their minds are so blinded that, although they have been often proved wrong and stand convicted by their own testimony, they still refuse to admit their folly.

The fundamental difference between the peoples of the East and Catholics is that the former, rashly and in contravention of decisions taken in preceding Councils, have come to the conclusion that an addition has been made to the Creed; namely, that the Holy Ghost proceeds from the Father and from the Son. However, the peoples of the East know from Scripture and the Greek Fathers that the Latins admit only one Origin, not two, and that they added these words ("and from the Son") in order to avoid the heretical opinions held by certain persons. Such a declaration was formerly necessary, because this error had not yet become manifest. The Popes who summoned the first councils and the Most Holy Greek Fathers who attended them have borne witness that the Holy Ghost proceeds from the Father and from the Son. This can be seen from the writings of Sts. Athanasius, Basil, Gregory of Nyssa, Chrysostom, and Anastasius, the Proceedings of the Council of Ephesus and elsewhere, all of which state with great eloquence that the Holy Ghost "is sent, proceeds, comes forth, and flows" from the Father and from the Son. The Most Holy Popes and Fathers of the Western Church approved this truth, and since these Fathers had cast their votes in favor of the true faith, the Fifth, Sixth and Seventh Councils enjoined the penalty of anathema upon those who refused to believe it.[7]

Certain people who do not know what they are talking about have the effrontery to assert that the Latins were excommunicated when the Council of Constantinople decreed anathema against anyone who held views or taught beliefs other than those approved by the Council or held by the Church at that time. The Council knew that the Latin Church had never believed or taught otherwise; it was against Macedonius[8] and Eunomius[9] and other such heretics, who held divergent views, that anathema was uttered. Each time the Greeks realized they had fallen into error they would, as I have pointed out, enter into agreement with the Western Church, as they did at the Council of Florence, and again as they had done more than 300 years ago at the General Council of Lyons in the pontificate of Gregory X, when the Greek bishops attending it publicly professed, in the name of all the Eastern peoples and the Emperor of Constantinople, that the Holy Ghost proceeds from Eternity from the Father and from the Son, not from two Origins but from one, and not from two Spirations but from one. At an assembly of all participants in the Council they intoned three times in Greek and three times in Latin the words: "In Accordance with the Scriptures, 'And From the Son.' "[10]

The next difference concerns the unleavened bread Latins use to celebrate the Divine Sacrament. The peoples of the East know that the Apostles Peter and Paul, inspired by the Holy Ghost, transmitted this observance to the Churches of the West. Although this is the best practice to follow, the Apostles did not interfere with the Eastern custom of celebrating with leavened bread, and for good reason. As Patriarch Gennadius says, as long as the things Christ instituted to celebrate the Eucharist -- the meal, the priest, the place, the intent and the words -- are present, nothing further is required. However, the Eastern peoples acknowledge that the Western Church has a good and sufficient reason for using unleavened bread; namely, that our Lord assumed the flesh without adulteration. Those who celebrate with leavened bread thereby imply that the Word of the Father is assumed in the flesh, and this means that there was both Perfect God and Perfect Man. No matter whether the Eucharist is celebrated with unleavened bread or leavened bread, we are taking the body of Our Lord and Savior; we must not believe that there are two Christs, one celebrated with unleavened bread and the other with leavened bread. When Christ consecrated the Supper of the Lamb with unleavened bread He was ordering us to do what He Himself did, and this prevents confusion with the Jewish ceremony. We are not following Jewish customs when we use water in the rite of Baptism even though the Jews use it in their baptisms. The Holy Council of Florence and Patriarch Gennadius (whose work I have given you in both Greek and Latin versions) have provided the firmest proofs that this is so from Scripture and the Fathers.

Purgatory is the fire in which souls make atonement; after this atonement they rise to Heaven until the Day of Judgment. Before the Day of Judgment the souls of the faithful enjoy heavenly bliss. The Apostle Peter entrusted the Roman Popes with the care of the Church Universal to the consummation of the world. This is so clearly expressed in Scripture and the Early Fathers that I am absolutely convinced that anyone who with God's mercy carefully reads the Proceedings of the Council of Florence or Gennadius, Patriarch of Constantinople, will recognize that the Roman Catholic faith is the one and most true faith; the gates of heavenly glory will never open to those who do not possess it. Since the Greeks knew this, they should have understood that the Holy See of Peter, and the Roman Catholic Church it controls, cannot err, and that the Holy Ghost received them from Christ Our Lord for the purpose of imparting true doctrine to the peoples.

It is a comparatively easy matter to dispose of all the ridiculous false statements and the lies and calumnies with which the Latins are assailed. The first one some Greeks have dared to make is that after the first Seven General Councils no further Council may be summoned. When did Christ ever say this? Can anyone prove it by Scriptural authority? Who has tried to muzzle the Holy Ghost, and in these days of burgeoning heresy and error who would deny the Church its constant right to strive for Christian Unity and to convoke General Councils to seek cures for the general malady? The Greeks realized that they would never be able to summon legitimate Councils unless they had the single visible Shepherd in whose hands Christ in His ineffable wisdom had necessarily left the

84

Church. Their inability to do so involved them in bitter quarrels and led to error, while they saw that the authority of the Roman Catholic Church to convoke and confirm General Councils remained unimpaired. This authority allowed the Apostolic Roman See, as I have said, to summon and confirm a number of other Councils after the first Seven, as, for example, the recent Council of Trent, which was called to condemn Lutherans and other heretics. The Greeks have tried to conceal the truth by pretending that the Seventh Council precluded, or had the power to preclude, the convocation of further Councils, as though God would abrogate what Christ Himself had conferred in perpetuity upon His Own Church.

In order to damage or denigrate the Cause, by emphasizing that Western rites differ from those of the East the Greeks thought they could take advantage of the fact that the Apostles, who understood that differences among peoples exist, wisely provided for diversity in church ritual. In passing, let us note that the East itself is a hotbed of ritual divergence; Syrians, Maronites,[11] Ethiopians, Armenians and Greeks all have different observances. It is easy to demonstrate that true Orthodoxy of faith only exists when a diocese preserves in love and unity the rites it received from its Apostles or their lawful successors.

The Greeks and Muscovites accomplish baptism by total corporal immersion, while in the West we merely sprinkle a few drops of water on the head, but in each instance the result is the same. Sts. Dionysius the Areopagite[12] and Cyril, Bishop of Jerusalem,[13] favored total immersion, while in the Apostolic Constitutions St. Clement supported sprinkling the head. If a Latin rebaptized a Greek child already baptized in the Greek rite, or a Greek rebaptized a Latin child already baptized in the rite of the Western Church, and anyone refused to believe that both had received the true baptism of Christ, his beliefs and actions would be very wicked. Certain Greeks also deny that there can be more than one Chrismatic Unction. This is an egregious error against Scripture, St. Clement and the Apostolic Constitutions, Sts. Dionysius the Areopagite and Cyril of Jerusalem, and the Sainted Pope and Martyr, Melchiades.[14] The Greeks fail to perform the Sacrament of Confirmation correctly; thus, it is not surprising that their faith is infirm and they have already suffered ruin at the hands of the perfidious Turks, the enemies of Christ.

A marriage in Christ and the Holy Universal Church remains indissoluble as long as both partners are living. The Greeks, however, permit divorce and allow a person to marry again while the first spouse is still alive. Thus it is not surprising that they divorced themselves from the Catholic Church, whose link with Christ, its Head, is manifestly an indissoluble marriage, of which the Apostle Paul says: "This is a great mystery" [Ephesians 5:32]. Greeks who marry before becoming priests may keep their wives after ordination. Latin priests are celibate, which is a better state for celebrating the Divine mysteries. Our priests are holy in body and spirit. They are not allowed to involve themselves in temporal affairs and the procreation of children, because they must be in an exceptional position to devote all their energies to the promotion of spiritual matters, helping their neighbors, and administering the Sacraments to the living and the dying at any time.

Some people in the East charge that Catholics have subtracted a week from the Great Fast, but it is a simple matter to show them that since the days of the Apostles Peter and Paul Catholics have observed a full Quadragesima, during which time they fast. This fast is held in order to imitate the life of Christ, as the Blessed Ignatius[15] writes to the Philippians, where he says that following the example of Christ Our Lord we are obliged, insofar as we are able, to fast for a like number of days. Anyone who wishes to add a week or even more to Quadragesima in order better to prepare for it is by all means free to do so; it is also commendable to celebrate not just one, but several Quadragesimae, a practice followed by many pious men among us. Pope Telesphorus[16] urged a fast of seven full weeks, which was the custom prior to his time. He wished clerics and monks to adopt this regimen, and many of them have done so, although it is not a formal requirement for everyone. Throughout all the Catholic Churches of the East and the West some begin their fast on Monday, others on Wednesday. There can be no quarrel with anyone about this as long as he fasts a full forty days in imitation of Christ (insofar as this is possible for mortals), since it was He who set the example, and we must do what He did. In the pamphlet on fasting he sent to Cometas, St. John Damascene[17] spoke of the Eastern mode of fasting which is still partially followed in the West and then said: "This is the rule and law of the Church, and we know that it is preserved in the Holy Resurrection of Christ. We should by all means encourage the faithful zealously to follow this worthy practice and *exuberare virtutem*,[18] that is, to brim over with virtue, for this is pleasing to God and sensible men. At the same time, we must not apply coercion or set up mandatory requirements. We should employ only a gentle urging, especially in difficult times. Today it is both expedient and essential for every man to enlarge his store of good and to refrain from violence." He adds: "Who would ordain that life should be one long fast? Admonition is one thing; legislation another. The prescription of the Holy Ghost is enough: *Admoneatur accretio, sive accessio boni*, that is, let the increase or growth of good be encouraged." This is what Damascene has to say on the subject.

Love is the final goal of the Lord's teachings, and all laws must be framed in its context. The institution of fasting was designed not to ruin health, but to curb the passions and exalt the mind to heavenly things; hence, there need not be the slightest hesitation to give the sick and the infirm, when they need it, food that would be forbidden to people in good health. St. Paul the Apostle says: "Godliness is profitable to all things" [I Timothy 4:8]. The sick are given food, not as food, but as medicine, since "God Almighty created it" [Ecclesiasticus 38:2], as Scripture says. The fact that people of the East fast longer during Quadragesima, or apparently have more fasts, which occur at different times of the year from the Latins, does not mean that they differ from the latter in the Faith. On the instructions of the Holy Ghost the Apostles and their successors allowed the Church the flexibility it needed to respond to the demands of particular times and places. Latins do not criticize the manner in which Greeks fast, although the Greeks sometimes fail to perform this observance properly. As Your Highness knows, they very often take food or drink other beverages besides water on fast days: no one should deceive others or himself be deceived by such spurious and superficial forms of abstinence. Latins fast during the Apostolic Vigils and on certain other days, particularly the Days of Our Savior and of the Virgin Mary, and on the following day they are more inclined to pray, perform good works, visit prisons and hospitals, console the afflicted, and attend the sick. In addition, twelve days are distributed through the four fast times of the year, including three in Quadragesima, when Latins fast after the manner of the earlier Apostles in order to assist their bishops to perform correctly the Ordination of spiritual workers in the same way as the Apostles themselves did, when, fasting and praying, they made Paul and Barnabas priests by the laying on of hands [cf. Acts 13:3]. Basing their contention on the Epistle of St. Ignatius to the Philippians, the Council of Gangra,[19] and the Apostolic Canons, the Greeks and others declare that there is no need to fast on the Lord's Sabbath Day. However, the Latins have shown that neglect of fasting on the Sabbath by the Eastern Churches corresponded in time with the appearance in the East of the Simonians,[20] who denied that the world, from the creation of which God rested on the Sabbath, is His work. It also resulted from the fact that God inspired the Apostles to foresee the heretics who would appear in the East, such as the Manichaeans,[21] Eustachians,[22] Marcionites,[23] Lampetians,[24] and the Messalians,[25] who appeared in Paphlagonia and only pretended to fast on the Sabbath in order to mock the Resurrection of Christ, which is generally considered to begin on the evening of the Sabbath, as Pope Leo the Great says in Chapter 1 of his 81st. Epistle. The Council of Gangra and St. Anastasius,[26] Patriarch of Antioch, indicated that one of their reasons for prohibiting Sabbath fasting was that heretics fasted on the Lord's Sabbath Day *ob simulatam abstinentiae exercitationem*, that is, to parody the practice of abstention. Since this problem did not arise in the West and this heresy did not flourish there, there was no reason to prohibit Sabbath fasting or any need to imply that a person could win praise for simply abstaining from meat. More will be said of this in due course.

Some are surprised that Latins do not fast or abstain from meat on Wednesday, but the Latins have explained that there are many people among them who observe this day with scrupulous abstinence. The Ancients proclaimed certain common fast days, which the Council of Gangra is said to have called *in commune*, but they have also been taught, so it is said, the need for individual fasts, which the Apostles permitted to occur on different days depending upon where people lived. The Eastern fast days are Wednesday and Friday; the Western ones are Friday and the Sabbath, and both Churches are enjoined to keep Quadragesima, or the Great Fast, in common. But whether it be East or West, abstinence is consistent with reason and graces the worship of God in the Church. Greeks fast on Wednesdays and Fridays because it was on those days the Bridegroom was taken away; on Wednesday Judas agreed to betray the Lord, and on Friday Our Most Benign Lord was crucified for our sake. The West fasts on Fridays for the same reason as the Greeks, and on the Sabbath because that was the day when He lay in the Sepulchre. The Jewish Day of Rest still remains a day of grief for us, and Christians show that they do not wish to keep the Jewish Sabbath for the most part by preparing themselves to celebrate Our Lord's festival and to receive the Communion of the Eucharist on the day following the Sabbath. It is wholly untrue that the Latin Church condemns the Eastern mode of fasting for this reason; on the contrary, we support the custom, insofar as it involves the Churches officially, just as the Blessed Augustine did in his work *Against Urbicus*, and Tertullian in his *Apology*. Whenever the Catholic Churches are able to discern high purpose in their institutions, they should observe them, provided that it can be shown that they have received these institutions from their common Head, Who is Christ Our Lord, in His Spirit. It makes no difference to faith that Eastern monks and bishops abstain from meat, while Western monks and Latin bishops do not impose this prohibition upon themselves, although it is certainly true that many of our monks do not eat meat. Except on fast days, all the Apostles sometimes ate meat, as did Christ, the Author and Source of all Perfection. Christ gives each person a measure of heavenly grace and then leaves him entirely free to choose the style of life each person considers appropriate for himself and which the Lord has called upon him to fulfill. Such forms of diversity are tolerable as expressions of faith, and they certainly can include the fact that during fasts in the Catholic Churches of both East and West some people take bread and water, others subsist entirely on dry foods, which the Greeks call *arida*. Some eat more, some less; some do not eat until evening, others eat in the afternoon, others at noon; some go a whole day without food, while others eat small amounts from time to time.

The Greeks charge that in contravention of Apostolic Decree we fail to abstain from strangled and bloody things. The Latins have explained to them that this prohibition was directed against the idol worshippers, who ate what had been sacrificed to idols or drank what the Apostle called "the cup of devils" [1 Cor. 10:2]. This decree must be observed, and it is observed by Catholics whenever they find themselves among peoples who worship idols and offer sacrifices to them. However, the decree merely forbids the consumption of sacrificial matter, not other things. Convincing testimony to this effect can be found in the Fourth Part of the Catechism of the Blessed Cyril of Jerusalem, Question 45 of Justin Martyr,[27] the Holy Easter Sermon of Gregory Nazianzus,[28] Origen's Eighth Book *Against Celsus*,[29] and in the earliest author to mention it, Magnetes,[30] in the Third Book of his Defense of the Gospel directed against Theostenes, that calumniator of the Gospel. All these highly authoritative Fathers lived in the East, and Tertullian, the African, in his *Apology* was one of the very first to approve this position.

We shall not spend too much time on the Sign of the Cross. The Muscovites complete it to the left, because they assume that by making the Sign to the right, when they name the Son, they are indicating that the Son sits to the right of the Father. We have a different way of making the Sign of the Holy Cross, which is awesome and full of mystery for us. Provided error is not present, we do not censure the Muscovite practice, but at the same time we cannot praise its piety, for those who make the Sign of the Cross to the left, according to what your people have told me, are moved to do so because they believe that the Holy Ghost sits to the left of the Father. Most Serene Prince, the Mystery of the Holy Trinity is far beyond human understanding and there are other things as well that fall outside our grasp, all of which we must accept on faith and authority. Here is the principle underlying our Sign. When we begin it from the head we are acknowledging the Father, the Head and Origin of all good and the Primary Source of the Other Persons of the Holy Trinity. When we lower the first three fingers of the right hand and invoke the name of the Son, we are remembering His Incarnation in the Virgin Mary, and with this remembrance (as the Apostle testifies) we bear witness to "the mystery which hath been hid from ages and from generations, but now is made manifest to his saints" [Colossians 1:26], and to the world, and which, as the greatest benefit of all, has been conferred upon us. When we touch the left and the right sides of the chest we are calling upon the name of the Holy Ghost, indicating that He proceeds from the Father and from the Son, as indeed He does so proceed, against the impious teachings of Eunomius and other heretics, professing that He is consubstantial with but distinct from Each of the Other Persons. We complete our Sign on the right, because in Holy Scripture right means perfection. We must always strive to achieve perfection, because that is what the Lord God, Who Himself is Ultimate Perfection, desires above all things.

Your Muscovites profess surprise that we do not adhere to their custom of inscribing our holy images with the names of the saints they represent. My view is that if inscriptions on images are the only way by which the holy saints can be identified, those who read the inscription no longer need the image. Everyone knows that Catholics can immediately recognize the representations of Christ on the Cross, the Virgin Mary, and a host of other Saints. What use is an inscription to illiterates, as almost all Muscovites are? Are not ikons intended to take the place of letters and writing for the laity? What if you were to say, as your people have said to me, that efficacy resides in the inscription? As a wise man you know that power and efficacy do not reside in letters, but in understanding and living faith. However, we shall not impugn a custom adopted by people who chose from religious motives, not superstition, to write names on ikons in order that they might teach others what they do not understand and show them how to tell holy ikons from profane ones. This is something that Latin Catholics often do as well.

Other Errors of the Muscovites, Who Have Followed the Eastern Schism Since the Greeks Sundered Themselves from the Church.

The Greeks err when they say that simple fornication is no sin. This contradicts what Christ Our Lord says: "For out of the heart proceed evil thoughts, murders, adulteries, fornications, thefts. . . the things which defile a man" [Matt. 15:19-20], against which Paul also speaks: "Neither fornicators, . . . nor adulterers, *etc.*, shall inherit the kingdom of God" [1 Cor. 6:9-10]. They err when they say that the Sacrament of the Eucharist is most effective when performed on the Day of the Lord's Supper, the Thursday of Holy Week, or that it is more powerful and efficacious when performed on that day than a celebration held on any other day. The power of God's Word is always the same when it is uttered by a priest in accordance with the Lord's teaching: "This is my body" [Matt. 26:26]. It is not a question of whether it is one day or another that imparts power and efficacy to the Sacrament, but the Institutions and Will of God, no matter when the rite is celebrated. They err when they say that sinners may not receive the Body of Christ Our Lord when they approach Our Lord's altar. Sinners may receive it, albeit unworthily, and as the Apostle says: "They receive judgment, not discerning the Lord's body" [cf. 1 Cor. 11:29]. They err in permitting a first marriage but condemning a second. When one spouse dies the other is free to remarry, as can clearly be discerned in the words of Christ Our Lord [cf. Matt. 19:9].

The Greeks err in refusing the Sacrament of Extreme Unction to the sick, since it sometimes helps their recovery, and it is invariably advantageous for the salvation of the sick person's soul. Such a doctrine is in contravention of Scripture, for concerning this Sacrament James the Apostle clearly states: "And the prayer of faith shall save the sick" [James 5:15], or, as the Greek text has it: "It will cure the sick, and will secure forgiveness for a man in sin."

The Greeks err in denying it is sinful to engage in usury. Christ Our Lord said: "Lend, hoping for nothing again" [Luke 6:35], and the Prophet David said: "He that putteth not out his money to usury . . . shall abide in thy tabernacle" [Psalms 15:1,5]. Anyone who lends money at interest and does not repent assuredly will not dwell in the Tabernacle of the Lord. They err in not believing it necessary to give back stolen goods in order to achieve life everlasting. It is written: "Thou shalt not steal" [Exodus 20:15], and "Bring forth therefore fruits worthy of repentance" [Luke 3:8]. Zaccheus said: "And if I have taken any thing from any man by false accusation, I restore *him* fourfold" [Luke 19:8]. How can there be fruits worthy of repentance unless the thing wrongfully taken is restored to its owner? In clear cases of usury, theft and robbery that priest is most seriously mistaken who thinks it sufficient merely to anoint the thief with oil, make him surrender a portion of his ill-gotten gains to the Church, and absolve him. God does not absolve such a person.

91

The Greeks err in thinking it is not permitted to make an image of Christ Our Lord. They fail to understand that God forbade the making of images solely to divert the Jews from idolatry, to which they were prone. The words, "Thou shalt not make unto thee any graven image" [Exodus 20:4], referred to those who worshipped idols like Beelzebub, Dagon and other devils, and offered sacrifices and incense to them. After the star of Christ arose on high, the practice of idolatry was completely abandoned, and now it is permitted to commemorate and recall the True God and Man, Jesus Christ, and His holy servants, the Saints, in any pious manner. When the Greeks assume that the first words of this Commandment prohibit making images of Saints, why do they not think that its next words prohibit the innumerable ikons Muscovites worship, which bear no resemblance to anything "that *is* in heaven above, or that is in the earth beneath" [*ibid*.]. Why do people have ikons of St. Nicholas all over the place, as we have seen with our own eyes, in the parts of Russia under your control?

It is a particularly abominable error to hold that a priest who has been duly consecrated is no longer a priest if his wife should die. All the Most Holy Fathers of East and West alike unanimously agree that once a bishop has imprinted the indelible mark of the priesthood on a man, he cannot lose his indelible rank of priest if his wife should chance to die. Can it perhaps be that it is his wife, and not Christ, who employs the bishop to make a man a priest? Or can it be that among the Muscovites priests are more important than bishops or monks, who have no wives and constitute the most convincing witness that the priesthood, instituted by Christ, does not depend on having a wife? Of course, it is most proper for Christian priests to be celibate.

However, by far the most egregious and palpable error held by Greeks and Muscovites alike is their assumption that they can achieve eternal salvation outside the Roman Catholic Church. No church can be a Christian Church unless its Order and Power have been instituted by Christ, or if it has failed to preserve them once they were conferred upon it. James says: "For whosoever shall keep the whole law, and yet offend in any one *point*, he is guilty of all" [James 2:15]; thus, anyone who denies that Christ Our Lord conferred authority and primacy on earth upon Peter, or who falsely and deceitfully thinks that these powers, against which the Gates of Hell shall never prevail, have been dissipated, stands already condemned, even though he may believe in all other things. God does not consider men who have not been confirmed by the Pope, His Vicar on Earth, to be Bishops

92

or Metropolitans; Christ Our Lord, Who is Truth, and God, Who does not lie, said to Peter: "Strengthen thy brethren" [Luke 22:32]. The Church that needed nurture, and the bishops, who as brothers required confirmation from Peter, have been destined to endure not just for Peter's own lifetime, but to the End of the World. St. John Chrysostom[31] was alluding to this in his 83rd. Homily on Matthew when he wrote: "He did not say, 'you will not deny,' but 'that thy faith fail not.' By His care and favor it came to pass that the faith of Peter did not completely disappear." In commenting on the 20th. Chapter of Luke, Theophylact[32] said: "Although you must soon be sifted, you possess hidden seeds of faith. The breath of the Invader may strip away the leaves, but the root survives, and your faith will fail not." In his Epistle to the Emperor of Constantinople, found as the Fourth Canon of the Sixth Council, and later universally approved at the Eighth Council, Pope Agatho said: "This is the rule of the True Faith to which the Apostolic Church of Christ has stoutly clung in prosperity and adversity alike. This Church, thanks to the Grace of God, has won acclaim because it has never strayed from the path of Apostolic tradition and has never been debased by, or fallen before, heretical innovations, because it was said to Peter: 'Simon, Simon, behold, Satan hath desired *to have* you that he may sift *you* as wheat: but I have prayed for thee, that thy faith fail not.' " [Luke 31:32].[33] From the testimony of such illustrious Fathers as these you can already see, and from the remarks that follow you will discern even more clearly, that your Metropolitan and these bishops of yours are not administering the Sacraments in a lawful and proper way, and that your people have strayed dangerously far from the correct path of Apostolic faith.

When the West, the East, or any other part of the Christian world falls into error, as has often happened, if there is no Visible Head of the Universal Church, who can pronounce on questions of faith? Who can confirm those chosen by chapters or nominated by rulers? Who will eradicate schisms? Who will condemn heresy? Who (I might add) has sufficient authority to restore amity among rulers? You yourself considered it highly important to ask the Pope to use his authority and good offices to end the war raging between you and Stefan, His Highness the King of Poland. Christ said: "Strengthen thy brethren." Without your confirmation your Senators could not render judgments or lawfully administer the provinces assigned to them. Who then would be so foolish as to think that the bishops of the Spiritual Kingdom of Christ, that is, the Church of the Living

God, could be confirmed by temporal rulers, or that nominations made by them could carry the slightest weight with Christ? "Lest by any means (he) should run, or had run, in vain" [Galatians 2:2], the Apostle Paul himself went up to Jerusalem to see Peter and James, in order to compare the Gospel he preached with theirs. He was "caught up into paradise, and heard unspeakable words, which it is not lawful for a man to utter" [II Cor. 12:4], and he firmly and truthfully bore witness that he had become one of the Elect not through man, or by man, but from God.

The Blessed Basil said in a letter to the Pope he gave to the Deacon Sabinus: "In truth he is worthy of that most exalted pronouncement in which he foretold that you would be blessed. The Lord has rewarded you for your piety, which enables you to discriminate between what is false and what is pure and unalloyed, and you preach the faith of the Fathers to the fullest degree."[34] At the Council of Ephesus 200 bishops drawn from many different dioceses wrote in a letter to Pope Celestine: "All of us, members of this very distinguished body, hold the opinion that you constitute the *fulcrum*, the central force, of the Churches."[35] Cyril, who later took the place of the Roman Pope as President of the Council, also wrote to Pope Celestine, after he came to the conclusion that it was necessary to consult him, as Head of the Church, concerning the Nestorian heresy: "Since God requires us to be vigilant in a matter such as this, *et diuturnae Ecclesiarum consuetudines persuadent, ut cum tua sanctitate haec communicentur*, that is, "and the longstanding constitutions of the Churches call for me to inform Your Holiness of these matters."[36]

In the Seventh Chapter of his Epistle to Anastasius,[37] the Sainted Pope Leo the Great followed Book 8, Chapter 4 of the Apostolic Constitution of St. Clement when he wrote: "The Metropolitan Bishop should refer the consecration of bishops and the question of harmony between clergy and laity to you, since the diocese has expressed a strong desire to have you informed, so that your authority may further strengthen ordinations that have been duly performed." A little later in the same Decretal he advised diocesan bishops to refer the election of Metropolitans to the Archbishop of Thessaloniki, the Pope's Vicar, for confirmation, based on the authority the Pope had delegated to him. This Epistle shows that, as we have just indicated, the Archbishop of Thessaloniki served as the Pope's Vicar in the churches of the East. In the name of the Pope, the Universal Shepherd, he visited remote dioceses and performed all other duties that reason and necessity required. He needed this delegated authority, because a journey to distant Rome would mean a long delay in confirming a bishop's ordination, but without authorization from the Successor of the Blessed Peter, the office had no validity, as St. Clement again testified in this work. The Blessed Peter provides that a bishop should be chosen by the elders and the people with the approval of the Metropolitan, who designates the new bishop as *electus*; if no objection is raised, the Metropolitan with the assistance of two other bishops ordains the bishop. The next step is to secure the authorization of Peter and his Successor, since both the election and the ordination are not valid without it. Sophronius of Jerusalem,[38] an Apostolic man during the time of the Emperor Heraclius, wrote in his Synodal Letter to Pope Honorius: "The ancient Apostolic tradition provides that those elected to the hierarchy (he means bishops) should in all honesty discuss their views and feelings concerning the faith (as Paul enjoined upon them) with those who have acquired or hold higher administrative office in the hierarchy, but they should do so *valde caute*, that is, very circumspectly, 'lest by any means (they) should run, or had run, in vain' " [Galatians 2:2]. He went on to say: "In keeping with this custom we are writing to you Theologi a profession of our faith *ut probetur*, that is, so that you may approve it. We write to you because you know how to discern *legitima dogmata ab adulterinis*, that is, right from wrong doctrine, and can *supplere, quae desunt*, that is, make good our deficiencies." As soon as he has received his Profession of Faith, Sophronius asks the Pope to reply with a letter, which he will be delighted to use when preaching the Gospel, for, as he says, "*Sanitas vestra a Deo data*, that is, the soundness God has given you is as the soundness of the faith." Sophronius would imitate the Apostle, who said: "that they may be sound in the faith" [Titus 1:13].

Peter, Patriarch of Constantinople,[39] imitated this example and followed the custom established by Apostolic tradition when more than 500 years ago he included a Profession of Faith in his Synodal Letter to Pope Leo IX, and asked the Pope to confirm both his faith and his See, which Pope Leo agreed to do. These are only a few examples I have chosen from among many to show you how the authority and ordinances of Christ are still vested in the Successors of Peter, so that (to emphasize what I mentioned earlier) you may understand that unless your Metropolitan and those bishops of yours receive confirmation in their faith and their Sees from this same Successor of Peter, God will not consider him a lawful Metropolitan or them lawful bishops, nor any of them persons fit to share in or to dispense the Heavenly Grace. After the Eastern patriarchs ceased receiving confirmation of the soundness of their faith from the heavenly soundness of Peter, their Head, or, in other words, when they no longer secured confirmation of their faith from the faith of the Roman Catholic Church regularly and formally set forth in Synodal letters, then, as we have said, they lost their faith, the authority of their Sees, and the freedom of life itself, when they became slaves to the Infidel.

Most Serene Prince, I have here shown you some of the basic differences that exist between our faiths, and described some of the errors in which the Greeks and your Muscovites have become involved. As I have said, you can learn more about these subjects from the five Treatises of Gennadius, Patriarch of Constantinople, which I have had conveyed to you. These bishops of yours will not be able to teach you much about so vital an issue as the Procession of the Holy Ghost from the Father and from the Son, because they have had no training in theology and you have no schools in which such questions could be studied. For this reason, in the hope of acquiring your favor and for the glory of God, I have arranged and simplified Gennadius' Treatises in such a way that you can easily use them in conjunction with the present work, as you will see in the accompanying document. May the Holy Ghost Himself illuminate you and may He implant in you an overwhelming desire to bring the many peoples under your rule into the light of the true Orthodox Catholic faith.

CHAPTER V

A Work Submitted by Antonio Possevino, S. J., to the Grand Prince of Muscovy After English Merchants Had Given the Latter a Book in Which a Heretic had Tried to Prove That the Pope is Antichrist.[1]

Most Serene Prince, it has come to my attention that recently, after my arrival in your country, some English merchants in Moscow gave you a book in which a heretic tried to prove that the Pope is Antichrist, and that you immediately ordered it to be translated into your language. I am saddened to reflect upon the snares of Satan, but I am encouraged to hope that the Divine Wisdom will use this clash between Catholic Truth and the efforts of heretics to strike a spark which will cause the Light to burst forth more splendidly over Russia for the glory of God than even it does at present. I am aware of the intensity with which you have persecuted the Lutheran heresy. Such blasphemous statements have appeared because you wrote last year to Stefan I, the King of Poland, saying that such things were one of the causes of the Livonian War. Others are circulated here by some Livonians, who, in sundering themselves from the See of the Blessed Peter and the Archbishop of Riga, their lawful Shepherd, lost their country, faith, freedom and churches, and have failed to see that you were but executing the just judgment of God when two years ago you ordered the destruction of the two churches they had built in Moscow.[2] Now the English merchants are thrusting wares of the same sort upon you, but you are a wise man and know that they are infected with the bane of Lutheranism, and Calvinism as well. You can come to your own conclusions concerning the purity of the water one can draw from this murky well of heresy. If they had offered you a complete edition of the Fathers and the ancient Councils they would not have insulted you in the way that they have done, but they want to boast and crow to their fellow English that the Calvinists, Anabaptists, and others of that sort, who are found here in some numbers, have easily been able to outwit you, and that the Grand Prince of Muscovy would rather hear a heretic say that the See of the Blessed Peter has changed into the See of Antichrist than to hear Christ Himself firmly declaring the See will last forever, and all the Councils recognizing it to be the most firm Rock, and the Holy Martyrs bearing witness to it with their blood. I must not avoid my responsibilities. Since the Pope sent me here to you not simply to mediate this peace, which has come about with Divine assistance, but for the sake of that Better Peace, in which we are to be united with God, I shall briefly explain the circumstances that led to the separation of England from the Apostolic See. A substantial portion of that island continues to preserve the Catholic Faith, and almost every day furnishes instances of those who are glad to endure martyrdom for the sake of it. There are two Colleges of English noblemen, one at Rheims in France and the other in Rome, where a constant stream of young men takes refuge, in order to learn and serve their ancestral faith. Both the Colleges are maintained at the Pope's expense, and your courtier Shevrigin saw the one in Rome.

Henry VIII, the King of England, once published a book attacking Luther, in which he refuted Luther's mad heresy, and for this reason the Pope gave him the title of Defender of the Catholic Faith. However, like Solomon, his heart was turned by women, for whose sake he abandoned the Catholic Faith and gradually lapsed into heresy. He wallowed in the blood of innocent people – monks, and others, and particulary Bishop John Fisher and Sir Thomas More, a man outstanding in faith, learning, and the conduct of affairs.

Henry fell in love with a woman and had the audacity to marry her and repudiate the sister of Charles V, and he tried to have his action ratified by Pope Clement VII and the Holy Apostolic See. This was contrary to Divine Law, but when he failed to obtain the sanction, he seceded from the Church, and doing something unheard of through the ages, had himself proclaimed Head of the English Church. But God is true and just: soon after Henry had introduced this woman he falsely called his wife into his bed she was taken in adultery and he had her put to death, although her only real adultery had consisted of going to bed with the adulterous king, who had forsaken his own chaste wife. There is no need to recount what happened later in this Island, for I am sure that reports concerning it have reached you.[3]

It is sufficient to say that the woman who now rules England has usurped the Headship and Primacy of the Church in England, and has added these epithets to her other titles. Strange prodigy! The English have spat upon Peter, and Peter's Successor duly established by Christ Our Lord, and subjected themselves to the rule of a woman (for that is all she really is) even in matters of religion, under unlucky auspices and with hasty counsel.

But the judgment of God is transcendent; He seizes the insolent and the crafty in the midst of their arrogance and guile. They are welcome to their woman as the Universal Shepherd of the Church in England: we shall keep the Successor of Peter, whom Christ the Shepherd instituted as the Visible Shepherd of His sheep and lambs!

In considering the argument contained in this book the English have given you, (leaving aside many other things) you must remember first that in Scripture the Holy Ghost presaged the advent of Antichrist with six clear signs: namely, the preaching of the Gospel throughout the entire world, the collapse and desolation of the Roman Empire, the coming of Enoch and Elijah, a persecution so savage and brutal that services could no longer be held at the altar, the death of Antichrist three and a half years later, and the end of the whole world. Although Catholics are now engaged in spreading the Light of the Gospel far away in the remote Indies, the bulk of the peoples of the world has not yet received the Word that will save them all. The Christian Catholic Caesar still surpasses all other kings and princes in his Imperial Roman majesty. We are still saying the Mass. Enoch and Elijah have not appeared, and they are supposed to come and be slain by Antichrist, as many, including the Greek Fathers, forcefully state; e.g., Origen, St. John Chrysostom in his Commentary on the Seventeenth Chapter of Matthew, Theodoretus[4] in his Commentary on the last chapter of Malachi, St. John Damascene in Chapter 28 of his Fourth Book, and St. Irenaeus[5] in his Fifth Book. Furthermore, the spiritual kingdom of the Pope has already endured for almost sixteen centuries; it cannot be demonstrated with any accuracy that someone else will rule for three and a half years and be considered Antichrist, and by denying that Christ was the True Son of God, try to make everyone believe that he is the true Christ promised by the Law and the Prophets and affirm that he is God. However, Scripture and the earliest Fathers, both Latin and Greek, as, for example, Irenaeus in Book Five, the Blessed Cyril of Jerusalem in Catechism Five, Theodoretus in his Second Epistle to the Thessalonicans, and many others, testify that Antichrist would do all these things, and also perform false miracles. When did the three miracles occur which St. John the Divine predicted in Revelation 13 at the coming of Antichrist: fire will descend from Heaven; an image of a Beast will speak, and Antichrist will seem to meet death and achieve resurrection, which will deceive many peoples and make them believe in him?

99

When did the Roman Pope invade, occupy and annex the kingdoms of Egypt, Libya and Ethiopia and kill their rulers, all of which Antichrist must do, as foretold in Chapter 7 of Daniel? What soldiers did the Sainted Pope Gregory the Great use to win England for Christ, or other Roman Popes use to plant the Cross Triumphant in the realms of the pagans? They have won the South, the East, and the Western Indies with nothing but the Word of Christ and the workers they have from time to time sent to those places. The heretics are accustomed to tell one lie after another, but although they try to call the Pope Antichrist because he has removed certain emperors and kings from their thrones, nevertheless they will be compelled to admit that the hand of Christ can be detected in such actions. The Pope received his power in Heaven and on Earth from the Father, and in His generosity God has allowed him to use as much of this power as he has needed in order to administer the Church and to free the Catholic faith from the impositions of tyrants. The Roman Popes have never tried to acquire control for themselves in the realms from which they have expelled base and wicked monarchs and where they have helped to bring pious and Christian rulers to the throne. Pope Gregory II deposed the Greek Emperor Leo III, an Iconoclast and a heretic;[6] Zacharias deposed Childeric, the King of France;[7] Gregory VII deposed the Roman Emperor Henry IV;[8] Innocent III deposed Otto IV,[9] and Innocent IV deposed Frederick II.[10] He did not lie Who said: "Whatsoever thou shalt bind on earth shall be bound in heaven" [Matt. 16:19], for all these rulers lost their kingdoms, and those rulers who did not actually lose their kingdoms were obliged to pay various severe penalties. As Gennadius, the Patriarch of Constantinople, following Nicephorus, observes, in the time of Photius Pope Nicholas I excommunicated the Greeks, and the validity of his action was everywhere accepted.[11] The Greeks became outcasts among all peoples, like the Jews, just as the Pope had said they would in his Bull. Earlier, Pope Innocent I had excommunicated the Empress Eudoxia for driving St. John Chrysostom into exile; her grave shook until the Saint was recalled and the ban was lifted by the Pope, when the trembling ceased.[12] The truth will out: Pope Nicholas V summoned the envoys of the Emperor Constantine, called Dragases, and handed them a letter that filled them with fear and dread. The Pope wrote this letter in 1451; Constantinople was captured in 1453. His letter contained these words: "You Greeks need not think that the Roman Pope and the whole Western Church are so deficient in intelligence as to fail to understand the deceit underlying your continued delays to respond to us; we understand it all too well. But we endure it and keep our eyes fixed on Jesus, the Eternal Priest and Lord, Who bade the sterile fig tree be preserved to the third year. The husbandman girt himself to chop the tree down because it bore no fruit; three years later its very dominion ceased to be."[13]

Prince, from these events you can see the sort of weapons the Apostolic See employs to overcome or chasten the stubborn. What has this got to do with the false and lying statements made by ignorant heretics? The English book slanders the Pope when it asserts that he sits in Rome (which once was rightly called Babylon, when it was ruled by pagan Emperors as the result of the universal errors of all the peoples) and does not preach the Word of God. In reality, every day the Pope deals with the most important affairs of the Christian Commonwealth, negotiating with Cardinals, Archbishops, Bishops and innumerable other persons. He has sent me to proclaim through the spoken and the written word and by pious example the Constant Truth to you. The English make ridiculous statements, such as: "You lost the keys to the kingdoms, which Peter gave to you, through your sins," or, "the Pope does not keep God's commandments." They cannot know or rightly say whether the Pope sins or not, and if committing sins were a ground for depriving rulers of their offices, there would be no rulers left in this world. The English charge that the Pope seeks excessive glory for himself; in reality he defers to the secular rulers, who have received their swords from God to exercise temporary sway over their subjects for an appropriate time, although he is by far the greatest among them. The English also say: "Whenever your name is pronounced one must stand up 600 times," and make all sorts of other statements concerning things we know nothing about, and which appear incredible to others as well. I tell you that all these are the fictions of Satan, who has been a liar from the beginning and has always longed to destroy the Apostolic See. He is extremely angry because the See (not the heretics) preserves the unity of the Church and duly performs the Divine mysteries. Incidentally, in addition to the current crop of heretics several centuries ago the Greeks did everything in their power to prevent this Divine Light of Truth from shining in the East.

It remains for me to dispose of the false charges brought against the Popes by these heretics, and by schismatics as well, that the Apostolic See has sometimes taught contrary to the Faith. Those who possess a true understanding know perfectly well that heretics have mistaken Orthodox Catholic doctrine for heretical opinion or have often utilized the slanderous views of Antipopes, those who had not yet become Popes, or those who never became Popes at all. The Roman Church has never strayed from the path of true Christian faith. Pope Agatho, whom you and your people deservedly esteem, in his Letter to the Emperor Constantine, which is found in the Fourth Canon of the Sixth Council of Constantinople and subsequently received general approval in the Eighth Canon, wrote: "This is the rule of the True Faith, which has been vigorously upheld and defended, in good times and in bad, by the Spiritual Mother of your most tranquil Empire, the Apostolic Church of Christ, which the Grace of Almighty God has never allowed to stray from the path of Apostolic Tradition, nor to be perverted and destroyed by the strange innovations of heretics. Since the time when the Christian faith first began, the Church has followed the precepts of its teachers, Christ's chief Apostles, and has remained firm and unshakeable in accordance with the Divine Promise made by Our Lord and Savior to His chief Disciple in the holy Churches: 'Simon, Simon, behold, Satan hath desired to have you, that he may sift you as wheat: but I have prayed for thee, that thy faith fail not: and when thou art converted, strengthen thy brethren' [Luke 22:31-32]. The Lord and Savior of everyone, Who is the Essence of Faith, and Who promised that Peter's faith would not fail, urged him to strengthen his brothers; Your Royal Highness should be aware that, as everyone knows, this is the policy which the Apostolic Popes, the predecessors of my humble self, have always followed." Here is what Pope Nicholas I wrote to Michael: "The privileges of this See are eternal; they were created and nurtured by the Divine Will; they can be modified, but they cannot be transferred. They existed before your Empire came to be and they have endured unimpaired to the present, thanks be to God; they will abide after we are gone, and they will always remain, as long as Christ's Name is professed." A little later he said: "Among other things, he who was chiefly responsible for having these privileges conferred upon us at his conversion heard the Lord say: 'Strengthen thy brethren.' "[14] I could speak at much greater length if I chose to cite what the Greek Fathers, such as Origen, Cyril and others were unanimous in affirming. For example, Theodoretus, in his Epistle to Renatus, a Roman Elder, wrote: "There are many reasons why this holy See holds the reins that guide the Churches of the whole world, but the chief one is that it has always been free from the taint of heresy."[15] This is the reason why those Eastern bishops whose championing of the True

Faith subjected them to persecution by the Emperors and the Greeks, sought refuge with the Roman Popes -- St. Athanasius with Julius,[16] St. John Chrysostom with Innocent I,[17] the third Ignatius with Nicholas,[18] Theodoretus with Leo,[19] Maximus with Martin,[20] and others as well. After obtaining letters from the Roman Popes, these men recovered their Sees. This shows how great is the power which Christ conferred upon the Successor of Peter.

The other Sees and the Eastern Patriarchs have not remained steadfast in the Faith, a fact that the Greeks themselves do not deny and the legitimate Councils have clearly demonstrated. In Jerusalem there sat as Patriarchs Eutychius, Irenaeus and Hilarius, who were Arians, and John, a follower of Origen. In Antioch there were Paul of Samosata,[21] a heresiarch, Peter Gnaphaeus, a Eutychian, Macharius, a Monothelite, and others such. In Alexandria there were George and Lucius, who were Arians, Dioscurus, an Eutychian, Cyrus, a Monothelite, and others such. In Constantinople there were Macedonius, Nestorius and Sergius,[22] heresiarchs all, and many others such down to the present. They withdrew from the bosom of the Holy Roman Church, and finally fell into the hands of the Turks. Now they have neither freedom nor the Orthodox Faith.

This book the English have given you, and your own Chronicles, or Tales, contain other material hostile to the Roman Popes. I know that Your Majesty, as a man of wisdom, will not easily permit your ears or your mind to be traduced by the calumnies of the disaffected, but your subjects have not been able to read the original records of the Greeks composed by reputable authorities because no one here knows the Greek language. Furthermore, they have not been exposed to the learning of the Latins, nor have they attended the Councils, which bring together peoples from virtually the whole world before the bar of Christ Our Lord, where they could learn what Isidor, the Metropolitan of Muscovy, came to recognize and believe to be the Truth when he attended the Council of Florence.[23] Of course, it is a regular practice of the Greeks to tamper with the Histories, Conciliar Proceedings, and Epistles of the Roman Popes: heretics inserted a fictitious correspondence between Pope Vigilius and Mennas, Patriarch of Constantinople, into the Canons of the Fifth General Council; their action was detected in the Sixth Council (Canons 12 and 14), when the Canons of the Fifth Council were reviewed and it was discovered that the heretics had inserted twelve full pages.[24] Similarly, those jealous of the Roman Church introduced remarks critical of Pope Honorius into the Canons of the Sixth Council, as Anastasius the Librarian[25] notes in his History, based on Theophanes, the Isaurian Greek. In his 83rd. Epistle to the Palestinians the Sainted Pope Leo I complained that the Greeks had tampered with his letter to Flavianus while he was still alive. The Sainted Pope Gregory the Great in his Epistle 15 (Book 5) to Narses asserted that the people of Constantinople had tampered with the Proceedings of the Council of Chalcedon and averred that he suspected the same was true of the Council of Ephesus. At any rate, the Roman Codices are far more truthful than the Greek, because, as Pope Gregory said, the Romans do not indulge in artifice or imposture. In his letter to the Emperor Michael Pope Nicholas I referred to the Epistle of Pope Hadrian I and said of it: "If it has not been falsified, which is the usual practice of the Greeks, but remains as the Apostolic See dispatched it, the Epistle should still be preserved in the Chancery of the Church of Constantinople."[26]

It is generally agreed that at the conclusion of the Sixth Council numerous bishops returned to Constantinople, where they published the Trullan Canons,[27] the chief purpose of which was to attack the Roman Church. You are welcome to compare any treatise which your people or those heretics may place before you with the pure clear source, the Ancient Fathers, and if the former fails to agree, then you ought to suspect it. In anticipation of the coming of the Institution created by Christ Our Lord Himself to Muscovy, you ought sometime to give serious thought to founding genuine Academies where sound training could dispel the darkness of error from the minds of your subjects. Otherwise Muscovy will become another Egypt, because the savagery of its peoples will never be mitigated until real piety and firm faith are introduced into the realm.

To return to the English, there is a certain irony in that, following naive and deceitful writers, they have claimed that an Englishwoman (who never existed) once assumed the name of John and became Pope,[28] and now they are revering a real woman as Pope in England. If they had given you the writings of the Sainted Pope Gregory the Great, from whom they received the Christian faith, they would have performed a true Christian action, for, as was once the case with Maurice, the Emperor of Constantinople, you would have clearly discerned the Truth from the writings of that Pope and the Apostolic See that will abide forever. The English know that the Pope is constantly striving to negotiate a treaty among the rulers directed against the inveterate enemies of Christ, and that you are now disposed to accept as proved that the Pope is not Antichrist. They also know that 56 years ago, during the reign of your father Vasilii, Pope Clement VII sent an envoy to arrange for peace between your father and Sigismund I, King of Poland, and that now again Pope Gregory XIII has employed his influence and good offices (which you yourself solicited by sending your Messenger to His Holiness), to end this most unfortunate war that has been raging between you and Stefan, King of Poland, for a number of years. Not Antichrist, but the Vicar of Christ has been able to end the shedding of Christian blood that has been going on for 22 years. Satan and his hordes are confounded at the fact that the Apostolic See of St. Peter has been able to render you this service, and because your Scythians and Tatars are hearing praise of the Pope and learning to pronounce his name. Heretics and the like could never have achieved true peace among Christians; instead they would have prevented it. Satan knows that the time he has left to ensnare souls is growing short; he is aware that the Prophecy made by Christ Our Lord that there will be but one Flock and one Shepherd is about to be fulfilled. If you join all the rest of the Christian rulers in the Flock, you will provide a mighty help in propagating the glory of God and the Church of Christ, and you will win everlasting honor for yourself.

CHAPTER VI

An Account of the Sessions Held Between The Envoys of Stefan I, His Highness The King of Poland, and of Ivan Vasil'evich, The Grand Prince of Muscovy, in the Presence of Antonio Possevino, S. J., and in the Name of Pope Gregory XIII, in December, 1581, at Kiverova Gora, near Iam Zapol'skii, in Muscovy.

Antonio Possevino asked Stefan, King of Poland, and the Grand Prince of Muscovy to send representatives to a particular place to conduct peace negotiations. The Grand Prince chose Iam Zapol'skii, a village some 45 miles from Velikie Luki and an equal distance from Pskov, but since the village had been destroyed earlier by the King's Cossack soldiers, another hamlet was selected as the conference site, five miles closer to Porkhov, between Paderovich and Iam, called Kiverova Gora by its inhabitants. The second part of this name means "little mountain," while the first part, Kiverova, is connected with the name of a certain noble family. Both sides conducted their meetings in the abode of Antonio Possevino. The Prince's envoys arrived on December 13, 1581, the day sacred to St. Lucy, the Virgin Martyr.

The King's envoys were Janusz Zbaracki, Wojewoda of Bracław, Albert Radziwiłł, Count of Ołyka and Nieśwież, Marshal of the Court in Lithuania and Captain of Kowno, both of whom were Catholics, and Michał Haraburda, the Royal Secretary, of the Muscovite faith, if what differs from the Catholic can be called a faith. Haraburda had often gone on missions to the Muscovites, and on occasion to the Tatars, and was an experienced man of affairs. He had entrusted his son's education to the College of our Order in Vilna. Antonio Possevino had asked the King to allow Krzystof Warszewicki[1] to attend the meetings as a favor to the Pope, who wanted to involve the King of Sweden in the negotiations. In this way Warszewicki would become familiar with the intricacies of the problem, and when he went to Sweden in the spring could negotiate with John III on behalf of the Polish King concerning the fortresses Sweden held in Livonia. He could thus dispose of a problem which had been a source of friction between the two rulers, and also, as a nobleman and a Catholic, advance the cause of the Catholic religion in Sweden. Antonio Possevino had carefully briefed him on the religious situation there, and he would be able to acquire further information from his brother, Stanisław Warszewicki, S. J., who had already spent two years at the court of the Queen of Sweden.

106

The Prince's representatives were Prince Dmitrii Petrovich Eletskii, Governor of Kashin and a courtier of the Grand Prince; Roman Vasil'evich Alfer'ev, Governor of Kozel'sk, a courtier of the Grand Prince and a cousin of Mikhailo Beznin, the Prince's Secretary, whom the Muscovites call a Notary, Nikita Basenka, son of Nikifor Vereshchagin, and the Assistant Secretary (or Vicenotary), Zakharii Sviiazev.

Having said Mass Antonio Possevino had just finished administering the Most Holy Eucharist to some members of his retinue, when the envoys of both sides suddenly appeared. After they were seated and one of the two interpreters he had brought to Muscovy was standing by, Antonio made a few preliminary remarks on the need for sincerity in such important negotiations and that all must keep their eyes firmly fixed on Christ, Who is our source of true peace, and then he asked the leaders of both delegations to produce and read their instructions. The Muscovites read first, and their instructions ran as follows:

Instructions to the Prince's Envoys, Written in the Russian, or Muscovite, Language.

The Divine Mercy and Clemency From on High guide our destinies in the East and direct our feet to the paths of peace. By the Mercy of God, Whom we humbly adore in the Trinity, we, Ivan Vasil'evich, Great Lord, Tsar (*i.e.*, King or Emperor), and Grand Prince of all Russia, Vladimir, Moscow, and Novgorod, Emperor of Kazan', and Emperor of Astrakhan', Lord of Pskov, and Grand Prince of Smolensk, Tver', Perm', Viatka, Bulgaria and other places, and Hereditary Lord of Livonia, have sent our Great Envoys, Prince Dmitrii Petrovich Eletskii, our courtier and Governor of Kashin, Roman Vasil'evich Alfer'ev, our courtier and Governor of Kozel'sk, our Secretary, Nikita Basenka, the son of Nikifor Vereshchagin, and our Assistant Secretary, Zakharii Sviiazev, to Stefan, by the Grace of God King of Poland and Grand Prince of Lithuania, Russia, Prussia, Samogitia, and Mazovia, Prince of Transylvania, and of other places, to negotiate with his envoys concerning peace. Whatever they say to his envoys at the meeting concerning our affairs is what we too say. Given in our palace in the fortress of Aleksandrovskaia Sloboda in the year of Our Lord 7090 from the Creation of the World, the month of November, the 10th. Indiction,[2] the 47th. year of our reign, the 35th. year of our rule over Russia, the 29th. over Kazan', and the 28th. over Astrakhan'.

Those who heard the instructions considered them inadequate. The King's envoys were rightly suspicious, and asked to hear the instructions the Prince had previously sent to the Polish king in the camp by Zakharii Boltin. These proved that the Prince had fully intended to send envoys with full powers to make a final settlement, as Antonio had asked him to do. Antonio had letters read which the Prince had written him concerning this matter and transmitted first by Boltin, and then by Andrzej Połoński, and they too were found to contain the same promises the Prince had made to the King. Further to underscore the inadequacy of the Prince's authorization, Michał Haraburda read out the King's instructions, which went as follows:

The Instructions of the King of Poland, Written in Polish and Sealed with the Seals of the Kingdom of Poland and the Grand Duchy of Lithuania.

We, Stefan, Great Lord, and by the Grace of God King of Poland, Grand Prince of Lithuania, Russia, Prussia, Samogitia, Mazovia, and Livonia, and Prince of Transylvania and of other places, affirm by this letter that the Great Lord, Ivan Vasil'evich, by the Grace of God Lord of Russia, and Grand Prince of Vladimir, Moscow, Novgorod, Kazan', Astrakhan', Pskov, Tver', Iugoria, Perm', Viatka, Bulgaria, and other places, sent a letter to us by his courier, Zakharii Boltin, stating that he had received a communication from the Reverend Antonio Possevino, representative of the Most Holy Shepherd, Gregory XIII, the Supreme Roman Pontiff, and written in the name of his Lord, which on the authority of the Most Holy Apostolic and Pastoral See, urged both of us to seek peace and harmony and for each side to send envoys to a place where they might be able to make peace between us with the help of the Pope's emissary. In response to the letter from the Pope's envoy the Grand Prince is sending envoys to a certain place, Iam Zapol'skii, located between Porkhov and Zavoloch'e on the road from Porkhov to Velikie Luki. Unwilling to behold the shedding of Christian blood we too have sent our envoys, Prince Janusz Zbaracki, Wojewoda of Bracław and Captain of Kremenec and Pinsk, Lord Albert Radziwiłł, Prince of Ołyka and Nieśwież, our Marshal of the Court in the Grand Duchy of Lithuania, and Captain of Kowno, and our Secretary in the Grand Duchy of Lithuania, Michał Haraburda, to Iam Zapol'skii. With this letter we have given them full powers to meet with the envoys of the Grand Prince of Muscovy and discuss amity and concord between ourselves and the Grand Prince of Muscovy, and between the chief men of both our countries. They may make and affirm decisions, in writing and with oaths, before the Envoy, the Reverend Possevino, and they may effect, accomplish and dispose of all matters without restriction. We intend to accept their dispositions, to be bound by them, and carry them out to the letter. Upon the advice of our Senators, who met with us at the time, we pledge our Royal word as King of Poland and Grand Prince of Lithuania that we shall firmly and fully carry out all the dispositions contained in the communications of our envoys, and we bind our successors in our realms and in the whole Republic to do the same. When the Grand Prince of Muscovy designates envoys to us, we shall sign the enabling documents drawn up by our envoys with our Royal name, seal them with our seal, confirm them with our Royal oath, and have his envoys take them back to the Grand Prince of Muscovy. The Grand Prince and his successors are to comport themselves in the same way towards us, our successors, and our chief men. We have consigned this letter to our designated envoys, signed by our Royal hand, and sealed with the signets of Our Majesty as King of Poland and Grand Prince of Lithuania. Given at our camp before Pskov, in the Year of Our Lord 1581, the 30th. day of the Month of November, in the sixth year of our reign.

After all the documents had been read, the King's envoys urgently requested the Muscovites to produce a fuller set of instructions, for they knew that they could not enter into serious negotiations with so inadequate a foundation as this, and to emphasize the point they read out the enabling clause of their own instructions once again. The Muscovites made excuses, declaring that what they had read constituted the formula the Grand Princes of Muscovy had always used in their instructions, and that in the letters he had written to the King and Antonio the Grand Prince had clearly demonstrated that he had granted his envoys sufficient power to negotiate all issues. They added that since they were in a position to guarantee their commitments, and the items under consideration were in urgent need of immediate adjudication, it was idle for the King's envoys to quibble about the wording in the Prince's instructions.

One argument led to another, with no easy solution in sight. Antonio advised the King's envoys to register a formal protest, which he would insert in the record, and suggested that the question be postponed to the following day. In the evening both sides were to provide him with copies of their instructions, and trusting in God he would examine them and speak privately with the Muscovites in an endeavor to ascertain whether they possessed another charter. This was done; Antonio discovered that the Muscovites had no other instructions, and the next day he addressed both groups of delegates.

December 14. Second Session of the Envoys.

"The Muscovite envoys say that they have no other instructions," said Antonio, "and therefore we must assume that the Grand Prince is acting in good faith, because he is

109

well aware that God and all Christians are closely watching the entire course of these negotiations." The Muscovites were then asked whether they were prepared to swear that the Grand Princes of Muscovy had never used any other forms of instruction save this, and when the question was put to the junior member of their delegation, Assistant Secretary Zakharii, he answered that he would swear to it, because he had gone back over the Acts of the Muscovite *Prikaz*[3] for the past 100 years and never found any other formula. The three other envoys agreed with this, and Roman Vasil'evich added that when he went as a Messenger to King Sigismund-Augustus twenty years ago to arrange for a five-year truce, the Grand Prince had given the Great Envoys exactly the same instructions. Antonio asked Michał Haraburda whether he had ever seen different sets of instructions, for if he had, as Secretary of the Grand Duchy of Lithuania he might very well have brought copies with him, but Haraburda replied that since he had never before participated in negotiations like the present ones, he had never seen any pertinent instructions. Antonio asked the King's envoys whether they had anything further to say before he expressed his own opinion. They stated that they adhered to their original position but would bow to the Pope's authority and begin negotiations. However, they made it clear that they would not leave the site until the Muscovites had made good on all their pledges.

Antonio said: "Neither side in these discussions stands to lose by beginning negotiations; on the contrary, both will benefit substantially. If either party negotiates in bad faith, its members responsible will incur eternal disgrace. The advantage of both rulers will best be served if their envoys negotiate honestly. I consider the time has come to get down to serious business, on the understanding that the negotiations do not infringe upon the reservations expressed by the King's envoys with respect to the Prince's instructions. The Muscovite envoys must realize that no other Christian rulers have ever employed a comparable formula." Turning to the King's envoys, Antonio asked them to say whether they had any objections to holding the negotiations in Iam Zapol'skii. One of them, Albert Radziwiłł, replied that the arrangement was entirely satisfactory to them. Antonio then declared that since the victor has the right to impose terms on the vanquished, and since this was the third delegation the Muscovites had sent to ask for peace, the King's envoys should be the first to propose terms. The Wojewoda of Bracław first thanked the Pope, and Antonio, the emissary of His Holiness, for undertaking the task of mediating the peace in a paternal spirit, and then eloquently and forcefully demanded the whole of Livonia, *i.e.*, all the parts of it still held by Muscovy, stating that without agreement on this issue there could be no further progress, and the negotiations would be broken off.

The Muscovites replied that this demand was excessive, and went on to make numerous general remarks designed to persuade the King's envoys, saying, for example, that blood should not be shed, or that true peace and brotherhood cannot exist without equality, but they did add Gov' to the list of the Livonian fortresses which three months earlier the Grand Prince had promised Antonio he would restore to the Poles. The Wojewoda rightly rejoined that the Muscovites were merely trying to force the King's envoys to reveal what concessions their instructions would allow them to make to the Grand Prince, while at the same time they were demanding the fortresses adjacent to Pskov, and all the other fortresses recently captured by King Stefan, such as Velikie Luki, Velizh, Zavoloch'e, Nevel', Kholm, *etc.*

The King's envoys said that their offer represented a substantial concession. It meant giving up Pskov and Novgorod, which the King was certain to capture, and allowing 40 miles of Muscovite territory to revert to the Grand Prince. After incurring enormous expense the Poles would be withdrawing an undefeated army, while the Muscovites had not fulfilled the promises their envoys had made earlier at Vilna. However, they did agree to restore to the Prince the four fortresses they held near Pskov.

In rebuttal the Muscovites said that there was no use negotiating further if they could not keep the fortresses they still held in Livonia, because the Grand Prince had paid too dearly for them to give them up without something in return. The King's troops had found out that Pskov was so strongly fortified that although the Poles had managed to take a few other fortresses they had not yet captured the city; they would never take it, nor any other towns either. The whole day was consumed in similar wrangling. The King's envoys kept insisting that Antonio should allow them to depart for the camp or go to the King, since the Muscovites obviously had no intention of surrendering Livonia. They made this suggestion designedly, in order to speed up the negotiations. Antonio declared he would dismiss the envoys at nightfall on condition that they return the next morning. The meeting was adjourned.

December 15. Third Session of the Envoys.

Since they were staying in Kiverova Gora the Muscovites appeared as soon as the King's envoys arrived from Iam Zapol'skii, about five miles away, where they were staying. Almost the whole day was spent in haggling over three particular points. The King's envoys angrily charged that the Muscovites were simply stalling in an effort to avoid ceding all of Livonia, and they added that they were formally requesting the Grand Prince to resign his title and rights to Livonia and to have the King of Sweden considered a party to the negotiations.[4] Then they said that, in addition to the fortresses near Pskov and the other Muscovite territory the King had seized this year, they were willing to restore the fortress of Kholm, which had been taken in the previous year. They declared this was a very substantial concession, because the delaying tactics practised by the Grand Prince had caused the Polish King to lose several Livonian fortresses, which had passed into other hands. Their instructions from the King demanded the quickest possible conclusion to the negotiations; thus, they were giving Antonio notice that they could not endure further delay; they would remain at the conference site no more than three or four days at most.

The Muscovite envoys rehearsed at length their previous remarks concerning equality, restraint of pride, and avoidance of bloodshed, and averred that the tactics adopted by the King's envoys would lead to massive bloodshed, for which they alone would be responsible. They pointed out that their instructions had nothing to say about the King of Sweden; if he wished to send envoys to the Grand Prince to discuss peace, they would be given a hearing. They reminded the Poles that when Haraburda and Gronostajski had once gone on a mission to the Grand Prince they had refused to discuss anything not found in their instructions; the King's envoys thus should understand that they were similarly obliged to remain within the limits specified in the instructions the Grand Prince had given them. They promised to turn over the Livonian fortresses of Pernau, Paida, Korstin, Huntecz, Kurslin and Porcholia to the King.

The King's envoys repeated their demands for restoration of the whole of Livonia and for the Grand Prince to abjure his title and rights to the region. Before Antonio left the camp at Pskov he had asked the King to impart to his emissaries his views concerning the status of the King of Sweden and the Grand Prince's abjuration of his title to and his rule of Livonia, and thus he already knew that the King's envoys had not received authorization to give up fortresses the King had captured unless they could obtain exceptionally favorable conditions in return. This led him to entreat the King's envoys by the blood of Christ and the obedience they owed the Apostolic See not to act rashly at so critical a juncture. He asked them to give him a little time to reflect on the issues and find answers to the problem in order to advance the cause of peace. They agreed, and Antonio said: "There will be no meeting tomorrow. The basic issue is the cession of the whole of Livonia. The Grand Prince's envoys have now offered six additional fortresses, but the King's envoys say they will not discuss anything further until the Prince's envoys surrender all the fortresses. Neither side is being open with the other. You should carefully go through your instructions to see exactly what commitments you can make and how far you can go, so that at our next session you can be prepared to state unequivocally what is the best offer each of you can make."

After the Poles withdrew, the Grand Prince's envoys remained with Antonio most of the night, as they very often did. In the interests of arranging peace more quickly he asked them to state frankly and confidentially what they were allowed to do concerning Livonia, and they revealed the extent of their instructions to him. He obtained their permission to place the whole matter before Jan Zamojski,[5] Supreme Chancellor and Captain-General of the Polish Kingdom, to whom the King had granted full powers to make a settlement, and he sent a letter by extraordinary courier that same night to him at the Polish camp. Zamojski's reply took all of four days to arrive; in the meantime Antonio had a good deal of difficulty allaying the suspicions harbored by the Muscovites towards the King's envoys. The latter constantly asserted that although their instructions granted them full powers to dispose of all issues, the Muscovites obviously possessed an even stronger mandate than they because it was set forth in so few words. Two days passed and Antonio invited the King's envoys to an informal meeting at which they could at least discuss the position of the King of Sweden. On December 18 they all assembled as usual at his place.

December 18. Fourth Session.

After reflecting on the problem, as the envoys had charged him, Antonio said that in his opinion the questions raised by the King's envoys concerning the position of the King of Sweden and the need for the Grand Prince to abjure his title to and rights in Livonia were both more important issues than they perhaps realized. He went on to say that the Pope had instructed him to look into the matter of the King of Sweden, who was a friend of the Holy See, and at Staritsa, in the name of both His Holiness and King Stefan, he had held five thorough discussions with the Grand Prince on the topic, which led the Prince to send a letter to the King of Sweden reviewing the whole issue. He was sure that King Stefan would be happy to assume this responsibility on behalf of his kinsman and spiritual brother, since it would do much to prevent wars in the future. He would be glad to hear any reply the Grand Prince's envoys might wish to make before taking up another topic.

The Muscovites replied that, as they had already said, their instructions from the Grand Prince contained no reference to this question, which ought properly to be directed to representatives of Sweden. They asked the King's envoys whether they held any authorization from the King of Sweden, and when they had to admit they did not, the Muscovites said: "Why do you keep trying to raise this issue? Even if we were permitted to discuss it, we could not make any firm commitments, particularly because there are other issues outstanding between our Grand Prince and the King of Sweden, who over the past two years has occupied Karelia, Ivangorod, Iam, and perhaps other places, as well as some fortresses in Livonia." Antonio praised the zeal with which the King's envoys were supporting the cause of the King of Sweden, but when he heard the Muscovites' reply, to which the King's envoys could not readily return an answer, he said that the only remaining alternative was to ask the King of Sweden and the Grand Prince of Muscovy, if they did not wish to meet personally, to designate representatives who could take up these issues at some future time. The Muscovites made no reply to this suggestion, as they had no instructions from the Prince on the matter. All the envoys unanimously agreed to drop the issue and proceed to the next item. The King's envoys were in fact quite pleased at the outcome, for their instructions said that failure to secure inclusion of Sweden was not to divert them from the task of concluding a peace. The next item was the demand for the Prince to surrender his title to and rights in Livonia. The only comment the Muscovite envoys had to make on the subject was that it seemed unfair to expel their Prince from Livonia. The session ended pending arrival of the letter Antonio and the King's envoys were expecting Zamojski to send from the camp, which would assist them in reaching a solution of the central issue.

December 20. Fifth Session.

Zamojski sent his relative, Stanisław Żółkiewski,[6] son of the Wojewoda of Bełsk, who arrived after the conclusion of the Fifth Session, bringing Antonio a letter of accreditation containing instructions that, in order to obtain a satisfactory peace, the Grand Prince's envoys would have to cede Neuhaus, and two other Livonian fortresses on the Narva River, which gave the Muscovites free access to the sea, while the fortresses taken by the King -- Velikie Luki, Zavoloch'e, Nevel' and Velizh -- would have to remain under Polish control. Zamojski implied that if the negotiations became absolutely deadlocked, Velikie Luki might possibly be returned, but no concessions were to be made to the Muscovites on Livonia. He had not received authorization of this procedure from the King,

114

but he hoped that both the King and the Estates would finally approve it. Antonio was considerably disturbed by this unexpected development. Zamojski had not written these instructions in his own hand, and Żółkiewski had said that the decision to allow the Muscovites to keep any fortresses in Livonia or to restore Velikie Luki would mainly depend upon Antonio and his reputation and judgment. However, a letter considered to be a holograph document conferring authority to do so was essential, in order to preserve a full account of what had occurred, in case future Polish authorities should demand an explanation. If the decision were subsequently reversed (which Antonio had known to happen more than once in other situations), or nullified for any serious reason by the King's envoys (who reiterated that they had received no authorization from the King to make any such arrangements), Antonio might be thought to have beguiled, or actually deceived, the Grand Prince's envoys with empty promises, and this would prove exceedingly unfortunate for the advancement of the worship of God in Muscovy. Although he personally lacked the power to surrender a single acre of Livonia, even if he wised to do so, Antonio was faced with the incessant demands on the part of the King for the cession of the whole of Livonia, a position to which the King was committed by the oath he had sworn, and a decree of both Estates of the Kingdom, a circumstance of which Antonio had been informed on numerous occasions, most recently by the eloquent and frequent speeches made by the King's envoys on the subject.

A few days earlier Antonio had written to the King and Zamojski, asking them whether, in the event the Prince refused to cede all of Livonia, he should return to Muscovy and try to arrange for representatives of the Prince to attend the sessions of the Diet scheduled to take place in Warsaw in March. The meetings of the Diet would reveal clearly whether the decree passed by the Estates of the Realm could be modified in any way, in order to leave some portion of Livonia in the Prince's hands, or whether it was the decision of the entire Republic to support the original position by continuing the war. If the latter, the Prince's delegates could witness the resolve of the Kingdom for themselves and thus more easily be inclined to accept the peace terms offered. There was no need to break off the present negotiations, which could continue through the balance of the winter. Zamojski replied in a letter dated December 13, which was delivered by a different courier the same day Żółkiewski arrived from the Polish camp with the Chancellor's second brief letter of instructions. In his reply Zamojski informed Antonio there was no question of modifying the decree. The views of the King and the Estates had not altered, and if the Prince refused to give up all of Livonia, the issue would be settled by force of arms.

When the King's envoys were apprised of all these developments, they decided that they should refuse to negotiate further concerning the fortresses in Livonia, or to make any more proposals at all. In their view, the Prince's envoys had by now had ample opportunity to see that King Stefan was determined to acquire all of Livonia; they had presented all their strongest arguments in favor of having it restored to the Prince, and now could only hope that attrition of the Polish position might lead the King to find some other territory to concede to their Prince. Furthermore, the King's envoys did not believe that peace could be made on the basis of the fortresses which, according to Żółkiewski's unsupported testimony, Zamojski was supposed to be offering, because the King did not control the fortresses which were being promised to the Prince in his name. They thought that Antonio should reply to Zamojski, and he sent the letter reproduced below. It contained a number of proposals which would contribute greatly to the expeditious conclusion of an honorable peace if the Chancellor would seize this splendid opportunity to indicate to Żółkiewski his private position, which he would not care to see publicly divulged. A part of this session was given over to these private negotiations, before the Muscovite envoys were asked to appear.

A Letter from Jan Zamojski, Supreme Chancellor and Captain-General of the Kingdom of Poland, to Antonio Possevino.

The information I gave your Lordship concerning the sortie made by the Muscovites and their defeat is true. I wish the information supplied by Piotr Koltowski were true, but I don't think it is. If peace is not made, I shall attack the enemy unless he attacks me first. But enough of these matters. I am sending your Lordship's letter to the King with all possible speed. In my opinion it is useless to debate ceding any part of Livonia at the Diet. No one with any regard for the future of his country would recommend it, even in the King's Privy Council. The situation has now become such that if the enemy fights us he risks losing Dorpat as well as all the rest of Livonia, for the Swedes hold half the country, are besieging Weissenstein, and closing in on Pernau and Fellin; Dorpat is the only place the Prince has any chance of keeping. What is the position of the Estates? They will have to appropriate more funds to outfit soldiers than they have up to now, and vote additional subsidies to carry us through August. What can happen in the meantime? The enemy now has all the foreign weapons he can import; how can he become more powerful later? I understand that these worthy envoys of the Muscovites are stalling. If they are waiting for new information they will obtain it from their courier, whom

116

I ordered escorted to the conference site. How seriously does this courier take his responsibilities? He said he would go to Porkhov and from there to Iam Zapol'skii to take a letter for your Lordship, but travelling only at night and not during the day, with men from Neuhaus as guides, he wandered off the Porkhov road, started out towards Pskov, and finally ended up no more than eight miles from our camp. Some of our soldiers found him there and set him back on the Porkhov road. Then he handed over his horse, that had a letter from the Prince to his envoys sewn under the saddle, to one of his companions and told the men to escape and he also told his three other companions to run away, although he had sworn he would not do this. This incident should certainly be carefully investigated to determine whether this man ought to be considered a courier or a traitor. I was willing to give him the benefit of the doubt, and so I provided him with guides and had him escorted to the conference site. I believe the new letter he is bringing so carefully concealed can be of real help to us in concluding the negotiations. Połoński is presently leading a more agreeable life than I am, as I have only one person who can handle the Muscovite language. I commend myself to your Lordship. Given in the camp before Pskov on December 13, 1581.

Second Letter from Jan Zamojski, Supreme Chancellor and Captain-General of the Kingdom of Poland, to Antonio Possevino.

I am sending your Lordship my kinsman, Lord Stanisław Żółkiewski, son of the Wojewoda of Bełsk. He will tell your Lordship what you wish to ascertain from me. You may trust what he says and be absolutely sure that he will not reveal any information you give him, and I give you my word that he will not do so at any time in the future. I commend myself to your Lordship. Given in the camp before Pskov on December 17, 1581.

Antonio Possevino's Reply to the Letters of Jan Zamojski.

Today I received two letters from Your Eminence. One was brought to me by the person escorting the Grand Prince's courier who had tarried on the road, or somewhere, for eight whole days. The other was delivered by Lord Stanisław Żółkiewski, Your Eminence's kinsman, who reported in some detail on the issue in which the King's envoys and I are vitally interested. With regard to what he said, if Your Eminence would be good enough to send us a letter written by your own hand and sealed with your personal seal, we could continue our work in the expectation of achieving an excellent peace. If you cannot

117

do so, whatever decisions we make will have to be taken on faith, and we shall have to account for our actions to the Republic, the Pope, the Grand Prince of Muscovy, and perhaps other rulers as well, to say nothing of our Order. Poland contains so many members of it that they might almost be considered hostages, and thus serious thought must be taken concerning them and their reputation. I am sure that Your Eminence's keen intellect has clearly grasped how desirable it is for the King to give his envoys the instructions he promised them written in his own hand, and similarly, other instructions should be circulated in such a way as not to prejudice so worthy a cause by creating the possibility of a delay caused by the need for close scrutiny of documents, as happens in this over-scrupulous age in which we live. I am delighted that Your Eminence approves of my conduct; I hope the time will never come when you will have occasion to find fault with it. May Jesus fortify Your Illustrious Eminence's hand and heart with Celestial Strength. Given at Kiverova Gora, in the evening of December 20, 1581.

When the Muscovite envoys were summoned to the meeting, they complained bitterly, as they had frequently done in other matters, that they were being treated like prisoners, their supplies stolen, and their men kidnapped or murdered. They further charged that the Grand Prince's courier bearing letters for Antonio and for them had been brought to the site under guard, his companions had been slain on the road, and their guide, a peasant, had been burned with torches (a common occurrence) to extract a confession. The courier had been given both written and verbal instructions from Zamojski to come straight to Antonio from the Polish camp, but notwithstanding this the King's envoys had instructed the Commander of the cavalry, Zebrzydowski (a high nobleman and an upright and brave Pole), to detain him for three days, and even after this long delay the Commander had been unwilling to restore the Grand Prince's letters to him. They declared that they had come from Muscovy to the meetings solely because the Grand Prince had trusted the Pope and his emissary Antonio, but in view of the insults and hostility to which they were exposed they would prefer to withdraw and terminate the negotiations. The King's envoys sought to refute the charges and began to rehearse the reasons for the delay that Zamojski had reported to Antonio. The latter, however, had questioned the courier and found out that he had been detained eight days en route for some unknown reason. He realized that any delays in transmitting communications sent by the King or the Prince would seriously retard the conclusion of the negotiations, and thus he earnestly entreated both sides by the authority of the Pope, to which they often said they deferred because the Pope had received it from God, and, above all, by the blood of Christ, not to abandon their efforts because of the crimes that Satan occasionally committed, for the longer they took, the more Christian blood would be shed. If the Muscovites' allegations were true he would accept full responsibility for the incident, and he would make due recompense at the appropriate time to either the King or the Prince, as the case might be.

They resumed their previous discussion in a better frame of mind. The chief issue was the single final proposal of the King's envoys, designed to prove to the Muscovites how extremely reluctant the King was to cause further bloodshed. It was for Antonio to select one of the four fortresses captured in the past two years and restore it to the Prince, provided that the Muscovites withdrew from all of Livonia and surrendered Sebezh, a fortress near Polotsk. The Prince's envoys replied that they would not agree to the proposal concerning Sebezh because the fortress had nothing to do with Livonia. They demanded the return of all their fortresses captured by the King, but were willing to add one other fortress in Livonia, called Lais. The King's envoys replied that Lais was in Swedish hands, and without another word they arose and withdrew. Their action ended the session for that day.

December 22. Sixth Session.

Both sides hurled at one another the same charges the envoys had often made at private sessions, and the Muscovites said over and over again that their Prince had not taken Livonia from the kings of Poland but from the Bishops and the Knights of the Sword. However, both sides said that reverence for the Holy See and the Pope had already led them to make many concessions, and they were prepared to abide by Antonio's ruling that one of two fortresses, Velikie Luki or Zavoloch'e, should be returned to the Grand Prince. At this juncture Piotrowski, a Polish nobleman, arrived from the camp with the following letter which Chancellor Zamojski had written to Antonio:

Jan Zamojski, Chancellor and Captain-General of the Kingdom, to Antonio Possevino.

Earlier I sent Żółkiewski to your Lordship to inform you what concessions we can make to the Muscovites in Livonia and under what circumstances, but later I decided to reduce the proposals to writing and send them to your Lordship. I am doing so now. You will obtain further information from Żółkiewski and particularly from our envoys. I wish your Lordship good health. Given at the camp before Pskov on December 19, in the Year of Our Lord, 1581.

First Conditions.

Velikie Luki and the fortresses of Zavoloch'e and Nevel' are to remain in His Majesty's hands. If Sebezh is returned to the Prince, Velizh must remain under Polish control, and the Prince's envoys are not to make an issue of it, since they never asked for the place in previous sessions. If the Muscovite envoys are empowered to arrange this at once, without having to request further instructions from their Prince, and further providing that in the interim Pernau is not lost (on which I should like a word from your Lordship), I will go so far as to cede the Livonian fortresses of Neuhaus, Serenets, Lais, Ostrov, Kholm, Krasnogorodok, Voronetz, and Vel'ia.

Second and Final Conditions.

If the Muscovite envoys have to send for further instructions from their Prince and lack the authority to accept immediately the fortresses of Neuhaus, Serenets, and Lais, to cede His Royal Highness Velikie Luki, Zavoloch'e, Nevel', and Velizh, and to give up Sebezh or at least have it destroyed, His Royal Highness will not allow me to cede the fortresses of Neuhaus, Lais, and Serenets. His Royal Highness will keep all of Livonia, restore or demolish Sebezh, and keep Zavoloch'e, Nevel', and Velizh, which is what he had empowered your Lordship and me to do, but he will restore Velikie Luki to the Prince in addition to the fortresses of Kholm, Ostrov, Krasnogorodok, Voronets and Vel'ia. The King will retain all of Livonia, as well as Neuhaus, Serenets, and Lais, in addition to the aforementioned fortresses of Zavoloch'e, Nevel', and Velizh, while Sebezh will be either restored or destroyed.

Antonio received no communication concerning these terms from the Polish envoys, and he realized this would give him more time to reflect about restoring either Velikie Luki or Zavoloch'e to the Prince. He also felt sure that after reading the letter Zamojski had sent them the King's envoys would come to the session next day better prepared to negotiate.

December 23. Seventh Session.

The envoys handed Antonio the peace conditions they had received and began to press him for an answer to give Zamojski, so that Piotrowski could leave the minute they handed the terms to him. Antonio felt that the time allowed was insufficient, but to avoid wasting the day he asked the Muscovite envoys whether they could restore Sebezh (a fortress in the Polotsk area) or whether they possessed authority to exchange it for the Livonian fortresses Zamojski had offered in the King's name. They replied that they would destroy Sebezh if King Stefan would destroy Drissa, but they must insist on the return of the other fortresses the King had captured. With the approval of the King's envoys and no opposition from the Muscovites, Antonio formulated a proposal to the effect that the Grand Prince would receive Velikie Luki on condition that he cede all of Livonia, while Zavoloch'e would remain in the King's hands. There were two further matters of business at the session. The Muscovites asserted that Serenets, one of the three Livonian fortresses offered by the King's envoys, was actually in Swedish hands, and Haraburda sought to prove to the Muscovites how the Grand Prince would benefit by making peace and withdrawing from Livonia. That day the Muscovites indicated privately that they would be satisfied with Neuhaus and Kerepets, on condition that the three other fortresses of Zavoloch'e, Nevel' and Velizh, were restored to them. Their final concession was to give even those up if the Grand Prince were allowed to keep Neuhaus and Kerepets. Then a second letter arrived from Chancellor Zamojski containing a third set of conditions. It ran as follows:

Jan Zamojski to Antonio Possevino.

I have instructed our Royal envoys to get in touch with you concerning the matters you referred to me through our Lord Żółkiewski. The solution of our problems has been rendered more difficult by the fact that the Prince did not discuss any of these fortresses (*e.g.*, Velizh) during our earlier negotiations. Your Lordship will learn more about this from our envoys, to whom, at their request, I have sent a handwritten memorandum specifying the places I consider can be ceded. My best regards to your Lordship. Given in the camp before Pskov, December 22, 1581.

Ultimate Conditions.

To achieve a good peace and to preserve your Lordship's work, which was specially undertaken in the name of the Pope, from failure, as a last resort I shall take it upon myself to offer the following terms: His Royal Highness will not cede the fortresses of Neuhaus, Lais, and Serenets; he will keep them along with all the rest of Livonia. He must have Velizh and Sebezh, or the latter must be destroyed, but he is willing to restore Velikie Luki, Zavoloch'e, Nevel', Kholm, Ostrov, Voronets, Krasnogorodok, and Vel'ia to the Grand Prince.

If these terms are rejected it will be clear that God does not wish us to make peace at this time. As God is my witness, I cannot and will not make further concessions. Your Lordship is not to blame; both His Royal Highness and I are fully convinced of your exceptional devotion and integrity, but I must satisfy my own conscience and discharge the obligation I owe to His Majesty and to our country. I swear to your Lordship by the Living God and by His Son, Jesus Christ, Whose awful mysteries you celebrate and Whose name you bear, that his Majesty would prefer to secure more advantageous terms and will not make more onerous concessions than these.

When the gist of this document was communicated to the King's envoys, it was decided that since the Muscovites had already promised to give up all of Livonia there was no need to reveal these Ultimate Conditions to them. For a number of reasons the next session was scheduled for the Most Holy Day of the Birth of Our Lord.

December 25. Eighth Session.

The Muscovites privately gave Antonio a document in which they had indicated that if the King would leave Neuhaus in the hands of the Grand Prince, the latter would abandon his claim to Velizh, and assured him that this arrangement would be satisfactory to them. The King's envoys stated that in addition to Velikie Luki they would give the Muscovites the rich territory of Rzhev, which had once belonged to Zavoloch'e. The Muscovites replied that the Rzhev lands were still a part of Zavoloch'e, and finally the King's envoys requested Antonio to decide which of the two fortresses, Nevel' or Zavoloch'e, he thought should be returned to the Prince. After hearing the position of the King's envoys he asked for a night to confer with the Muscovites and adjourned the session. That evening a courier arrived posthaste from Muscovy bearing the Grand Prince's reply to a letter Antonio had sent him a few days earlier from Biskovits and another letter for his envoys. At their request Antonio secured the agreement of the King's envoys not to hold a session the next day. The interval was spent in intense discussions with the Muscovite envoys in an attempt to find a way to break the deadlock in the negotiations. Antonio passed on the letter he had received from the Prince to the King's envoys in an effort to preserve scrupulous neutrality. Antonio told the Muscovites that if they were afraid to take any initiatives, such as leaving Nevel' and Velizh under the King's control, without consulting the Prince, he would go surety with his own life before the Prince rather than see the negotiations fail, but they took their solemn oaths that they could not assume such responsibility, for, they added, even if each envoy had ten heads, on their return the Prince would cut off every single one of them if they did so. Antonio dispatched a courier with all speed to Zamojski to inform him of the latest terms, and the following day the King's envoys returned to the conference as agreed.

December 28. Ninth Session.

Antonio called on both sides to conclude peace at that session, which the King's envoys had announced was the last one they would attend. Earlier he had spoken at some length to the King's envoys on the considerable effort he had been expending to achieve this goal, but in reply they had stated only that they intended to adhere to the proposals they had already made. They went on to argue that by leading them to believe he could achieve peace Antonio with his activity had merely served to delay the Polish army before Pskov for two months. Now they were under orders to return to the camp, and thus they had no business to offer further concessions until they had made an accounting to the King and the Republic, to which they had sworn their oaths. At the end of their address they stated publicly and in Antonio's presence that the conclusion of peace did not depend upon them alone, and as a final request they asked Antonio to testify to their devotion to the Republic and the Kingdom at the sessions of the Diet meeting in Warsaw in March, by which time he would probably have returned from Muscovy. They concluded by saying that they were offering their hands in farewell to the Muscovite envoys, and would take leave of Antonio by letter the next day.

The Muscovite envoys made an address to Antonio which, though short, nevertheless revealed the extent of their disquiet. They said that they had acceded to his demand to surrender Livonia, and Michał Haraburda should now appreciate how much truth was contained in the opening statement he made calling upon them to give up Livonia, in which he had said: "Once the stumbling-block of Livonia is removed, the remaining road to peace will be smooth." They were ceding Livonia: they had acted, while the King's envoys had only talked. They called on God as their witness that "the conclusion of peace did not depend on them alone;" they knew who would be responsible for the terrible

123

new bloodshed that was imminent. In rebuttal Michał Haraburda repeated some of the previous arguments, and then Antonio said that it meant a very great deal to him to see peace made, but as he had been unable to persuade either side to show sufficient trust in the other's ruler, he was now proposing that King Stefan return Zavoloch'e, since he had not yet irrevocably committed himself to holding it. He hoped this concession might achieve the desired result, but if it failed to do so, it meant that the time had not yet come for the parties to be considered worthy of enjoying true peace. If neither side would give in over these two small fortresses, the King's envoys should consider granting the Muscovites ten days in order for them to obtain an answer on the issue from the Grand Prince, as they were willing to do. The King's envoys declared that they could not agree to this, while the Muscovites rejoined that they had already exceeded their authority by promising to surrender Dorpat and other places; they could only regret that when some 40 fortresses were to change hands the whole peace should founder merely because of two. The King's envoys said: "You say you have made promises exceeding your authority; make good on them. Let both sides abide by Antonio's decision concerning the two fortresses at issue, and later we can justify our actions, you to the Grand Prince and we to the King." Antonio begged the King's envoys to give the Muscovites one more night for deliberation. They agreed, but only on condition that Antonio must inform them before daybreak whether the Muscovites would agree; if they did so, the King's envoys would return to the conference table, but otherwise they would depart without further ado. That night the Muscovite envoys explained that it was utterly impossible for them to cede Velizh; however, if the King's envoys would agree, they would give up all the rest of Livonia and keep only Neuhaus, while the King's envoys would retain Velizh, with both sides fully reserving their rights until the expected replies from both rulers arrived. With this proposal the meeting ended. The representations Antonio made to the envoys and others in order to keep the negotiations going can be found in the memoranda he wrote to the King's envoys and the King; they are of considerable assistance in affording insight into the whole problem.

December 28. Tenth Session.

This was the day the King's envoys had fixed for their departure. The night before the Muscovite envoys on two occasions spent considerable time with Antonio, weeping, and asking him what they should decide concerning Velizh; if they allowed the King to keep it the Prince would make them pay with their lives, but if the peace were aborted over this single fortress they knew that the carnage would be frightful when the war broke

124

out again. Antonio declared that at this critical juncture the only thing he could think of left to do in order to save their lives was to give each of the envoys a document written in his own hand and sealed with his personal seal, in which he would state under oath that he had compelled them to make this decision, and he offered his life to the Prince to do with as he pleased if the latter decided that Antonio had acted rashly in his zeal to prevent a new outbreak of the conflict. If all else failed, he would sound out the King's envoys as to the possibility of obtaining equal compensation for Velizh. The Muscovites said that they would entrust their safety and the final solution of the problem of Velizh to Antonio, but they begged him to do all in his power to see to it that their action should not cause the Grand Prince to put them to death.

After this discussion the King's envoys appeared, for they had been delaying their departure in order to take leave of Antonio. When they heard his proposal they promised to place Velizh under Antonio's personal jurisdiction. He would have to assume full responsibility and assign a member of his own entourage to guarantee that either it remained in the King's hands or his alternative proposal was accepted. They said that they did not have to fear for their lives if in this matter they exceeded the King's instructions, but their position would be highly compromised unless Antonio testified personally and publicly before the King and the Diet that was to meet in Warsaw that they had taken this action solely in the interest of the general good. Antonio agreed to do so, and the conference resumed. The King's envoys asked for Sebezh to be handed over to the King, while the Muscovites countered by saying they would leave Velizh alone if Sebezh were similarly treated, and if the Grand Prince retained Dorpat they would be satisfied if the Prince destroyed Sebezh and the King destroyed Drissa. A great controversy arose over this, and the question was put off to the next day on the proviso, formulated by the King's envoys, that the intervening time be used to dispatch a courier to the camp to ascertain from Zamojski more fully what the King's views were.

To a question from the King's envoys the Muscovites replied that they were fully empowered to surrender fortresses in Livonia held by the Grand Prince, but they could do nothing about those in the hands of the King of Sweden. Then the King's envoys said that the one point all their Envoys and Messengers had emphasized over and over again, both in speeches and in writing, was that King Stefan insisted on having the whole of Livonia. This meant that the Prince's envoys must state whether they would renounce the Prince's title to and jurisdiction in the area. If not, a spark would remain which could touch off a new war, because King Stefan intended to acquire the fortresses held by the King of Sweden peacefully on the grounds of kinship, or else he would discover some other means to obtain them. If the Prince now refused formally to renounce all claim to Livonia and the King should decide to fight the King of Sweden in order to recover these fortresses, the war between King Stefan and the Prince would break out again.

Antonio had other reasons for approving of these sentiments; he said that both sides would make a firmer and truer settlement if they were carefully to eliminate all possible causes of future conflict. The Muscovite envoys replied that they would list all the fortresses held by the Grand Prince in the Treaty, surrender legal possession of them to the King, and confirm the entire transaction with an oath. However, they said, the King's envoys should stop demanding places over which the Prince had no control nor possession, and no mention of the King of Sweden could be made in the Treaty.

Antonio observed that if it was possible for them to decide all other questions by mutual agreement, the envoys should by all means draw up a provision whereby, in the event the King and the Grand Prince should clash over a fortress, the Grand Prince should not invade the territory of Livonia under the King's control, the Kingdom of Poland, the Grand Duchy of Lithuania, and Prussia, while the King should not invade the realm belonging to the Grand Prince. The King's envoys informed Antonio they desired to lodge a formal protest over this, which they wished him to take down in his own hand and sign with his seal. Antonio replied that he would do so on the understanding that the protest was made without prejudice to the King, the Grand Prince, or any other person, and constituted no diminution of their rights. He added that he would accompany the protest with his own stated opinion to the effect that although both sides possessed a legitimate right to protest jurisdiction and title, the issue could not constitute valid grounds for war, and he took this action within the hour. He stated his intention to call upon the envoys to do all they could in the way of moderate representation with both rulers to minimize this issue as a source of future contention. The King's envoys registered their protest through Michał Haraburda, and then they served a formal demand on Antonio for inclusion of it in the record. Even the King, as he had himself told Antonio in the camp, knew that the fortresses could not be surrendered without leaving the Muscovites some room in which to manoeuvre, but at least his envoys had eloquently placed the Muscovite envoys on notice that he was determined to acquire the fortresses the King of Sweden had seized in the war. The last question concerned whether the artillery in the fortresses under Muscovite control should be handed over along with the fortresses

126

themselves, for the King's envoys claimed that the previous Muscovite envoys, who had been in Vilna, had promised to do this. The Muscovites answered that they would immediately summon courtiers from Novgorod, and if the King's envoys would be patient there would be no difficulty about the artillery. This ended the session, and another was called for the following day.

December 29. Eleventh Session.

The Muscovite envoys began the session with the question of Sebezh, and a long and involved discussion ensued. The King's envoys urged the problem be referred to Antonio, who would in course refer it to both rulers without prejudice to the rest of the treaty. The Muscovites reminded them that it was only because of Antonio they had ceded Velizh, allowed it to remain intact in the King's hands, and were no longer insisting it be destroyed: they did not think that the King's envoys should continue to demand further concessions. Using the analogy of a piece of metal which, if not removed, would infest the entire body, they declared that unless the problem of Sebezh were solved, the entire peace negotiations would become infected and poisoned by it. If the King's envoys wished to postpone consideration of the matter temporarily, they would agree, since this would permit them to consult the Grand Prince and do all that they could to prevent contention from arising among future generations. Supporting the position of the King's envoys, Antonio urged both sides to tackle the other issues, leaving this one aside, since he was familiar with the King's views on the subject and was awaiting Zamojski's reply to the questions he had asked him. The Muscovites taxed the King's envoys with failing to carry out the promise to withdraw the Polish army besieging Pskov which Zakharii Boltin had brought to the Grand Prince, and which the King had promised Antonio to do in a few days. The King's envoys replied that all the King had promised Antonio was not to attempt to storm the city; the army would not be withdrawn until a peace treaty had been devised, drawn up and attested with the proper oaths. When the King's envoys asked how the fortresses would be surrendered, the Muscovites said: "We are reasonable men. Our Great Lord has given us no instructions. He is a Christian Prince and has ordered us to act in an honorable Christian manner. We are acting in this way towards you, just as we would with our own people. We want you to know that the minute we reach a decision regarding Sebezh we shall summon courtiers from Novgorod, whose rank is as high as our own, and who have been assigned the task of surrendering the fortresses. One of them is Ivan Zherebovin, the Voievoda of Porkhov." The Muscovites demanded that no more of their peasants be carried off to Lithuania; the King's envoys stated that the practice had been forbidden by the King, and as soon as they made peace further incidents of this sort would not occur. The Muscovites then declared that they would be ready to surrender the fortresses on or about the day of the Annunciation of the Virgin Mary [March 25]. In spite of the objections voiced by the King's envoys, they arranged that both sides should restore each other's artillery on the sensible basis of markings or notations on the weapons that identified them as the property of either the King or the Grand Prince.

The next issue was prisoners. The Muscovites asked both rulers to display their generosity by releasing all of them, but the King's envoys said that the only way to do it was to follow the procedure the King had described to Antonio: a soldier should be exchanged for a soldier, an officer for an officer, and a commander for a commander; any prisoners left over could either be ransomed, or exchanged for the Livonians held in Muscovy. Furthermore, the King's envoys stipulated that the Prince must free those merchants whom he was holding contrary to all law, Christian custom, and the convenants and agreements into which the rulers had previously entered, to the effect that merchants should not suffer in the event of war. The King had named two merchants of Vilna, Zareski and Marcin Mammonicz, as individuals whom he wished the Prince to release. The Muscovites replied that Christian blood should not be for sale, and they said that the merchants were not prisoners under restraint; the Prince had assigned them a *Pristav* merely to prevent anything from happening to them. This discussion lasted to evening, and other matters were put off to the next session.

New Year's Day, 1582. Twelfth Session.

The Muscovite envoys spent much of the night with Antonio. They told him he would give their Great Lord true pleasure if the documents he was to compose concerning the peace referred to the Prince as Tsar of Kazan' and Astrakhan', for in his eyes none of the fortresses he was preparing to surrender to the King remotely compared in importance with this salutation. Antonio took advantage of this opportunity to speak to the envoys at length about the single Emperor of the Christians, a title requiring confirmation by the Apostolic See, which was brought to the West at the time when the Byzantine Emperors began showing less loyalty to the Catholic Church than they should. If the Grand Prince of Muscovy desired to have a valid title and to enjoy a legitimate dignity, he should first negotiate with the Pope, like the rest of the Christian rulers, who were well aware that the acquisition of Kazan' and Astrakhan' was not sufficient to warrant the addition of a new title, such as "The Other Caesar," which means Emperor, or King. If the Prince tried to call himself Caesar, everyone would know that this title meant only Tsar, not Caesar, and that it was an oddity borrowed from the Tatars in an effort to approximate the title held by other Kings.

The Muscovites replied that Honorius and Arcadius had sent an Imperial crown from Rome to Vladimir, the first prince of Muscovy, and the Pope had sent a certain bishop, Cyprian, to confirm it, and other nonsense of this sort.[7] Antonio explained that Honorius and Arcadius had lived 500 years before Vladimir, but the envoys in their ignorance said they meant another Honorius and Arcadius, who had lived at the same time as Vladimir. They again urged Antonio, because they had called the Pope the Shepherd of Universal Christianity, not to let the King cheat the Prince out of his proper title of Tsar of Kazan' and Astrakhan', and the King should also allow him to keep his title of Lord of Livonia. Antonio replied: "It is proper for you to call the Pope the Shepherd of Universal Christianity, since it was Christ Our Lord Who instituted this custom. The Pope himself is little concerned with this title, save insofar as it serves to promote the unity of the Church and the glory of God, and prefers to call himself the Servant of the Servants of God. How can your Prince expect to keep his title to Livonia when he has to hand the fortresses over to the King? If you take off the clothes you are wearing and give them to me, have you any right to claim that you still possess them?"

This exchange of views had some effect on the subsequent course of the negotiations, when the King's envoys returned and the discussion resumed concerning Sebezh and the duration of the peace. That day the King's envoys agreed that Sebezh could remain in the hands of the Grand Prince, while the Muscovites agreed that the peace should last for eight years, and they observed that they would spend the evening considering whether they needed to add anything further. The King's envoys asked the Prince for a guarantee not to harm any peasants who had pledged loyalty to the King, and the Muscovites replied that they would be glad to give their word on this. On the question of the way in which the fortresses should be restored, both sides agreed on a statement to the effect that Dorpat and other major fortresses should be restored first. The Muscovites asked the King to provide an escort when the *Vladiki* and *Popy* (their priests) were leaving and removing

129

religious equipment, particularly the holy ikons, to prevent any of it from falling into the hands of the King of Sweden. The King's envoys were not particularly disposed to grant this request, but Antonio observed that it was only fair for religious objects to be withdrawn in safety, especially since the Poles were unwilling to have the Muscovites send detachments to escort their people home. At this point the session came to an end.

January 2, 1582. Thirteenth Session.

The leader of the King's delegation and Michał Haraburda were the only ones in attendance that day: they said that Albert Radziwiłł had stayed behind because of illness. Antonio asked them whether they could make decisions in his absence and when they declared that they could, he summoned the Muscovite envoys and asked them what they thought the duration of the peace should be. They added another year to make it nine years, and the King's envoys agreed to this. Previously advised by Zamojski, they called on the Muscovite envoys to cede Livonia "in its entirety," and sought to insert a codicil in the treaty committing the Muscovites to a tacit acceptance of "cession in entirety," even though the phrase did not explicitly appear anywhere in the document. Antonio did not approve of this ambiguous mode of procedure and felt moved to say privately to the King's envoys: "Ask for Livonia in its entirety clearly and openly, and avoid the appearance of trying to trick your future brothers." The Muscovites said: "Five days ago we told you that we would freely cede all of Livonia controlled by the Grand Prince, but that we could say nothing about the fortresses in the hands of the King of Sweden. If you start raising new issues now, you will manage only to prolong the negotiations, and it will be more than a year before we finish the treaty."

Michał Haraburda had already entered a protest on this issue in the name of the King's envoys, as has been noted, and asked Antonio to accept it; he had drawn up the protest in proper form and conveyed it to Antonio, and the matter had been considered settled. Now he asked to have it back, although Antonio kept a copy, and next, acting under instructions, the King's envoys wrote out the whole protest in their own hand and sealed it with their seal. All this delay in drawing up the peace treaty could have been avoided if the Muscovites had only been willing to abjure the Prince's title and rights to Livonia.

One speech followed another until finally Antonio said to the King's envoys that since no one had apparently foreseen the difficulties they were presently experiencing, it might be a good idea to define and describe by name all the fortresses to which the Grand Prince claimed title and submit a list. Any other fortresses that were subsequently discovered still to be in Muscovite hands could be surrendered later. If they chose, they could insert an operative clause into the document to the effect that the Grand Prince should no longer be referred to by the title of Lord of Livonia, and that all other issues had been adequately arranged in accordance with the instructions issued by the King. Next, both sides made an attempt to define the boundaries of Livonia. The Muscovites wanted to defer this matter until the delegation to ratify the peace treaty arrived, but the King's envoys insisted that the present groups must decide the question, in order to eliminate every possible ground for controversy. The Muscovite envoys declared: "If we cannot reach agreement because we do not know what all the boundaries are, we ought to refer the matter to our rulers." Both sides did manage to agree that the boundaries of Pskov should be restored to their original limits. The King's envoys wished to insert a clause into the treaty calling upon both rulers to have their envoys negotiate within the year to exchange Sebezh (belonging to the Grand Prince) for Velizh (belonging to the King). The Muscovites replied that they would not agree under any circumstances; the King had no right to impose more restrictions upon the Grand Prince's possession of Sebezh than the Grand Prince had imposed upon the King's possession of Velizh. The King's envoys thought that acquisition of Velizh might open the door to their winning Livonia "in its entirety," and so they began backtracking and stalling. They demanded and obtained the number and names of the fortresses still held by the Prince. Then they asked for the names of the fortresses held by the King of Sweden, and finally they said that they would have to discuss matters with Prince Albert Radziwiłł and would make a statement at the next session.

Names of the Fortresses to be Surrendered by the Prince.

Lennewarden, Asheraden, Kokenhuzen, Kreuzburg, Behrson, Kudun, Seswegen, Luza, Rositen, Walck, Wolmar, Roroni, Goroia, Trikaten, Marienburg, Pürkel, Kirchholm, Neuhaus, Krynpäh, Dorpat, Falkenau, Randen, Ringen, Kongedahl, Kawelecht, Kurslow, Lais, Tarwast, Polczew, Paida (Weissenstein), Fellin, Old Pernau and New Pernau.

Names of the Fortresses Under the Control of the King of Sweden.

Narva, Serenets, Borkholm, Tolsborg, Rakoboz, Reval, Padis, Kolower, Likhover, Habsal, and Wyholumisa.

January 5. Fourteenth Session.

Both sides took turns making complaints. The Muscovites said that the King's envoys were stalling, while the Poles and Lithuanians were removing the peasants and prisoners and destroying all the adjacent territory. The King's envoys asserted that while the Muscovites were procrastinating and refusing to address themselves to the issues, the fighting continued and would grow worse until they accepted the peace terms. They added that no peasants and prisoners were being abducted; they were merely being taken to the winter camps to which each of them had been assigned. A dispute arose concerning Serenets, a Livonian fortress which the Muscovites asserted had been seized by the King of Sweden, while the King's envoys claimed it was still held by the Grand Prince. The truth of the matter could not be ascertained, but the King's envoys said they were very anxious to have it, and the Muscovites replied that they would certainly surrender it if the King of Sweden had not occupied it. The King's envoys again read out the name of every single fortress held by the Prince or captured by the King of Sweden. Then at last, after a great deal of vain sparring, an agreement was reached whereby the Prince would surrender to the King all his possessions in Livonia, including fortresses, villages, fields and all other immovable objects pertaining thereto, while the King would restore to the Grand Prince all the fortresses, except Velizh, he had captured which had formerly belonged to the Prince, together with all villages, fields, and other immovable objects pertaining thereto. For the duration of the peace neither side was to wage war against the other: the Prince was not to try and take Velizh or Livonia, and the King was not to attack Velikie Luki, Zavoloch'e, Nevel', Kholm, Sebezh, or the fortresses around Pskov. Both sides requested Antonio's secretary and the interpreter to copy down these terms. Sharp contention arose concerning how and when the Muscovites were to remove their artillery, *Vladiki, Popy* and ikons from the fortresses and how and when the King was to lift the siege of Pskov, and as evening was approaching discussion of these items was deferred to the next session.

The Day of Holy Epiphany [January 6]. Fifteenth Session.

The King's envoys asked why the persons whom the Grand Prince had sent to Novgorod to supervise the surrender of the fortresses had gone away. The Muscovites answered that the Prince had assigned others to perform this task and there would be no delay in surrendering the fortresses as soon as peace was declared. It was agreed that once the King's troops and the Prince's representatives had entered the fortresses, both sides would

132

authorize a period of eight days in which the Commanders, *Vladiki, Popy,* and merchants would withdraw with the ikons and all the rest of their movable goods. If stocks of food and other such items could not be removed within this period of time, a few Muscovites might return to finish the task. It was further decreed that all the Livonian fortresses the King was to receive were to be handed over to him within a period of eight weeks from that day, and during this time the King's forces were also to restore to the Muscovites what had been assigned to them. The question of artillery came up again. Both sides agreed to swear an oath and kiss the cross thereto that they would restore all artillery found inside the fortresses. Michał Haraburda as Secretary for the King, and Nikita Basenka for the Grand Prince listed the number and names of the pieces and exchanged copies of their lists, prepared in their own handwriting. The King's envoys lodged another protest with Antonio, asking for Serenets; the Muscovites merely reiterated their previous statement to the effect that it was held by the King of Sweden.

A furious controversy again arose concerning prisoners. The King's envoys now demanded the two fortresses of Sebezh and Opokha, but the Muscovite envoys asserted that Christian blood should not be sold for money and fortresses. The King's envoys countered this charge by alleging that the Grand Prince had once asked the Polish King for the fortresses of Uświaty and Jezierzyszcza as ransom for prisoners, and that in exchange for Chlebowicz, a noble Lithuanian, he had tried to obtain three prisoners, and a sum of money as well, and that there had been other instances of this sort besides. It was finally decided to refer the entire issue to different envoys of both rulers. The King's envoys had asked Antonio to mediate the question, but the latter replied that he was unwilling to do so because of a difficulty he had once experienced in the Polish camp. The King had promised to hand over a Muscovite prisoner to him, but the King's orders had not been obeyed. Antonio had thus decided that it would not be well to have the name and reputation of the Pope involved in every instance when Muscovites were captured by foreigners and not returned to the Grand Prince.

The Muscovite envoys urged the King to take the initiative by sending delegates to Muscovy to ratify the peace, but the King's envoys replied that it was enough for the representatives of both rulers to approach the boundary of their respective jurisdictions simultaneously. One delegation would go to the King, the other to the Prince, or the King's representatives might assemble first in Smolensk. The Muscovites refused to accept this plan on the grounds that their people were inexperienced in such matters. The question was left in abeyance

133

and postponed to a future session. That day both his envoys and Antonio received a letter from the Grand Prince containing a second and stronger grant of authority. A dispute arose between Antonio and the King's envoys as to whether the Prince was serious in the quest for peace. The letter was read in their presence, and ran as follows:

Copy of the Second Authorization by the Grand Prince.

By the Divine Grace and Mercy that have guided us in the East from ancient times and direct our footsteps to the path of peace; by the Mercy of Him Who is Our God adored in the Trinity, we, Ivan Vasil'evich, Great Lord, Emperor and Grand Prince of all Russia, Vladimir, Moscow, and Novgorod, Emperor of Kazan' and Emperor of Astrakhan', Lord of Pskov, and Grand Prince of Smolensk, Tver', Iugoria, Perm', Viatka, Bulgaria and other places, and Hereditary Lord of the Livonian Land, etc., greet Stefan, by the Grace of God, King of Poland, and Grand Prince of Lithuania, Russia, Prussia, Mazovia, and Samogitia, Prince of Transylvania, and of other regions, etc. Antonio Possevino, the Envoy of Gregory XIII, the Pope of Rome, wrote to us about the need to make peace in order to prevent the shedding of Christian blood and to stop the war, and he asked us to send envoys to a particular site, who, in the presence of the Pope's Envoy, might arrange a peace Treaty between us. In order to obtain a Christian peace, we have sent as our envoys the courtier and Governor of Kashin, Prince Dmitrii Petrovich Eletskii, the courtier and Governor of Kozel'sk, Roman Vasil'evich Alfer'ev, the Secretary, Nikita Nikiforovich Basenka Vereshchagin, and the Assistant Secretary, Zakharii Sviiazev, to Iam Zapol'skii, or any other suitable place between Zavoloch'e and Porkhov, to meet and achieve the peace. I have given them full instructions on how to meet with the envoys, discuss worthwhile undertakings, and arrange a Christian peace, in the presence of the Papal Envoy, between ourselves and you, King Stefan. We are forever to be bound by any decisions they make, as they make them, and by any peace terms which either side proposes and ratifies by covenant and by kissing the cross. King Stefan, you have assigned envoys to negotiate with us on these issues, while we are required to write an authorization for our envoys in our own name and seal it with our own seal, and we shall send this same authorization, confirmed by our kissing the cross, by your same envoys to you, King Stefan. Similarly, King Stefan, you are required to send us, by our envoys, whom we have assigned to negotiate with you, the same authorization, prepared in your own name and sealed with your own seal. We have given this mandate to our envoys under our seal, written in our realm at the palace, in our citaedel at Moscow, in the year 7090

134

from the Creation of the World, the month of December, the Tenth Indiction, the 47th. year of our reign, the 35th. over Russia, and the 29th. over Kazan', and the 28th. over Astrakhan'.

January 7. Sixteenth Session.

After all the envoys had again assembled, they chose the times at which to exchange ratifying bodies: the King's representatives should go to Muscovy on the day sacred to the Holy Trinity [May 15], while the Muscovites were to proceed to the Polish King on the Day of the Assumption of the Virgin Mary [August 15]. They would take up the question of prisoners with both rulers in person, and thus consideration of that issue was postponed to these later occasions. The Muscovites began trying, at first covertly, later openly and most insistently, to have their Prince referred to in these documents by the titles of "Lord, Great Emperor, Grand Prince," etc. When the King's envoys steadily refused, the preceding night (as he had often done) Antonio sought out the Muscovites on this issue and tried to dissuade them, on the grounds that Christians recognized only one Emperor, and that such modes of address lacked all validity without the sanction of the Pope, who would not allow even the Caesar of the Romans to display such effrontery. The Muscovites abandoned this project, but next they brought intense pressure to have the Prince called Tsar of Kazan' and Tsar of Astrakhan'. This too they failed to obtain. The King's envoys denied their assertion that the Prince had been accorded those titles by Sigismund-Augustus. When Antonio inquired the reason why they had not brought a letter from King Sigismund, which would have gone far to substantiate their claim, they replied that none could be found. Michał Haraburda showed them some old treaties, displaying the King's seal, none of which contained any such titles. Thus the session ended.

January 8. Seventeenth Session.

The Muscovites still continued stubbornly to insist that the Grand Prince at least be given the title of Tsar of Kazan' and Tsar of Astrakhan'. The whole question was finally referred to Antonio. The King's envoys declared their instructions from the King contained no mention of this, and that he could clear the matter up with the Prince in person when he returned to Moscow. Antonio turned to the Muscovite envoys and said that, as far as he could determine, there were three ways to approach the problem. The first was

135

to have the King's envoys call the Prince "Lord of Kazan' and Astrakhan', " for although the Muscovites did not appear to set much store by this, the King's envoys had parenthetically agreed to do so when they observed that the Kings of Poland could never be induced to allow Christians to call a Christian ruler by a Tatar or Turkish title like "Tsar of the Tatars." The second alternative was for the Muscovite envoys to lodge a formal protest, which he was prepared to accept without prejudice to either ruler or as a detriment to the peace treaty, now so near to realization. The Muscovites replied that they knew nothing about protests and the principle of utilizing them did not exist among their people. The third possibility was for Antonio to promise personally to take the matter up with the King, and, if need be, with the Pope, as befitting an honorable and Christian man. The pressure which the Muscovite envoys brought to bear on this point was unrelenting, and Antonio later complained to them that the Grand Prince had never mentioned this matter to him during the course of the detailed discussions he had held with the Senators at Staritsa, nor had the Prince included this item in the letters he had written to Antonio, while the latter was in the Polish camp before Pskov, concerning the basic issues in the peace negotiations. It was something they, the Muscovite envoys, had kept completely hidden from sight until now, and thus they had only themselves to blame if time to negotiate it had now run out. Antonio's representations persuaded the Muscovite envoys to permit their letter to the King to be drawn up without these titles. Then, after this matter was settled, they began insisting that the Grand Duchy of Smolensk, which the Muscovites had once taken from the Lithuanians, lay within their jurisdiction, and that the Prince's title to that at least must be included in the treaty. The King's envoys firmly refused to agree, saying that they were merely following the traditional mode of drafting treaties. At this point both sides recessed.

January 9. Eighteenth Session.

In the absence of Albert Radziwiłł both sides chose to spend the day going over and correcting the draft treaty. It was proposed to follow prior models, listing each fortress by name and specifically delimiting all their boundaries. This request (like so many others) came from the King's envoys, and was opposed by the Muscovites, who preferred a generalized document, containing a proviso to the effect that Lithuania and Livonia were not to attack Muscovy, and Muscovy was not to attack them. The King's envoys stuck to their position but finally accepted Antonio's suggestion to state in the treaty that the Prince was not to attack the Lithuanian fortresses of Kiev, Kanev, and Cherkasy, and others adjacent to them, nor the fortresses in Livonia he had surrendered, while the King was not to proceed against other Muscovite fortresses; in the case of both rulers, the territory originally comprehended by the fortresses was to be restored. This discussion brought the session to an end, and it was decided to devote the next session to drawing up the treaty.

Sessions of January 10 and 11.

The King's envoys spent two days scrutinizing the Muscovite version of the draft treaty and reviewing the authorizations given by the King and the Grand Prince, where they discerned the unequivocal stipulation that the peace negotiations must be carried to completion in Antonio's presence. In their opinion, if a statement certifying to this were not included in the treaty its provisions would be invalid. Considerable controversy between them and the Muscovite envoys arose concerning this interpretation, but the view of the King's envoys ultimately prevailed.[8] Thinking that everything was now settled, the Muscovite envoys requested a codicil inserted in the treaty to the effect that, in addition to the fortresses, their Grand Prince was surrendering Riga and Curland, places which he had never possessed. The King's envoys categorically rejected this, but when the Muscovites absolutely refused to yield on the point, Antonio ordered this item to be postponed to the next meeting. The King's envoys protested to Antonio that they were not obliged to obey the Pope in all matters, no matter how legitimate. The point at issue (which was generally understood) was the Prince's desire to retain some kind of legal title to Livonia, which he considered he was only ceding at most for the ten-year period which the peace had to run, after which time he would try and reclaim it. The justifiable suspicions of the King's envoys were increased by the fact that for two days the courier whom the Muscovite envoys had appointed to summon the commanders from Novgorod had not yet departed. They contrived delays, declaring that the treaty was not yet finished, even though scarcely any differences of opinion concerning its provisions remained. Even after they had been asked to leave, first one, then another, and finally all the Muscovite envoys came back to Antonio's abode and told him such things as that they were not authorized to make peace unless the cession of Riga were included in the treaty, or that their relationship with their Prince differed from that of other subjects to other rulers, as could be seen from the fact that they were not allowed to change a single syllable in the instructions they had been given. They requested a period of ten days to obtain an answer from their Prince, and finally asked Antonio's advice as to how they should proceed. Antonio had become accustomed to their devious manner of speaking throughout the long course of the negotiations, and now he expressed himself more openly. He said that he was concerned for fear that the Muscovite envoys had adopted their present stance in a desire to delude the King's forces and wear them down; thus, he said, they should either promise in writing to abide by the existing agreements and omit all mention of Riga, or else they should go that very evening to the King's envoys, read the peace treaty, and tomorrow swear a most solemn oath to uphold it; if they did nothing the King's envoys would be certain to withdraw. Following their invariable practice the Muscovite envoys said they would do whatever Antonio advised, make no reference to Riga, and spend the night drafting the treaty. They asked for Michał Haraburda to help them. Antonio sent for him, and a little after nightfall both he and the Wojewoda of Bracław came from the village to which they had retired. All of them spent almost the entire night and much of the following day examining the draft treaty. At Antonio's instigation the King's envoys asked whether the Muscovites would be willing to insert a clause in the treaty to the effect that any peasants who wanted to go over to the King after the treaty became effective would not be subject to reprisal from the Muscovites. At first the Muscovites refused to agree, but then they gave their word to Antonio and promised the King's envoys that the Prince would not harm the peasants in any way; they recognized that they had sworn an oath to the King concerning the peasants, who were like sheep and had every reason to be terrified when they saw others of their number slaughtered. A further year was added to the nine, and the peace was decreed to endure for ten years. The Muscovite envoys asked for a list containing the number and names of all their artillery pieces located in the fortresses captured by the King, although this matter had already been dealt with. The Wojewoda of Bracław responded by handing them one list, the Catalog for Nevel', but the Muscovites insisted that the King's envoys transmit a complete set to them, since they had given them all of theirs. Men were dispatched to obtain them as quickly as possible. The position of the King's envoys was better taken, but they had failed to support their cause with as much care and foresight as the Muscovites had done.

January 15. The Final Session.

A very serious dispute between the two delegations had again arisen in the course of the two preceding days. The Muscovites demanded that their copy of the treaty at any rate should show that the fortresses surrendered to the King constituted a diminution

138

from the sum total of the Grand Prince's patrimony. The King's envoys were vigorously opposed, saying that the Prince would employ this device as a legal pretext to lay claim to the part of Livonia he had not surrendered to the King. They again told the Muscovite envoys to return to Moscow before the treaty was signed, unless they were willing to abandon this proposal. The Muscovites begged Antonio to employ his good offices to achieve this purpose and restrain the King's envoys, who had threatened to leave. Antonio did what was necessary to persuade the Muscovites to remove this wording from their version of the treaty. Then both delegations assembled to read each other's drafts and exchange authorizations from their respective rulers in the traditional way; the Grand Prince's Mandate was deposited with the King's envoys, and the King's Rescript was held by the Muscovite envoys. The secretaries of both delegations present at the conference, Michał Haraburda and Nikita Basenka, signed documents containing lists of the artillery and other munitions in the fortresses. The King's envoys lodged a formal protest with Antonio concerning the remainder of Livonia. Finally, in Antonio's abode, and in Antonio's presence, they consecrated the peace treaty by swearing oaths, signed the documents with their own hands, and kissed the Cross. For the Glory of God, Amen. Dated at Kiverova Gora, January 15, 1582.

NOTES TO THE CHAPTERS

CHAPTER I

[1] Possevino has not included this earlier Commentary in this, the 1587 Antwerp edition of the *Moscovia*, which bears some marks of hasty compilation. Chapter I might more logically be considered the "Second Commentary," since it is based on material prepared after Possevino had completed his entire mission, while he composed Chapter II in 1581, on his way to the Polish Camp, before he had met with the envoys to mediate the peace or visited Moscow to discuss religion and other matters with the Tsar.

[2] Two sons of Gustavus I Vasa controlled Swedish affairs during this period. Eric XIV was King of Sweden to 1569, when a *coup d'état* placed his half-brother, John III (1537-1592), upon the throne. Formerly the Duke of Finland, he was married to Katerina Jagiellonka, of the royal house of Poland that came to an end when King Sigismund-Augustus died without direct issue in 1572. John's accession aroused the Church to hope for a Catholic restoration in Sweden, and Possevino himself received his initiation into the complex politics of the eastern Baltic region in the course of two missions he undertook to the Swedish court in 1577-1578 and 1579-1580 respectively, which, although ably conceived and executed, did not prove to be ultimately successful. John's son Sigismund was brought up a staunch Catholic, and made good his claim to the Polish throne in 1587.

Stefan Batory, a Hungarian, was born in 1533, the son of the Commander of Transylvania, and educated in Italy. Although Transylvania was a vassal state of the Turkish Sultan, Batory acquired his formidable reputation as a military leader in operations against the pretensions of the Habsburgs in the region. This circumstance in turn drew the attention of the anti-Habsburg and anti-Imperial forces in Poland to him, and they managed to secure, in 1576, his accession to the Polish throne to end the interregnum that had occurred in the aftermath of the precipitate departure of Henry of Valois. Rapidly establishing his authority against those who still championed the Austrian candidate, Batory consolidated a strong position, and became the principal architect of the Polish policy of winning substantial territorial gains at the expense of the Grand Duchy of Muscovy. He died suddenly in 1586, at the height of his career.

[3] Ivan IV, the Terrible, was born in 1530, not 1528. His father, Vasilii III, died suddenly in 1533, and his mother, Elena Glinskaia, acted as regent during his minority to her own death in 1538. The leading Boyar families, neglecting the young ruler, engaged in constant and sometimes violent intrigues. In 1547, at the age of seventeen, Ivan asserted his authority and had himself crowned with the formal title of Tsar.

[4] Circassia lay between the western end of the Greater Caucasus range and the Kuban' river, and its inhabitants formed two groups, the Adygei or Cherkes, and the Kabardians. These tribes lived a comparatively peaceful, semi-nomadic and pastoral existence until the 1550's when the Crimean Tatars began systematically to harass them. In search of support they turned to Muscovy, and with his interest in the south growing as the result of his capture of Kazan' (1552) and Astrakhan' (1554), Ivan was pleased to respond to their appeal.

[5] Near Derbent, the chief city of Dagestan, located on the southwest coast of the Caspian Sea, was a pass known as the Iron Gate, the possession of which afforded control of the narrow coastal route linking Transoxania and Asia Minor. The Ottoman Empire, the champion of the orthodox form of Islam, coveted the region as a means of communication with its coreligionists in Central Asia and as a vantage point in its struggle with the Shi'i Muslims of Persia. Capitalizing on internecine rivalries then besetting the Safavid house of Persia, the Empire declared war in 1578. Possevino may be confusing Sultan Selim II (1566-1574) with Murad III (1574-1595); the actual Turkish commander who captured the Iron Gate in 1578 and held it to 1583 was the redoubtable warrior Osman Pasha.

[6] Mikhail Temriukovich, son of Temriuk Aidaiovich, the prince who had been Ivan's strongest supporter among the Circassian chiefs, took service with Moscow in 1558, and with his own force of 5,000 men participated in the Livonian War. In 1561, to cement the alliance, Ivan married his sister Kuchenei, who became known as Mariia. She died in 1569, and Mikhail was executed in 1570, but relations between Muscovy and Circassia, resting on their common hostility to the Crimean Tatars, were not seriously impaired.

[7] The Kabardians sent an embassy to Ivan in 1578 asking him to help them build a fortified stronghold on the river Terek at the point where the Sundzha flows into it. Ivan agreed and dispatched a small force of masons and artillerymen to protect them under the command of Luka Novosil'tsev.

[8] The Great Nogai Horde occupied the lower reaches of the southern steppes east of the Volga. Its capital was Saraichik, situated at the mouth of the Iaik River, where it enters the Caspian Sea. They constituted a somewhat irrational factor in the area, for although they regularly and frequently raided and plundered Muscovite territory, sometimes they cooperated with Moscow in her undertakings, as, for example, in the capture of Astrakhan'.

[9] The Tauric Chersonese was the name ancient geographers employed to denote the Crimean Peninsula, the home of the Crimean Tatars, who, under the protection of the Sultan, continued to pose a threat to Russia to the time of Catherine the Great. In the present instance, on his return to Moscow after mediating the Truce of Iam Zapol'skii, Possevino brought the Tsar a letter from Batory calling upon him to joing the king in an attack on the Crimea. Due to the exhausted state of his country's resources, of which Possevino here paints a grim and graphic picture, Ivan was in no mood to provoke the Khan, Mahomet-Girei, and thus hastened to point out that his ambassador, Prince Vasilii Mosal'skii, after spending several years in the Crimea, had just managed to conclude an agreement with the Khan leading to a cessation of hostilities. The Khan was also glad of a respite because of the long struggle with Persia and also because of the strained relations that then existed with his suzerain, the Ottoman Sultan.

[10] Wolther von Plettenberg, the last independent Master of the Livonian Order, assumed office in 1494 and held it to his death in 1535. The Battle of Pskov was not a "total disaster," but it did constitute a defeat for the Muscovite forces. Fought in September, 1502, it led to a series of truces, successively renewed in 1509, 1522, 1531 and 1552, when Ivan chose to abrogate the agreement and began arranging for his campaign to annex Livonia.

[11] This work, known as *Livoniae Commentarius*, appeared in Riga in 1852.

[12] The formation of the *Strel'tsy* ("Shooters"), who came into existence in the 1550's, was the first attempt to create a permanent military establishment in Muscovy as opposed to the irregular levies of serving-men that made up the bulk of the Muscovite forces. They proved their worth in the campaign against Kazan' in 1552. When not in the field they engaged in a variety of civilian occupations, and they continued to constitute Muscovy's only permanent, hereditary armed corps until their ranks were decimated by Peter the Great after their revolt in 1698.

[13] It is surprising that most foreign visitors say that plagues were virtually unknown in Muscovy. In reality local chronicles are filled with references to the ravages of plague.

[14] In May, 1571 (ten, not twelve years earlier) the Khan of the Crimean Tatars, Devlet-Girei (1551-1577), took advantage of Ivan's preoccupation with internal problems and the Livonian War to sack Moscow in a daring and successful raid. Possevino's narrative furnished authentic and dramatic testimony to the severity of the devastation.

[15] Philip II of Spain (1527-1598).

[16] The respect which was shown at the time for the slight treatise of Paolo Giovio, *De Legatione Basilii Magni Principis Moscoviae ad Clementem VII Pontificem Maximum Liber*, is illustrative of the ignorance concerning Muscovy on the part of even highly informed persons in contemporary Western Europe. As Possevino notes, Giovio never visited Muscovy. He met a certain Dmitrii Gerasimov, an envoy Vasilii III had sent to Pope Clement VII in 1525, asked him questions, and merely set down as best he could what Dmitrii told him. The work first appeared in 1527.

[17] Alberto Campense, like Giovio, was more significant for what he wrote than for who he was. He too never visited Muscovy, but his father and brother had; drawing upon their experience, he sent a letter to Pope Clement VII in 1523 in which he drew specific attention to the size and power of Muscovy in terms of the contemporary configuration of European states, and informed the Pope that Muscovy would have to constitute an essential ingredient in any proposed league against the Turks.

[18] Certain contemporary observers were inclined to place the population of Moscow at no less than 80,000 people, and some modern scholars would make it even higher. Possevino was a careful observer; if his estimate of 30,000 is considered low, it serves as a useful corrective to more exuberant statistics. Some English visitors compared the population of Moscow with that of London, which then contained approximately 50,000 inhabitants.

[19] A second reference to Devlet-Girei's sack of Moscow in 1571.

[20] It was not Ivan's father, Vasilii III, but his grandfather, Ivan III the Great, who invited Pietro Antonio Solari to come from Milan to Moscow in 1490, where he built a number of important edifices in the Kremlin. The inscription, which merely states that Ivan III had commissioned Solari to undertake certain tasks, was preserved over the Spasskii Gate leading through the fortifications (on which Solari also worked) to the interior of the structure. Perhaps one of the reasons why the Kremlin found favor in Possevino's eyes, in contrast with much else he saw in Muscovy, was because it presented a somewhat Italian appearance.

²¹ This person is otherwise unknown. Possevino could scarcely be referring to the famous Aristotele Fioravanti, whom Ivan III summoned from Bologna in 1475 to build the Cathedral of the Dormition in the Moscow Kremlin. He is the only Italian architect known to have visited Novgorod, but his appearance there was occasioned by Ivan's desire to use Fioravanti's engineering skills in the Muscovite attack on Novgorod in 1486.

²² This section clearly alludes to the parsimony for which the Grand Princes of Muscovy had been noted since the fourteenth century. The rise of Moscow had put an end to the right of the various appanage rulers to strike their own coins and the last two such mints, in Novgorod and Pskov, ceased functioning early in the sixteenth century. In 1534 occurred the so-called Reform of Elena Glinskaia, which standardized the Muscovite coinage by striking a silver *Kopek*, or *Denga*, which was also known as a *Moskovka*. Possevino is evidence for the fact that by 1581 other coins beside the official *Denga* had come into circulation.

²³ The initial foray of the Muscovites into Livonia in 1558 was one of their most successful campaigns. The Tsar's maternal uncle, Mikhail Vasil'evich Glinskii, was one of the two commanders.

²⁴ The beginnings of a foreign colony in Moscow date from Ivan's reign and the Livonian War. The Tsar generally looked rather favorably on the Livonians he resettled in his kingdom. In 1565, when he transferred a number of families from Dorpat to various towns in Muscovy, he did not harass them in any way and permitted a Protestant pastor to make regular visits to them. However, in 1578, a feeling that the Livonian inhabitants of the suburb of Nalivki, which constituted the nucleus of what eventually became the "German Suburb" of Moscow, were displaying too great pride and ostentation, Ivan ordered a raid upon them. The raiding party behaved in a cruel manner and did much damage to property, but the suburb itself was not destroyed and its religious privileges were not cancelled. Possevino's compressed account of the history of Livonia is, of course, highly partisan and tendentious.

²⁵ Possevino's derivation of the word is accurate, and so is his observation that the *D'iaki* had by this time come to assume entirely secular functions. Originally officials of low rank, they had managed to acquire great power and influence by virtue of the fact that they possessed the ability to read and write, skills that were as highly prized as they were rare in sixteenth-century Muscovy.

²⁶ The war between the Ottoman Empire and Safavid Persia, which had begun in 1578.

²⁷ Possevino employs terms more familiar to him in discussing the constitution of the Boyar Duma, which was now composed both of members of the hereditary nobility and of previously obscure persons who had been rewarded with high rank and trust by gaining the favor of the Tsar. The term Senator did not come into regular use in Russia until the time of Peter the Great.

²⁸ Prince Ivan Fedorovich Mstislavskii. His house began its rise to prominence when the father of Ivan, Prince Fedor Mikhailovich Mstislavskii, came from Lithuania to take service with Vasilii III in 1526, and was rewarded with a huge estate in the Iaroslavl' area. Ivan

Fedorovich was born in 1530, attained the rank of Boyar in 1549, and participated as a leading commander in most of the major military actions during Ivan's reign. Also, as illustrative of the way in which civilian and military assignments were indiscriminately mingled in the Russia of Ivan's time, he was one of the nobles who went to Aleksandrovskaia Sloboda in 1564 to negotiate with the Tsar over his apparent "abdication proclamation," and he was named one of the two joint heads of the *Zemshchina*, the term collectively applied to all the lands which were not placed in the *Oprichnina*, Muscovite territory under the Tsar's personal supervision, during the time that institution existed. He was Governor of Novgorod, and it is a sign of the strength of his position that he was able to survive two accusations of treachery that were laid against him before the suspicious and vengeful Tsar. He was one of the leading figures in the Pentarchy that governed Russia after Ivan's death in 1584, but Boris Godunov, considering him a potential rival in his own bid for the throne, forced him to enter a monastery in 1592, where he died the following year.

[29] Fedor Ivanovich Mstislavskii, the son of Ivan Fedorovich, also had a most distinguished career. He became a Boyar in 1576, and held many top military posts, including command of the entire Muscovite army from 1588 to 1591. He also served as First Councillor of the Boyar Duma. Godunov did not eliminate him; he opposed and then supported the first False Dmitrii, and was prominently mentioned as a candidate for the throne in 1606, although the choice finally fell upon Vasilii Shuiskii. He took part in the Assembly that elected Mikhail Romanov to the throne in 1613, and died in 1622.

[30] Ivan Fedorovich Mstislavskii had no son named Simeon, but his daughter Anastasiia was married to Simeon Bekbulatovich; it is highly probable that it is to him Possevino is referring. Simeon, a lineal descendant of the Khans of the Golden Horde, to 1570 as Sain-Bulat was the ruler of the Kasimov Tatars, loyal supporters of Muscovy since the middle of the fifteenth century, and he served with distinction in many of Ivan's military campaigns. In 1573 he was received into the Orthodox church and given the name of Simeon after baptism. The extent of the trust the Tsar felt he could repose in Simeon is very strikingly revealed by the fact that he allowed him, for obscure reasons of Ivan's own, to function for a period of some six months in 1575-1576 as Tsar, while Ivan remained behind the scenes. Simeon was subsequently made Governor of Tver', and it frequently has been alleged that this appointment constituted a form of honorable exile. However, Possevino's allusion to the fact that Simeon was apparently performing governmental functions on the highest level in 1582 shows that the Tsar had not forgotten him, and renders more understandable Godunov's concern after Ivan's death that Simeon might possibly put in a claim to the throne, an action he forestalled by having Simeon swear a special oath of fealty to Tsar Fedor.

[31] Nikita Romanovich Iur'ev rose to a position of the greatest power, as Possevino says, by virtue of the fact that his sister Anastasiia had been Tsar Ivan's first wife. He remained one of the Tsar's closest confidants throughout the latter's entire lifetime. He was made Boyar in 1565, named Governor of Tver', and carried out many civilian and military tasks of the utmost importance and delicacy. He died in 1585. He was the father of the future Patriarch, Filaret, and the grandfather of Mikhail, the first Romanov Tsar.

[32] The career of Andrei Iakovlevich Shchelkalov affords a classic illustration of the way in which a *D'iak* could rise to positions of great importance. Andrei was first a Secretary, which gave him the rank of Junior Court Boyar. By 1570 he had become a Secretary-Councillor, and then he assumed the office of Great Secretary, when he presided over the highly important Military Records Bureau to 1577. He came in contact with Possevino in his capacity as Secretary of the Foreign Bureau, which he headed from 1571 to 1594. He held numerous other responsible positions, and, in charge of the Bureau that administered all the newly-acquired lands along the Volga from Kazan' to Astrakhan' he became one of the most influential and powerful men in Muscovy, fully deserving of the title of Chancellor that Possevino gives to him. He died in 1597.

[33] Andrei's brother, Vasilii Iakovlevich Shchelkalov, became a Secretary-Councillor in 1571. He presided over the Military Records Bureau from 1577 to 1594, and was in charge of the Foreign Bureau to 1601. He died in 1611.

[34] The many members of the Bel'skii family who rose to prominence in the latter half of the sixteenth century furnish an excellent example of the way in which heretofore undistinguished serving-people could advance with great rapidity by acquiring Tsar Ivan's favor. The most outstanding representative of this family was Bogdan Iakovlevich Bel'skii, a young kinsman of Maliuta Skuratov, who had acquired an unsavory reputation as the man the Tsar most often called upon to carry out the sentence of execution he had decreed upon those whom he suspected of disloyalty. Bogdan entered the Tsar's service in 1570, and immediately attracted Ivan's attention and favor, which he retained without interruption till the end of the ruler's life. He held the office of Chamberlain, in personal attendance upon the Tsar, and in 1578 obtained the post of Royal Armorer. He was also Governor of Rzhev. Popular with the people, he was one of the five most influential men in the kingdom at Ivan's death, and he continued to play a prominent role in affairs during the Time of Troubles, often in opposition to Boris Godunov. He first intrigued in support of Dmitrii of Uglich, Ivan's son who died under mysterious circumstances in 1591, and this led to his being exiled to Nizhnii Novgorod by Godunov. Upon his return, he became one of the strongest partisans of the first False Dmitrii, and was sent into a kind of unofficial exile in Kazan' by Tsar Vasilii Shuiskii, where he was killed in a Tatar raid in 1611.

[35] The reference is very probably to Bogdan Bel'skii's cousin, Grigorii Mikhailovich Nevezhin Skuratov, who had taken service with the Tsar in 1570, and thus could have risen to a position of prominence by 1581. His career, however, was otherwise undistinguished.

[36] Vasilii Grigor'evich Zuzin (Possevino has rendered his patronymic incorrectly) came originally from a Boyar family of Tver', and, upon his return from Lithuania won the Tsar's confidence through loyal service in a variety of capacities. He commanded one of the detachments Ivan sent on his punitive raid against Novgorod in 1569-70, and was rewarded with confiscated estates in that region. At the time when his knowledge of Latin facilitated his negotiations with Possevino he held the rank of Equerry, and was Governor of Suzdal'.

[37] Ignatii Petrovich Tatishchev had held army commands in the 1550's, and was rewarded with a grant of lands in the Dmitrov region. By 1581 he had attained the rank of Privy Councillor.

[38] Oboim Voeikov did not himself have a prominent career, but he was a member of an old and distinguished house that originated in the time of Dmitrii Donskoi. Its most famous member was Ivan Vasil'evich Voeikov Men'shoi, who assassinated the first False Dmitrii in 1606.

[39] Mikhailo Andreevich Beznin had served with distinction in the Livonian War from its outset, and thus managed to survive a period when he was officially under the Tsar's displeasure in 1576. By 1581 he had attained the rank of Privy Councillor.

[40] Petr Ivanovich Golovin was a member of an old and distinguished family. After a stint of military service, he performed the functions of Treasurer on a sustained basis until his disgrace and death, which occurred in 1584 in the aftermath of Tsar Ivan's death.

[41] Fedor was born in 1557, became Tsar in 1584, and died in 1598. Since he was not in full possession of his faculties, his brother-in-law, Boris Godunov, held the actual power during his reign, and succeeded him upon his death. Ivan Ivanovich was born in 1554, which would make him 27, not 20, at the time of his death.

[42] Dmitrii, Ivan's first son by Anastasiia, was born in 1552. The next year Ivan became seriously ill and asked the Boyars to swear allegiance to this son, but many of them preferred Dmitrii's paternal uncle, Prince Vasilli Andreevich Staritskii, an incident Ivan never forgot nor forgave. Shortly after Ivan's recovery that year the young prince Dmitrii died. In 1563 Mariia Temriukovna bore Ivan a son, Vasilii, but he died within five weeks. The other son was Dmitrii of Uglich, whose mother was Ivan's last wife, Mariia Nagaia. Dmitrii was born in 1582 and died in 1591. His death was used by Boris Godunov's opponents in an attempt to discredit him by hinting that he had secretly given orders to have Dmitrii murdered, but Godunov's complicity in the affair has never been fully established.

[43] Possevino's first interpreter had been a Polonized Lithuanian, Andrzej Połoński, who died after the conclusion of the Truce of Iam Zapol'skii in mid-January and Possevino's return to Moscow in February, 1582. He then obtained the services of another Lithuanian, Vasilii Zamaski, a convert to Catholicism, who had previously been in the Tsar's service.

[44] Tsarevich Ivan's first two wives had been Evdokiia Saburova and Praksevna Solovaia, who were forced to take the veil and lived in nunneries, the former in Suzdal', the latter in Beloozero, until their simultaneous deaths in 1620. His third wife was Elena Sheremeteva.

[45] One has only to think of the classic painting by Repin to realize that Possevino is alluding to one of the most celebrated incidents in Russian history. Arriving in Moscow only two months after the event occurred, Possevino constitutes a primary source, and thus his account must be weighed very carefully. A different view, for which some inferential supports exists, is that Tsarevich Ivan led a kind of "war-party," which demanded strenuous efforts be made to relieve Pskov, hold Livonia, and drive back the Poles. By this time Tsar Ivan was totally committed to ending the war by negotiation and whatever concessions to Batory were necessary. The Tsarevich's overt opposition to this view made Ivan so angry that he struck his son down. The incident took place on November 14, 1581, and by November 19 the Tsarevich was dead.

[46] This is in error. No formal arrangement had ever existed in the Grand Duchy of Muscovy whereby the succession would pass to the Master of the Horse in the event of the ruler's demise. No significance thus attaches to the fact that the last Master of the Horse, Ivan Petrovich Fedorov-Cheliadnin, was killed in 1568, rather than 30 years earlier.

[47] Baron Sigismund von Herberstein (1486-1566) the author of *Rerum Moscoviticarum Commentarii*, perhaps the most famous single work on sixteenth-century Muscovy, conducted two missions there during the reign of Vasilii III. The first was undertaken on behalf of Emperor Maximilian I in 1517-18; the second, for King Ferdinand I in 1526-27. In both Herberstein sought, in the interest of the Habsburg monarchy, to make peace between Poland and Muscovy and then to unite them with other European nations in a campaign against the Ottoman Empire. His first mission failed in its objective; the second produced a truce of five months, but before any further steps could be taken the Turks had decisively defeated Hungary at the battle of Mohács. Herberstein gathered a mass of information on all phases of Muscovite life during his visits, and this subsequently formed the basis for his Commentary. The work proved enormously popular from the time of its first appearance in 1549. It has run through innumerable editions and been translated into a variety of languages. It is not too much to say that systematic study of Russia in the West originated with Herberstein.

[48] Archbishop David. However, his disgrace occurred in 1583, and there is no evidence to connect this directly with any acceptance of Possevino's views.

[49] Probably an error in the text, for Possevino is usually accurate in indicating distances. Pskov is situated approximately 400 miles northwest of Moscow, and at the time lay some sixty miles inside the territory over which the Polish King claimed jurisdiction.

[50] Possevino's chief associates on his mission to Muscovy were Father Paolo Campano and Brother Michele Moreno, Italians from Reggio Emilia and Milan respectively, Father Stefan Drenocki, a Croatian from Zagreb, and Brother Andrei Modestyn, a Czech. While he was at the Polish camp before Pskov Possevino left Drenocki and Moreno in Moscow, and gave the former detailed instructions, complete with ample quotations from Scripture and the Fathers, on how to conduct himself among the Muscovites and how to engage in proselytization. The precautions taken by the Tsar forestalled such activity.

[51] A good example of the Aesopian language employed in Moscow during Ivan's reign; the phrase is, of course, a euphemism for the Tsar's death.

[52] Father Campano, who had become seriously ill as a result of the rigors of the climate and the journey, returned to Italy before the truce negotiations began in December, 1581. He too has left an interesting account of his experiences. L. N. Godovikova, "Svedeniia o Rossii kontsa XVI v. v Paolo Kampani," *Vestnik moskovskogo universiteta, seriia istorii* 6 (1969), pp. 80-84 has translated Campano's brief report on Russia, without notes or commentary. The present author has translated and edited Campano's remarks and Possevino's introduction to them: "The *Missio Muscovitica*," *Canadian-American Slavic Studies* 6 3 (1972), pp. 437-477.

[53] The Spanish possessions in America.

[54] In 1534 the Portuguese established an enclave in Goa, on the west coast of India some 200 miles south of Bombay, and Goa's first bishop, appointed in 1537, was a Franciscan, João Albuquerque. St. Francis Xavier arrived there in 1542; as a result of his labors Goa acquired jurisdiction over all Catholic missionary activities in the Far East and became a Metropolitan See in 1557. By 1570 some three quarters of the 200,000 inhabitants of the enclave had become Christians, but this marked the high point in its development.

Christianity failed to put down firm roots in the Indian subcontinent, and the See of Goa went into a steady decline. For Jesuit missionary activity in Ethiopia cf. Note 18, Chapter II on the career of Andrew of Oviedo.

[55] Western travellers uniformly refer to the dominions of the Grand Prince as Muscovy, not Russia. The latter term was used to denote the possessions of the Polish King, who was also Grand Prince of Lithuania. Possevino regularly adheres to this practice.

[56] See chapter 6 *passim* for the names and titles of these individuals.

[57] Andrzej Połoński, from Lithuania. He served as interpreter at Possevino's meetings with Ivan at Staritsa in Summer, 1581. When Possevino went to Iam Zapol'skii in late November he had to leave Połoński behind in the Polish camp, as he had become ill. He died there soon afterwards.

[58] On the mission Ivan sent to Italy, his courier, Istoma Shevrigin, was accompanied by two interpreters. From Moscow Shevrigin had brought Wilhelm Popler, of Livonian origin, born a Catholic, later a Lutheran, who became Orthodox and was known as Fedor Filipov. He knew Russian and German. In Lübeck Shevrigin obtained the assistance of Francesco Pallavicino, a Milanese merchant who had visited and served Muscovy. He knew German and Italian. Popler translated Shevrigin's remarks into German; next Pallavicino rendered them into Italian. Considerable ill-feeling apparently existed between the two men. On their way back from Italy, in a private altercation Popler assaulted Pallavicino, who died of his wounds shortly afterwards.

[59] This was more than a courtesy call to Archduke Karl von Steiermark. Possevino wished him to take more vigorous measures against the Protestants in his realm, and also hoped to arrange a marriage between this branch of the House of Habsburg and the Swedish royal house, part of Possevino's own plan to forge a strong Catholic bloc in central and northeastern Europe involving Poland, to which the Swedish crown had good pretensions.

[60] The Ottoman Empire.

[61] The Prus legend constituted one phase in the development of Muscovite identity in the sixteenth century, as the rulers sought to devise a pedigree giving them comparable prestige to that enjoyed by other European monarchs. The Communication of the monk Spiridon-Savva (quoted in R. P. Dmitrieva, *Skazanie o kniaz'iakh vladimirskikh*, Moscow-Leningrad, 1955, pp. 161-162) contains a succinct formulation of it: "Augustus began to distribute the whole world. He set up his brother.... Prus on the banks of the river Vistula, and in the towns called Malbork, Toruń, and glorious Gdańsk, and many other towns on the river called Neman, which falls into the sea.... Prus ruled a long time.... and to this day the land is called 'Prussian,' after his name." Next came the link with Novgorod and Kiev, the axis of the first Russian state, which was always considered a part of the Grand Princes' patrimony, in spite of the fact that Poland-Lithuania controlled the territory the Kievan State had formerly occupied: "And at the time a certain Voievoda in Novgorod called Gostomysl' was at the end of his life; he called those ruling with him in Novgorod and said: 'I give you some advice; send to the Prussian land and summon a prince from among those dwelling there who are from the line of Augustus, the Roman Tsar.' They went to the Prussian land and found there a certain prince named Riurik, who

was descended from the line of the Roman Tsar Augustus, and entreated him in the name of all the people of Novgorod. Prince Riurik came to them in Novgorod and brought his brothers with him, Truvor and Sineus, and a third kinsman, called Oleg. And henceforward Novgorod was called the Great, and Grand Prince Riurik ruled it." Grand Prince Vladimir, who brought Christianity to Kiev from Constantinople, was said to be fourth in line of descent from Riurik, and the Byzantine Emperor Constantine IX Monomachos was supposed to have given the Imperial insignia (that Ivan used at his own coronation in 1547) to his grandson, Vladimir Monomakh, eighth in line from Riurik.

[62] At Iam Zapol'skii (cf. Chapter VI) Ivan consistently endeavored to insert formulations such as "Hereditary Ruler of Livonia," *etc.* into the treaty in order to have a pretext for future claims against the region. Muscovy's inability to wage aggressive war against Germany is patent from Possevino's own writings; Ivan's negotiations with the Habsburgs were designed to create a diversion by arousing them against Batory. Nevertheless, this statement by Possevino constitutes perhaps the first formulation of a concept that has had a very long history.

[63] An allusion to the theory of Moscow the Third Rome, first formulated in a letter from Filofei, an elder of the Eleazar Monastery in Pskov, to Grand Prince Vasilii III in 1510. However, Possevino's juxtaposition is misleading, for the question was not one of political dominion but rather of spiritual awareness, part of a general movement that presaged and culminated in the appointment of an independent Russian Patriarch in 1589.

[64] The death of Sigismund II Augustus in 1572 brought the Jagiellon dynasty in Poland to an end; the period from 1572 to 1576 confirmed the principle of elective monarchy. Various candidates vied for the throne, and certain elements, particularly among the petty gentry of Lithuania, favored Ivan, in the belief that he would champion Orthodoxy and curb the great lords, as he was thought to have done in his own kingdom. However, tales of his capricious cruelty cooled enthusiasms, and as a compromise some advocated offering the throne to Ivan's younger son Fedor. In 1572 Ivan discussed the position, indicating a willingness to accept the throne, with the Polish envoy who brought him official news of Sigismund's death. In 1573 the Lithuanian *Rada*, acting independently of the Polish *Sejm*, sent Michał Haraburda (cf. Chapter VI) to ask Ivan for a definitive answer. Ivan attached unacceptable conditions to Fedor's candidacy and stressed his own availability. He refused, however, to campaign among the electors, and the pro-French party succeeded in electing Henry of Valois. Upon Henry's precipitate vacation of the throne in 1575, Ivan was once more solicited, but again refused to campaign, and in 1576 the throne passed to Stefan Batory, who had conducted himself energetically. It is to these negotiations Ivan refers, but Possevino exaggerates when he says that the issue was the overthrow of the Polish kingdom. The Habsburgs had asked Ivan to support the candidacy of the Archduke Ernst, a son of the Emperor Maximilian II, to the Polish throne, offering to join him in a drive to oust the Turks from Europe, whereby Ivan would acquire Constantinople and be proclaimed Emperor of the East, and there were implications that the Habsburgs were not averse to a "partition" giving Austria control of Poland and Muscovy control of Lithuania. Such a project was premature, but Ivan chose to support the Archduke's unsuccessful candidacy, as he correctly assumed that the election of Batory would prove inimical to his own interests.

[65] A reference to Maximilian II (1527-1576), who became Emperor in 1564. Faced with the need to conciliate the Protestants in his realm, and fearing the possibility of the kind of uprising which the Duke of Alva was attempting to suppress in the Low Countries, in 1568 he informed Pope Pius V of his intention to allow the Protestant nobles and gentry of Lower Austria, Hungary and Bohemia free exercise of their religion in accordance with the terms of the Confession of Augsburg, arrived at in 1530. It was not a question of a plot on the part of the Emperor deliberately to diffuse Protestantism in his dominions; Maximilian considered his position sufficiently serious to resist the heaviest pressure against his decision which the Pope was capable of bringing to bear.

[66] The Donatists, a Christian sect that arose in North Africa during the fourth century A.D. and endured there until the victory of Islam, believed that the Church consisted of a penitential elect devoted to fighting pagans while awaiting the imminent end of the world. Intensely opposed to state interference in church affairs, people who often sought a martyr's crown, they attracted many peasants by their millenial program of social reform. As the Catholic church became more institutionalized and hieratical, in the eyes of the Donatists it had taken the place of the Roman officialdom they hated.

[67] Although Christianity was the official religion of Ethiopia, it occupied a highly tenuous position between the powerful counterforces of paganism and Islam. The Ethiopian church had formed close ties with the Coptic Church of Egypt, and firmly espoused a Monophysite position. Reaction to Jesuit efforts at penetration and organization were deeply resented, and contributed substantially to the steady decline of Catholic influence in Ethiopia from the sixteenth century onwards. There was never any question of asserting Papal domination over the Ethiopian Church.

[68] Jan Hus (1369-1415), Rector of the University of Prague, influenced by the teachings of Wyclif took advantage of anti-Catholic reaction to the sale of Indulgences in Bohemia in the early fifteenth century to lead a reform movement. He was martyred at the Council of Constance, an incident that led to the creation of an autonomous Hussite Church. The Hussites split into two camps, the moderate Utraquists and the radical Taborites, but neither one voluntarily sought a rapprochement with the Church; on the contrary, they were united in their opposition to it.

[69] Possevino is misleading. The Armenian Church, founded in the second century A.D. by Gregory the Illuminator, came to adopt a strongly Monophysite position, whereas Nestorius (Bishop of Constantinople from 428 to his condemnation at the Council of Ephesus in 431) championed a form of dyophysitism and advocated a concept in which Christ was considered as Two Persons, human and divine, which were closely and inseparably linked together, but yet distinct.

[70] Possevino has chosen to cloak the person of King Stefan Batory himself under the soubriquet of "a certain N."

[71] Muhammed Sokolli (1505-1579), originally from Bosnia and taken into the Janissaries by the *Devshirme* (child-empressment), was a successful military commander and rose to become what many consider to be one of the greatest Grand Viziers of the Ottoman Empire. He served under Suleiman the Magnificent (1520-1566), his son Selim II (1562-1574), and Murad III (1574-1595). Suleiman was thus the grandfather of the ruling Sultan.

[72] Possevino is alluding to a complex series of negotiations from memory, not always accurately, nor in chronological order. The thread that links all of them together is the persistent efforts of Papal diplomacy to erect an anti-Turkish league. The specific issue in this instance was whether it was possible to include Muscovy in the league, a question complicated by the fact that a state of chronic hostility existed between Muscovy and Poland, resolution of which was considered an essential preliminary to further negotiations. In 1561 Cardinal Hosius, Pope Pius V's chief representative in Central Europe, recommended that a distinguished layman from Bologna, who had carried out successful missions for the Pope elsewhere, Giovanni-Francesco Mazza di Canobio (whom Possevino confuses with Alessandro Canobio), be assigned the task of composing the current hostilities between the two countries. That summer Canobio tried to proceed through Poland to Moscow and reached Vilna, but certain Royal councillors argued that it was detrimental to Polish interests to have Muscovy emerge from her isolation, and the Protestants of the region were suspicious of the part played by Rome in the affair. These forces prevailed upon the King to deny Canobio permission to proceed further. As Turkish strength in the Eastern Mediterranean steadily grew in the late 1560's, Pius V became even more anxious to involve Muscovy in an anti-Turkish league. In 1570 he issued instructions to the Papal Nuncio in Poland, Vicenzo del Portico, to proceed to Moscow in person in order to recruit the Grand Prince for the league; in return the Pope offered to send a few artists and preachers to Moscow. The Pope's plan shows considerable naïveté, as well as lack of knowledge of conditions in Muscovy. This was the time of Ivan's assault on Novgorod and the worst wave of executions, and the sack of Moscow by the Crimean Tatars was imminent. Portico, who possessed somewhat better information concerning these matters than the Pope, delayed and passed on what he heard to Rome. At the end of 1571 the Pope abandoned the project. His revised estimate of Ivan's character and temperament may have contributed to his decision, but it is far more likely that the optimism engendered by the victory over the Turks at Lepanto had led the Holy See to consider an alliance with Muscovy as of much less pressing moment than before. In the next few years Grand Vizier Sokolli displayed remarkable skill in restoring Turkish military strength, and this correspondingly revived Papal interest in Muscovy. Furthermore, in 1575-1576 Johann Kobentzl went to Moscow to seek Ivan's support for the candidacy of Archduke Ernst to the Polish throne, and in the report he issued, which was widely circulated, he spoke in awed terms of the Grand Prince's financial resources and military power, and of Ivan's great desire to join an anti-Turkish league. These circumstances aroused Pope Gregory XIII to instruct Cardinal Morone, then Papal Nuncio in Poland, to make new overtures to Ivan. Morone was attending the Diet of Ratisbon, to which two Muscovite envoys had come in the hope of concluding an alliance with the Emperor prejudicial to Batory's interests. The Cardinal selected Rudolph Clenck for the task. A man of vigorous piety, he had some knowledge of Slavic languages and had visited Muscovy on a previous occasion. However, forces in the Imperial court prevailed on the Emperor to prevent Clenck's departure by the expedient of declaring that his mission could only take place as part of a general embassy made up of representatives from all interested countries. The Habsburgs, like the Poles, were unwilling to allow the Papacy to establish special relations with Muscovy which they could not control. Clenck died in the summer of 1578; his death was not the proximate cause of the mission's failure. Anxious to try again, in 1579 the Pope asked the Nuncio, now Andrea Caligari (subsequently Bishop of Bertinoro) to persuade King Stefan and his chief coadjutor, Jan Zamojski, Captain-General of the Kingdom, of the need for peace with Muscovy as an essential preliminary to any concerted action against the Ottoman Empire. Caligari had no success; the King, the

Chancellor, and the Estates all favored a policy of war with Muscovy. For two decades Papal policy towards Muscovy, which was founded on illusion, had produced no results. It is uncertain what Rome's next move might have been, for in March, 1581 Shevrigin reached Rome to request an audience with the Pope. In the light of the foregoing the alacrity with which the Holy See responded to Ivan's appeal becomes much more understandable.

[73] The first five works constitute a compendium of writings by ecclesiastical personages identified with the concept of Papal sovreignty.

[74] George Scholarius (1405-1472) was a very broken reed for Possevino to lean upon. As a learned layman at the Imperial court of Constantinople he had composed certain treatises friendly to Rome and had participated in the Council of Florence as a moderate Unionist. However, in 1445, at the dying request of Mark of Ephesus, the most adamant opponent of union, he reversed his position and became the leader of the anti-unionist forces. In 1450, after the death of his patron, Emperor John VIII Paleologus (1392-1448), he became a monk under the name of Gennadius, and was appointed Patriarch of the Orthodox Church by Sultan Muhammed the Conqueror after the Ottoman capture of Constantinople. He was a voluminous writer; unionists and anti-unionists alike can find quotations apposite to their views in his writings. Also cf. *supra*: Note 5 to the *Note on the Text*.

[75] Sakran wrote "An Illumination of the Errors Found in the Orthodox Ritual," a slight two-page pamphlet. It was included in a popular compendium compiled by Jan Łasicki and published in Spires in 1582, *De Russorum Moscovitarum et Tartarorum religione, sacrificiis, nuptiarum funerum ritu e diversis scriptoribus, quorum nomina versa pagina indicat.*

[76] Nicholas Sander (1530-1581), an English Jesuit, graduated from Oxford and went to Rome *ca.* 1559. He travelled throughout Europe on Papal business and is thought to have died in Ireland while trying to incite an unsuccessful rebellion against England. He was a prolific writer: Possevino refers to his best known work, *On the Visible Monarchy of the Church*, composed in 1571.

[77] Francesco Turriano (Francisco Torres, 1509-1584), a Spanish Jesuit, who entered the Order in 1566 and did missionary work in Germany. A passionate champion of Papal supremacy, he constantly assailed the Protestants, sometimes intemperately. An indefatigable author, his bibliography comprises some 58 substantial treatises.

[78] Piotr Skarga (1536-1612) was the most eminent of the early Polish Jesuits. He enjoyed a distinguished and influential career. After studying in Rome from 1564 to 1571 he began his activity in Poland as a teacher. He soon became involved in preaching and missionary work, and was responsible for the founding of many Jesuit colleges throughout Poland and Lithuania, since he was a firm believer in the power of education to serve the cause of the Church. He was very interested in the Eastern dominions of Poland, and served as the first rector of the Jesuit Academy at Vilna, from 1579-1584. His most famous work is *O Jedności Kościoła Bożego pod Jednym Pasterzem*, which appeared in 1577.

[79]Thomas Stapleton (1535-1598), another English Catholic, went into exile in Belgium soon after receiving an Oxford degree in 1556. He was long associated with the English College at Douai. He became a Jesuit in 1584, but ill-health caused him to withdraw from the Order shortly afterwards. At the end of his life he served as Rector of the University of Louvain. A vigorous controversialist and polemicist, his best-known work is *A Defense of the Authority of the Church*.

[80]Cardinal Hosius had proved remarkably successful in recruiting an able band of clerics to advance the cause of the Counterreformation in Poland in the second half of the sixteenth century. Among his supporters was Father Stanisław Sokołowski, a preacher famed for his rhetoric and apologetics. He was especially concerned with promoting Catholicism in the Orthodox portion of Poland's eastern dominions by the device of criticizing what he considered to be deficiencies in Orthodox ritual (as here), and by interdicting communication between leading Protestant theologians and the Patriarchate of Constantinople.

[81]St. Robert Bellarmine (1542-1621) entered the Jesuit College at Rome when he joined the Order in 1560. In 1569 he became the first Jesuit professor at the University of Louvain. His main work, the *Controversies*, was directed against the Protestants, and constituted a major contribution to the developing synthesis of the Catholic position. He was summoned back to Rome in 1588, where Pope Clement VIII created him a Cardinal in 1599. Bellarmine forcefully upheld the high mediaeval position that the Pope's power was primarily spiritual, but also temporal, since spiritual power is greater than temporal power; thus, the Pope was at liberty to intervene in secular affairs whenever he thought they might infringe upon his spiritual prerogatives.

[82]Johann Faber (1478-1541) in 1524 became Chaplain and Confessor to the Archduke Ferdinand, and Bishop of Vienna in 1530. He acquired his reputation from the polemics he composed attacking Protestants; in 1526 he published a brief pamphlet on the Muscovite religion derived entirely from secondary sources, called *Ad serenissimum principem Ferdinandum Archiducem Austriae, Muscovitarum iuxta mare glaciale religio à D. Ioanne Fabri aedita*.

[83]Alessandro Guagnini, whose work appeared in 1578, an Italian soldier of fortune from Verona, served as a military commander in the Polish fortress of Vitebsk on the Muscovite frontier, and thus his account merits attention, although his tendency toward sensationalism somewhat detracts from its credibility.

[84]The word *slavicus* assumes different meanings in the various contexts in which Possevino employs it. When directly opposed to the Muscovite vernacular, as it is in the present instance, it serves as a reminder that the language of church ritual and writ had become markedly different from the spoken language of the sixteenth century.

Notes To Chapter II

[1] Possevino gathered the material for this Chapter on his first visit to Muscovy, of which the chronology was as follows: he entered Muscovite territory at Smolensk early in August, 1581, and reached Staritsa, where Ivan was making his headquarters at the time, by the middle of the month. He spent 28 days there, engaged in protracted negotiations, had a final meeting with the Tsar on September 12, and arranged for Drenocki and Moreno to go to Moscow, while he returned to the Polish camp before Pskov, which he reached on October 5.

[2] Possevino is guilty of some exaggeration. The Metropolitans who held office before, during, and after Ivan's reign were: Makarii (1542-1564), Afanasii (1564-1566), Filipp (1566-1568), Kirill (1568-1572), Antonii (1572-1581), and Dionisii (1581-1587). Of these, only Metropolitan Filipp met with a violent end. He had remonstrated privately with the Tsar over what he considered to be the latter's personal and administrative excesses, and then publicly refused to give the Tsar his blessing. He was deposed by a Council, confined to a monastery, and, at the end of 1568, reportedly strangled by Maliuta Skuratov, one of Ivan's chief henchmen.

[3] Maksim the Greek (Michael Triboles, 1475-1556) was born in Greece and studied there and in Italy. For 10 years he was an inmate of the Vatoped Monastery on Mt. Athos, whence he was summoned in 1518 to Moscow by Vasilii III in order to translate church books from Greek into Old Church Slavonic. Possessed of an ascetic nature, he found the views of the Trans-Volga Elders, who opposed church involvement in secular affairs, more congenial than the materialistic attitude held by the other, and more influential party, known as the Josephites. Of a forceful and assertive disposition, Maksim became associated with various reformers and criticized the luxurious lives led by many of the Muscovite clergy, as well as other current practices. A church inquiry against him was held in 1525, which brought about his incarceration in a monastery in Moscow. While there he continued his discussions with dissidents, and this finally led, in 1531, to another hearing on charges that he had deliberately mistranslated devotional literature and intrigued with a Turkish envoy. He was removed to a monastery in Tver', and ultimately, in 1551, to the Trinity Monastery, where he died five years later.

[4] Possevino is rendering the Slavic word *Vladyka*. The word is associated with the verb *vladet'* ("to possess, control"), and is stronger than the meaning he gives to it. It can refer to an Emperor, or a Chief Administrator, or, in religious context, to an Archpriest. With the qualifying adjective *nebesnyi* ("heavenly"), it can refer to God.

[5] Ivan's seven wives: Anastasiia Romanova (d.1560), Mariia Temriukovna, Marfa Sobakina, Anna Kol'tovskaia, who was sent to a convent in 1575 and survived to 1626, Anna Vasil'chikova, Vasilisa Melent'eva, sent to a convent in 1577, who lived to 1611, and his last wife, Mariia Nagaia, who outlived him.

[6] The details concerning Tsarevich Ivan are repeated. cf. Chapter I, Notes 41 and 44.

[7] Elsewhere Possevino states that he "learned a great deal" from conversations with Shevrigin in the course of their journey.

[8] Another partisan reference to the events described in Note 24, Chapter I.

[9] Not included.

[10] Known in Wallachian records as Alexander II (1568-1577).

[11] Not included.

[12] References concerning a festival, held on May 9 of each year, in honor of St. Nicholas go very far back. It was designed to commemorate the transference of the saint's relics from Myra, a city in Asia Minor, to the south Italian town of Bari in 1089. The exact reason for the continuing and widespread popularity of St. Nicholas' cult in Muscovy is not clear.

[13] Possevino prints this Polonized version in his text. The "curved" week resulted from the elimination of Christmas Day from ordinary calendrical calculations.

[14] Boris and Gleb were the younger sons of Vladimir Sviatoslavich, Grand Prince of Kiev. When internecine war broke out in 1015 on their father's death, their elder brother, Sviatopolk, ordered the two young men put to death. They did not resist his verdict, and came to be regarded as martyrs. In 1071 Prince Iziaslav built an elaborate tomb to house their remains in the town of Vyshgorod; this was the beginning of a cult that culminated in the young princes' canonization as the first saints of the Russian Orthodox Church.

[15] Metropolitans Peter and Aleksei are Saints of the Russian Orthodox church. Peter, born in Volynia in the second half of the thirteenth century, immediately after being confirmed as Metropolitan by the Patriarch of Constantinople in 1305, took up residence in Vladimir. On his arrival he found a struggle for primacy in the region between Moscow and Tver'; in the contest Peter supported Moscow. He fostered good relations with the Khan of the Golden Horde, and when a second struggle with Tver' broke out in 1325, at the beginning of Ivan Kalita's reign, Peter's support was so unswerving that he transferred the Metropolitan See, with all the prestige attached to it, from Vladimir to Moscow. He died in 1326. Aleksei continued Peter's policies. Born in the 1290's, he became bishop of Vladimir in 1345 and Metropolitan at Moscow in 1354. He encouraged the princes in their struggle with the Tatars, and his loyalty to the regime was such that he was given a number of important administrative tasks, including the virtual governance of the Grand Duchy during the minority of Dmitrii Donskoi, leader of the united forces in the first successful contest with the Tatars at Kulikovo Pole in 1380. Metropolitans Peter and Aleksei firmly established the principal of church-state cooperation that remained characteristic both of the Grand Duchy of Muscovy and the Russian Empire.

[16] Sergei (ca. 1314-1392) was made a saint of the Orthodox Church in 1452. In 1337 in the village of Radonezh he founded and served as the first abbot of what ultimately became the Troitso-Sergeev Monastery, the largest and most influential in Muscovy. He too supported the Muscovite Grand Princes in their struggle against the Tatars, and in particular encouraged Dmitrii Donskoi before the latter took the field at Kulikovo. Possevino makes a mistake of 170 years in reporting the date of Sergei's death.

¹⁷The prescience of these observations by Possevino should be noticed. He anticipated the problem, first posed by the activities of Maksim the Greek, but which did not become acute until nearly a century later, during the reign of Tsar Aleksei Mikhailovich. Changes in the ritual and corrections in the church books decreed by Patriarch Nikon led to the convocation of a Church Council in 1656 that censured Nikon, and to the Schism of the Old Believers, which seriously split the Orthodox Church.

¹⁸Ethiopia was thought to be the site of the fabulous kingdom of Prester John. Asnaf, the Negus, or ruler, of Ethiopia, wished to obtain Portuguese support to strengthen his position against the forces of Islam. The price, which he was not anxious to pay, was permission for Jesuit missionary activity in his realm. In 1555 three Spanish Jesuits, Nunhes, Carnero and Oviedo, were given the title of Patriarch and Suffragan Bishops respectively, and dispatched to Ethiopia. Oviedo alone succeeded in reaching their destination. At first he was made welcome, but when Asnaf was killed in a battle with his opponents in 1559, his successor drove Oviedo and his small band of converts out of the capital. The Jesuit took refuge in the desert of Adowa, where he labored under most difficult conditions for the next twenty years, completely cut off from civilization, until his death in 1577. Possevino's language artfully conceals the true state of affairs.

¹⁹Even if the results of his activity were minimal, St. Francis Xavier (1506-1552) remains one of the greatest missionaries in the history of the Church. Making Goa, which he reached from Lisbon in 1542, his headquarters, he labored for three years in Malaysia, two years in Japan, and, in the last year of his life, attempted to enter China. He landed on an offshore island and was seeking permission to proceed to Canton when he died. St. Francis' extraordinary career has been productive of legend; the story of his deliberately selling himself into slavery to an Indian in order to enter China falls into this category.

²⁰The chief base of operations for the Ostrogski family was Volynia, and its leading figure in the sixteenth century was Prince Konstantin Ostrogski (1526-1608). A man of enormous wealth and huge landholdings, he used the freedom characteristic of the great Magnate families of Poland to champion Orthodoxy and combat Catholic encroachment. Observing how the Jesuits were making effective use of seminaries and academies to advance the Counterreformation in Poland, he became convinced that education was the best means by which to improve the Orthodox position, and founded a number of schools at his own expense. The most outstanding institution he established was an Academy, located in the town of Ostrog, which constituted the first attempt to teach the Trivium and the Quadrivium in an Orthodox context. He also set up three printing-presses, which turned out Orthodox devotional literature and anti-Catholic propaganda. The Stucki family vigorously fostered Orthodox interests in Belorussia. There is little in the activities of these two families to support Possevino's contention that the Orthodox gentry in Poland's Eastern dominions was ready for mass conversion to Catholicism.

Notes To Chapter III

[1] Cf. Appendix for the Muscovite version of these public discussions.

[2] What Ivan had actually written to King Stefan runs, in part, as follows (*Poslaniia Ivana Groznogo*, D. S. Likhachev and Ia. S. Lur'e, edd., Moscow, 1952, pp. 229-230): "...the Pope and all the Romans and Latins say the same, that the Greek and Latin faiths are identical. When a Council assembled in Rome in the days of Pope Eugene.... it enacted that the Greek and Roman faiths were one and the same. So how can your Lords complain that Livonia is now in the sphere of the Greek faith? ....although the Pope enacted that the Greek and Latin faiths are one, they seek to overturn this and direct people from the Greek faith to the Latin faith. Is this Christian behavior? There are some people in our country who follow the Latin faith, and we do not apply any pressure to direct them away from it....and they profess whatever faith they wish."

[3] St. Andrew, the brother of St. Peter, enjoyed enormous prestige among the original Apostles. In his missionary travels he was supposed to have preached to the "Scythians," Greeks and others inhabiting the northern Black Séa region. Legend had him visit the future site of Kiev, plant a cross there, and proceed northward to Novgorod. It is understandable that Possevino should assume that Ivan was simply prevaricating. He failed to realize that the legendary visit of the Apostle Andrew constituted yet another example of the contemporary Muscovite desire for an ancient and prestigious pedigree.

[4] Prominent early Popes from Clement I of Rome, who probably lived towards the end of the first century in the reign of the Emperor Domitian, to Agatho (Pope 678-681), a leading champion of Orthodox views at the close of the Monothelite controversy.

[5] Eight books of the purported sayings and exhortations of the Apostles, as taken down by their disciple, Clement of Rome. The inaccuracies and anachronisms contained in them made Possevino's contemporary, St. Robert Bellarmine, suspicious of their authenticity. They are thought to belong to the fifth or sixth centuries.

[6] Presumably the assemblage of Orthodox leaders convoked by Metropolitan Dionisii to assist the Tsar in his disputation with Possevino.

[7] In 1569 some Swedish envoys had come to Moscow to negotiate a truce. Ivan proposed harsh terms. When the envoys hesitated, he had them imprisoned, exposed to the fury of a mob, and threatened with torture and death. The incident rankled and had not been forgotten.

[8] An ikon representing the Virgin and Child in austere mode, known as the *Hodigitria*, which was said to have been painted by St. Luke and blessed by the Virgin herself, had long existed in Constantinople, but was destroyed at the time of the Turkish conquest. Representations of it were occasionally made in Muscovy; in Ivan's time one was located in the Cathedral of the Archangel Michael in the Kremlin. Its author is unknown, but many details of the work, including a certain relaxation in austerity, mark it as a typical product of the contemporary Moscow school of ikon-painting.

157

⁹Metropolitan Dionisii succeeded Metropolitan Antonii in February, 1581, less than a month prior to Possevino's arrival in Moscow, after Antonii had died a natural death.

¹⁰Another reference to Metropolitan Filipp.

[1] Iakov Molvianinov (cf. Chapter I). He was accompanied on his mission by a Vicenotary, Tishina Vasil'ev.

[2] Leo I (the Great, Pope 440-461) was one of the earliest Popes strongly to support the advancement of Papal power. Leo opposed the growing influence of Constantinople in Illyria. In 444 he wrote to the bishops there that Peter had received the primacy from Christ and the Popes were Peter's legitimate successors; thus, it behooved the bishops to refer all matters of importance to the Roman Pontiff for final decision. Leo enjoyed some success with his policy, but after his time political considerations constrained Constantinople to assert its authority in this area on its own borders.

[3] Not the Fifth, but the Third Canon of the Second Ecumenical Council, held in Constantinople in 381, stated: "The Bishop of Constantinople is to have honorable preeminence next to the Bishop of Rome, because the former city is the New Rome."

[4] Not the 16th, but the famous 28th. Canon of the Fourth Ecumenical Council, held at Chalcedon in 451, stated in part: "The Fathers have been right in granting the See of Old Rome its privileges because this city used to be the Imperial City. Similarly, privileges have also been conferred upon the New Rome, which is honored because it is the domicile of the Emperor and the Senate. Since it enjoys the same privileges as the Old City, it must possess the same advantages in the ecclesiastical order, and be second after it." This wording aroused strong opposition on the part of subsequent Popes.

[5] John the Faster, Patriarch of Constantinople (582-595) presided over a Synod in the capital in 588 at which he was addressed as *Archbishop* and *Ecumenical Patriarch*. This brought forth a denunciation from Pope Gregory the Great, who declared that no churchman should display such arrogance and pride as to permit himself to be addressed thus. However, certain earlier Popes and Patriarchs had been so called, and the term could well mean simply "Imperial Patriarch," a phrase devoid of the pretensions which Gregory chose to read into it.

[6] The events leading up to the formal Schism between the two halves of the Church which occurred in 1054 A.D., when Patriarch Michael Cerularius and Pope Leo IX mutually excommunicated one another, constituted the culmination of a long and complex process. The basic issue was the secular political pretensions of the Papacy; the intellectual groundwork had been laid during the career of Patriarch Photius.

[7] The *Filioque* controversy split the Church. This addition to the Creed first appeared in 589 at the Third Council of Toledo, and from Spain it spread to France, where a Synod convoked by Charlemagne at Aachen in 809 gave it official sanction. Since, however, the ecumenical Councils of Fourth Constantinople and Second Nicaea had not alluded to this phraseology, Pope Leo III, when asked to ratify the proceedings at Aachen, adopted an ambivalent attitude. Patriarch Photius made the addition of the *Filoque* a cardinal charge in his indictment of the Papacy, and the word was not formally employed until the year 1014, when Pope Benedict VIII used it in consecrating King Henry II.

[8] Macedonius was a Bishop of Constantinople in the latter half of the fourth century, the details of whose life are very obscure. The view he is thought to have upheld is that the Holy Ghost was not originally a Divine but a created being. Like many comparable figures in the pre-Nicene period, he was influenced by Arian concepts.

[9] Eunomius, Bishop of Cyzicus *ca*. 360, advocated the view that the Father was utterly unlike the Son, the Energy of the Father had produced the Son, and subsequently the Energy of the Son had produced the Holy Ghost.

[10] The Council of Lyons, held in 1274 during the pontificate of Gregory X, was attended by Byzantine dignitaries concerned with minimizing the threatening stance adopted towards the empire by the West. Since the Eastern position was menaced both by Western anger over the loss of the preeminence it had acquired during the existence of the Latin Empire of Constantinople, and by the Saracens, it is not surprising that the Emperor Michael Paleologus brought heavy pressure to bear on his reluctant ecclesiastics to accept binding formulations, including the *Filioque* and acknowledgment of the primacy of the Pope, in the hope of diverting the ominous Western combination headed by Charles of Anjou.

[11] The Maronite Church, which takes its name from a semi-legendary founder, Bishop John Maron, was unknown prior to the seventh century. It managed to preserve a distinctive form of Christianity within the Islamic world, observing its own ritual and customs. Originally attracted to Monothelitism, the Maronite Church, when exposed to Crusading influence, in 1182 renounced all doctrinal deviation in favour of an association with the Pope and Catholic Christianity.

[12] St. Dionysius the Areopagite was supposed to have been converted to Christianity by St. Paul, served as the first Bishop of Athens, and be the author of a series of treatises on Christian mysticism, as well as ten pastoral letters. There are no references to St. Dionysius before the sixth century, and Italian humanist critics were among the first to question the original stories concerning the author. However, the influence of this work as a prime foundation for the mystical tradition in Christianity remains very substantial.

[13] St. Cyril, Bishop of Jerusalem (d.386) was a prominent theologian among the early Church Fathers, and a devout supporter of Nicaean Orthodoxy. He had no pronounced views on the primacy of the Pope; he held that the existing Church was the one intended by Christ as fulfilment of the Church predicted in the Old Testament. He composed a series of catechetal letters for Christian neophytes.

[14] Little is known about the career of Melchiades (Pope 310-314), but his pontificate saw the occupation of Rome by Constantine the Great, and it is said that Melchiades was given the responsibility of deciding whether Donatus or Caecilianus should be confirmed as Bishop of Africa. His decision in favour of the latter inaugurated the Schism of the Donatists.

[15]Little is known about the life of St. Ignatius, for whom no sure dates can be given. Tradition makes him a disciple of the original Apostles and second bishop of Antioch, and assigns him a martyr's crown. There is further dispute over the authenticity of the letters he is thought to have written. If genuine, they afford much valuable information concerning Church organization and governance during the reign of the Emperor Trajan.

[16]Telesphorus (Pope 127-137) was perhaps a martyr. Tradition had him establish the 40 day period of Lenten fasting.

[17]St. John Damascene (ca. 700-754) remains one of the most distinguished and authoritative Greek Fathers of the Church. He was an outstanding synthesizer and compiler of Christian doctrine rather than an original theologian.

[18]Latin equivalents are given for the Greek phrases Possevino employs in this and similar passages.

[19]The minor Synod of Gangra (ca. 340) took up questions of ritual, because it had to inquire into complaints against certain persons who had interpreted the Scriptural injunctions concerning asceticism too literally.

[20]Possevino would certainly call members of the following sects heretical, but in reality their views do no more than reflect the multiplicity of doctrinal opinion that existed prior to the establishment of Christianity as the official religion of the Roman Empire and the legislation of belief attempted by the major Church Councils. The Simonians were the followers of the figure of Simon Magus, whose career is extremely difficult to reconstruct, and who was the subject of highly involved and complex controversies. Simon was called "a magician of Samaria" in the Gospel; he appears as a false Messiah in certain Apocryphal books, and by the end of the second century innumerable stories, including many to the effect that he claimed to be God, were in circulation. He was supposed to have devised a cosmogony, in which the primordial element was fire, and a theory of the creation of the world and man that differed markedly from the account in Genesis. It was also alleged that Simon offered the Apostles payment to receive the power conferred by the Holy Ghost – the reputed origin of the term "simony." It is a moot question whether the host of ideas gathered around Simon can rightly be called a Christian heresy, and whatever followers the sect may have acquired had virtually disappeared by the fourth century.

[21]Manichaeism, a movement that began in Babylonia in the mid-third century, proved extremely popular, especially in the army, spread throughout the Roman Empire, and for a time was a serious rival with Christianity itself. Its founder, the Persian Manes, contended that the world was the scene of an intense and constant struggle between the forces of Light and Darkness, or God and Satan, both regarded as positive entities. The human estate lies in the domain of Satan, but contains within it potentialities of light. It is the duty of every individual to strive to the utmost for the liberation of these potentialities, so that they can return to their native habitat. In the after-life, reward and punishment are meted out in accordance with one's behaviour on earth. Although Manichaeism began to decline after the triumph of Christianity, it was a force to be reckoned with, especially in certain Eastern areas, for a thousand years, and it would constantly reappear in a variety of forms.

161

²²The followers of Eustathius of Sebaste. They, not Bishop Eustathius (d. *ca.* 378), were censured by the Synod of Gangra for their excessive asceticism, that sought, among other things, to separate husbands from wives.

²³Marcion came to Rome as an enthusiastic Christian convert in 140, but soon devised a distinctive theology of his own. He contrasted a God of the Old Testament with a God of the New Testament, whom he considered different from and greater than his Predecessor. After positing two Godheads, he similarly postulated two Christs: Jesus was not the Messiah foretold in the Old Testament, as this figure had not yet appeared. His followers, the Marcionites, were noted for their austere and moral lives. The sect at first flourished but began to die out soon after Constantine granted official recognition to the Church. Marcion himself died probably in the second decade of the third century.

²⁴Lampetians: another name for Messalians.

²⁵The Messalians, also known as Euchites and by others names, constituted a sect that arose in Mesopotamia, spread to Syria, and thence to Paphlagonia. They held the view that sin could be overcome and perfection attained by perpetual prayer. They were numerous from the mid-fourth to the mid-sixth centuries. They believed that people were infested with powerful spirits, to overcome which they sometimes received the assistance of the Fire of the Holy Ghost, and that everyone possessed Divine properties within himself. They did not think that the Sacraments of the Church enjoyed special efficacity. They held that their enthusiastic practices were necessary to exorcise the marked propensity to evil that mankind had acquired at the fall of Adam and Eve. The Messalians were frequently attacked by the Church.

²⁶Anastasius I, Patriarch of Antioch 559-599, was a friend of Gregory the Great, an opponent of the Emperor Justinian's various excursions into theology, and the author of a number of popular Church compendia.

²⁷St. Justin Martyr was an influential and highly-regarded Christian apologist. Born in Palestine *ca.* 114, he was martyred in Rome in the 160's. Trained in Greek philosophy, he was one of the first Christians to expound the faith in a speculative way.

²⁸Gregory of Nazianzus, a town in Cappadocia (*ca.* 329-390), was an ascetic, a great preacher, and an effective exponent of Orthodox views. He held a number of bishoprics in Asia Minor, and in 379 appeared at the Council of Constantinople as an avowed champion of the Nicene position against those who continued to espouse Arian views. He composed 45 orations, usually in honour of the Christian holidays, over 200 epistles, and a number of poems.

²⁹Origen (182-251) was the most famous teacher and prolific author of the early Church. He presided over a very popular school of Christian learning in Alexandria; an ascetic, he went so far as to perform an act of self-castration in order to avoid the slightest possibility of scandal at his school. His voluminous writings were mainly concerned with Biblical exegesis and systematic theology. Origen was very much of a Platonist in his views,

and fond of articulating an abstract and idealized concept of the Deity, although his Eight Books *against Celsus* constituted an attack on the Neoplatonist position. The 4th and 6th centuries saw numerous disputes about his work, and charges of heresy were sometimes made against him.

[30] Marcarius Magnes (here written *Magnetes*), late fourth-early fifth centuries, about whose life and career virtually nothing is known, was the author of the *Apocriticus*, a lengthy disputation with an imaginary opponent called Theostenes, who represented the Neo-Platonist position. Francisco Torres made extensive use of the dialogue, and Possevino undoubtedly considered it an authentic historical document.

[31] A paraphrase based on a section of Homily 82 (not 83), in which Chrysostom, commenting on Matt. 26: 33, emphasizes the importance of Peter as First Apostle in order to stress the grievousness of his fall, not his leadership of the Church. Cf. J-P Migne, ed., *Patrologiae Cursus Completus: Patrologia Graeca* (161 vols.), Paris, 1844-1866, 58, Col. 741 [*PG*].

[32] Theophylact, a learned Greek and Archbishop of Okhrid 1078-*post* 1081, made extensive exegeses of the Bible. His Commentary on the 20th. Chapter of Luke (*PG*. 123, Cols. 1038-1047) discusses the Parable of the Vine, but nothing in it bears any resemblance to Possevino's present quotation.

[33] From the First Epistle of Pope Agatho to the Emperor Constantine IV Pogonatus (J-P Migne, ed., *Patrologiae Cursus Completus: Patrologia Latina* (221 vols.), Paris, 1844-1864 [*PL*], 87, Cols. 1169 & 1170). Possevino's quotation is abridged. In context the issue was the Pope's desire to prove to the Emperor that Rome had never favored the Monothelites, not the Primacy of Peter. The Pope's letter received a sympathetic hearing at the First Trullan Council (680-681) since the loss of the Empire's Eastern provinces to the forces of Islam had largely obviated the need for the Monothelite compromise.

[34] St. Basil (330-379) became Bishop of Caesarea in 370. Prior to that he had lived the life of an ascetic and a hermit. Highly enthusiastic for monastic life, he drew up regulations prescribing and governing the forms of individual and coenobitic monasticism that the Eastern Church has followed ever since. The present citation is quoted from Basil's Epistle 92 (*PG*. 32, Col. 483), which he wrote, not to Pope Damasus, but to "the Bishops of Italy and Gaul." He was not acknowledging the Pope as Head of the Church, but rather soliciting spiritual backing from as many Western bishops as possible in order to counter the power of the Arians, who at the time enjoyed the support of the Emperor Valens. Dated in 372, the letter was conveyed by Sabinus, a papal representative, who was returning to Italy after bringing messages from the Pope to various prominent churchmen in the East.

[35] The voluminous material emanating from the Council of Ephesus contains but one letter sent in the collective name of the bishops to Pope Celestine (J.D. Mansi, *Sacrorum Conciliorum Nova, et Amplissima Collectio*, Florence, 1760, Vol. IV, Cols. 1330-1338). The letter does not contain the sentence Possevino quotes here and constitutes a factual account of the actions the Council took against Nestorius. Its tone is one of informing an esteemed and valued colleague; the claims to preeminence for the Pope made by his legates at the Council are pointedly ignored.

³⁶St. Cyril, Archbishop of Alexandria (370's-444), the leading opponent of Nestorius at the Council of Ephesus, wrote in the preamble of his Ninth Epistle to St. Celestine I (Pope 422-432) (*PG*. 77, Col. 80) as he is quoted here, but in a somewhat different context. Alluding to the desirability of tranquility as opposed to turbulence in the affairs of men, he regretted that the agitation of the partisans of Nestorius had become so intense that he was obliged to disturb the Pope over the matter.

³⁷The Anastasius to whom St. Leo the Great directed several epistles assumed his duties as Bishop of Thessaloniki in January, 446. In Chapter 6 (not 7) of his Epistle 14 (*PL*. 54, Col. 673) the Pope is asking, not ordering, Anastasius to take the procedural steps he recommends.

³⁸St. Sophronius of Jerusalem is also thought to be a certain Sophronius the Sophist. His Synodal Letter (*PG*. 87, Cols. 3149-3152) is primarily concerned with the condemnation of heretics, particularly Monothelites, is full of rhetorical devices and embellishments, is usually dedicated to Sergius, Patriarch of Constantinople, not Pope Honorius, and in it the *You* to whom constant reference is made is a literal, not a Royal plural. As such, it is difficult to consider this document a testimony to the leadership of the Pope in the affairs of the Church.

³⁹Michael Cerularius, who presided over the final rupture with Rome, became Patriarch of Constantinople in 1042, and St. Leo IX was Pope 1049-1054. The person presently referred to is Peter, Patriarch of Antioch, who assumed office in 1052, and sent a Synodal Letter to Rome, to which Pope Leo replied early in 1053 in highly flattering terms. Each side was sedulously seeking support for its position in the tense situation that existed at that time.

Notes To Chapter V

[1] This work is known only through Possevino's present reference to it.

[2] Cf. Chapter I, Note 24.

[3] Possevino's version of major events in the reign of Henry VIII (1491-1547). Himself a seasoned diplomat, he must have been aware that it was dynastic considerations which motivated Henry's actions. The king had married Catherine of Aragon (the widow of his deceased brother Arthur) in 1509, but she was unable to produce a male heir to the throne. Eventually Henry sought sanction to divorce Catherine from Pope Clement VII, who was moved to deny it in 1529 under pressure from the Emperor, Charles V. Parliament supported the King, who had little difficulty in obtaining the Act of Supremacy, which cleared the way for his repudiation of Catherine and his marriage with Anne Boleyn in 1533. Anne's similar failure to produce a male heir led to charges of adultery against her, which may or may not have been true, and to her execution in 1536.

[4] For Theodoretus, cf. *infra*, Note 15.

[5] St. Irenaeus (*ca.* 137-190) came from Asia Minor to serve as one of the first Bishops of Lyons, in Gaul. A good organizer and effective leader, his writings on a variety of subjects throw valuable light on the affairs of the Church in the second century.

[6] It is little short of ridiculous to assert that Gregory II (Pope 715-731) deposed Leo III Isaurian (Emperor 717-741), one of the greatest rulers of Byzantium. In the first year of his reign Leo repulsed the heaviest attack the Arabs had yet mounted against the city of Constantinople. The first Iconoclast Emperor, Leo issued a series of increasingly uncompromising decrees against the veneration of images. The European dominions of the Empire generally took strong exception to his position, and in this the Papacy supported them. However, although Leo's edicts provoked sporadic outbursts of violence, the Popes, including Gregory II, remained politically loyal to their Imperial overlord, as they needed his protection against the Lombards.

[7] Zacharias (Pope 741-752) had very little to do with the deposition of Childeric III (743-751). Childeric was the last representative of the Merovingian dynasty in France, where power had for some time been vested in the Mayors of the Palace. However, a revolt of the lords in 741 on the death of Charles Martel had convinced the latter's sons, Pepin the Short and Carloman, of the need for keeping a Merovingian figurehead on the throne a little longer. When Pepin felt strong enough to assert his prerogatives he secured his own election and removed Childeric to a monastery.

[8] Hildebrand (Gregory VII, Pope 1073-1085) came into conflict with Henry IV (1050-1106), King of Germany and Holy Roman Emperor. To regenerate the Church Hildebrand tried to curtail the process of lay investiture, and Henry was aroused to oppose him, because the royal power largely depended on the monarch's ability to control the great feudal bishops and abbots. Among the highlights of the contest between these two powerful figures were Hildebrand's excommunication of Henry in 1076 in retaliation for

the latter's attempt to depose him, Henry's Humiliation at Canossa, the creation of an anti-King, Rudolph of Swabia, Hildebrand's second excommunication of Henry in 1080, and Henry's deposition of Hildebrand and election of an anti-Pope, Clement III, whom Henry installed in Rome by force in 1084. Hildebrand invoked the support of Robert Guiscard, the Norman king of Sicily, who forced Henry to retire. The Normans then subjected Rome to pillage; Hildebrand received much of the blame for this, and in 1085 was obliged to accompany the Norman army southward, where he died at Salerno. It would perhaps be more accurate to say that Henry IV succeeded in deposing Pope Gregory VII.

[9] Innocent III (Pope 1189-1216) held office at a time when the mediaeval Papacy enjoyed great power to influence the course of temporal events. Two kings had simultaneously been elected in Germany; Philip of Hohenstaufen and the Duke of Brunswick, subsequently known as Otto IV (*ca*. 1182-1218). Innocent at first favored Otto, but when Philip began to prevail over his rival, the Papal attitude altered. However, Philip was murdered in 1208; Innocent then agreed to crown Otto as Emperor, and did so in Rome in 1209. When Otto showed no disposition to fulfill the agreements he had made with the Pope, Innocent excommunicated him in 1210 and renewed the sentence in 1211. Otto ignored this and continued his striving to unite the Kingdom of Sicily with Germany under his rule, a policy which the Pope was determined to thwart, since such a united principality would outflank the Papal power base in central Italy. In what was rapidly becoming a pan-European conflagration, Otto and his forces were defeated in 1214 at the Battle of Bouvines, in which the French and English kings participated, and he was forced to retire to his ancestral domain of Brunswick, where he died in 1218. The Papacy certainly influenced the course of events, but Otto's defeat and withdrawal to his own realm were not caused by the actions of Pope Innocent III.

[10] Innocent IV (Pope 1243-1254) went as far as any Pope had ventured to go in asserting the temporal side of Papal prerogatives, and in doing so he blunted the effectiveness of excommunication as a weapon in the struggle and emptied the Papal treasury. His opponent was Frederick II Hohenstaufen (Emperor 1220-1250), who succeeded in uniting Sicily with Germany. Frederick further sought to assert his hegemony over the north Italian cities, and this policy greatly alarmed the Papacy. Innocent's predecessor, Gregory IX, had excommunicated Frederick in 1227 because the Pope felt that the Emperor had shown himself tardy in going on a crusade. The sentence was lifted, but when Frederick continued to pursue his policy of aggrandisement in northern Italy to the detriment of the position of the Papal States, Gregory excommunicated him again in 1239, and Innocent, relying on French support, declared Frederick both excommunicated and deposed in 1245. Frederick paid no attention to the Popes' fulminations and continued to pursue his policies to the time of his death. There can be no doubt that Papal actions complicated the Emperor's position and contributed to the collapse of the dynasty after his death, but in many respects Innocent IV's inability to enforce his mandates marked the beginning of the Papacy's decline as the preponderant political force in European affairs.

[11] St. Nicholas I the Great (Pope 858-867) was a major early champion of the concept of the primacy of Rome among the Metropolitan Sees, and, more particularly, of the personal preeminence of the Pope. In the present instance he undertook to interfere directly in the internal affairs of Constantinople, where a power struggle had brought about the deposition of Patriarch Ignatius and the elevation to that office of the learned layman Photius, the architect of the definitive theological position the Eastern Church was to occupy henceforward. Ignatius and his supporters asked Pope Nicholas to intervene. The Papal legates approved Ignatius' deposition at a Synod held in Constantinople in 861, but Nicholas repudiated their action and, at a Synod convoked in Rome in 863, declared Photius excommunicated and deposed. The Pope's action aroused public opinion in Constantinople in favor of Photius, who in turn summoned a Synod in 867 which called the Pope a heretic because of his approval of the *Filioque*, and declared him deposed and anathematized.

[12] Innocent I (Pope 402-417) was interested in extending Papal power, and clerical celibacy. He sought to mediate the dispute involving St. John Chrysostom and the Empress Eudoxia, but there is no evidence that he excommunicated the Empress. The story of the earth's trembling belongs to the realm of legend.

[13] This is rather a paraphrase of than a translation from the Pope's letter (Migne, *PG*. 160, Col. 1209). The original conveys a much milder impression and does not prophesy the imminent capture of Constantinople. It is a courteous, if a trifle impatient, request that the Emperor implement the decrees of the Council.

[14] Possevino repeats, with amplification, the observations made by Pope Agatho quoted above, and supplements them with a close paraphrase of Pope Nicholas' Epistle 83 to the Emperor Michael III Amorian, written in 865 (PL. 119, Cols. 948 & 950), in which the Pope was merely affirming what he believed to be true to those who refused to accept it. The immediate outcome of the Photian-Ignatian controversy was not determined by the Pope, but by the fall of Caesar Bardas, and the rise of Basil I Macedonian (867-886), who murdered Michael, the last of the Amorians, in order to seize the throne.

[15] Possevino had previously cited St. Cyril of Alexandria with enthusiasm, and here he quotes with approval Theodoretus, one of Cyril's opponents at the Council of Ephesus. Theodoretus (d.*ca*. 457) had suffered deprivation of his episcopal see because of his refusal to condemn Nestorius, and in his anxiety to regain it, petitioned all who he thought might be useful to him for that purpose. Renatus was a Papal legate who, in 449, had vainly tried to read Pope Leo's Rescript to the "Robber Council" of Ephesus. In this Epistle 116 (*PG*. 83, Cols. 1324-1325) Theodoretus indulges in fulsome praise and flattery of Renatus, asking him to intervene with the Imperial authorities on his behalf, but apparently to no avail, for Theodoretus was not restored to office until he had recanted at the Council of Chalcedon, after the death of the Emperor Theodosius II.

[16] In the course of his stormy career St. Athanasius, Bishop of Alexandria (293-373), one of the most famous and controversial figures in the history of early Christianity, was obliged to go into exile five times. During his second exile he was received by Julius I (Pope 337-352), who sided with him in the Arian controversy.

[17] On becoming Patriarch of Constantinople in 398 St. John Chrysostom (*ca.* 347-407) displayed great reforming zeal. He criticized and incurred the wrath of the powerful Empress Eudoxia, who encouraged the Patriarch's enemies in the hierarchy to depose him at a Synod held in 403. Chrysostom had to go into exile, but popular pressures led to his recall. Nothing chastened by his experience, he singled the Empress out for personal attack and was again sent into exile. Violence occurred in the capital, and Chrysostom's followers asked Pope Innocent I to support him. Both the Pope and the Western Emperor Honorius sought to intervene, but their efforts to revoke the decree of banishment failed, and Chrysostom died in a remote part of Armenia.

[18] As mentioned above, Ignatius' second Patriarchate (867-877) did not depend upon the efforts of the Pope expended on his behalf, but on the change of dynasty at the Imperial court.

[19] As noted above, Theodoretus' attempts to regain his office were not successful until he had recanted at the Council of Chalcedon.

[20] St. Martin I (Pope 649-653) and Maximus the Confessor (580-662) were unable to prevail against determined Imperial opposition. Maximus, of Constantinople, was a leading opponent of Monothelitism, and took it upon himself to arouse the West and North Africa against it. He persuaded Martin at his accession to condemn the *Typus*, an edict of Constantine IV forbidding discussion of the Monothelite question. Imperial legates arrested Maximus in Rome in 653 and took him to Constantinople to answer charges, after which he was reportedly mutilated and sent into exile, where he died. The Emperor also arrested Pope Martin, who was likewise, after an inquiry in the capital, sent into exile in the Crimea, where he too died.

[21] Paul of Samosata was Bishop of Antioch in the second half of the third century. He taught what was known as Adoptionism, the theory that a man could become divine, as opposed to the Orthodox concept (upheld against Paul at a Synod *ca.* 268) of God become man. The dualistic possibilities inherent in Paul's views may readily be appreciated, and the Paulicians, who later were severely to vex the Byzantine Empire, took their name from him.

[22] The Emperor Heraclius (610-641) was extremely hard pressed by the military success of the Persians. One problem was the disaffection of the population in the vulnerable Asiatic provinces of the Empire, which were largely Monophysite in sentiment. Patriarch Sergius (610-638) proposed Monothelitism, a compromise between official Orthodoxy and Monophysitism, which, it was hoped, might mollify the Monophysites and conciliate their loyalty. The policy met with some success, but it inflamed old Christological controversies. Sergius first enunciated it in 633, and his initial opponent was St. Sophronius of Jerusalem.

[23] Catholic apologists have unanimously stressed the fact that Isidor, the Metropolitan of Moscow, had shown himself to be one of the most ardent champions of church union at the Council of Florence, and thus it behooved the Muscovites to accept the Council's decisions. It is often forgotten that Isidor was the last Greek to hold office as Metropolitan in Muscovy. Born in Thessaloniki, he had not occupied his position long when he persuaded Grand Prince Vasilii Temnyi to permit him to attend the Council. To reward his zeal the Pope made him a Cardinal and Apostolic Legate to the Northern Lands. Isidor returned

to Moscow in 1441 and celebrated a Uniate High Mass in the Cathedral of the Dormition. This provoked a great outcry; Vasilii rejected the Union and had Isidor arrested. After a Church Council had formally condemned the Union, the Metropolitan left Russia and made his way to Rome. He participated in the final defense of Constantinople in 1453. His career reveals that he was poorly informed concerning the realities of the Muscovite church in his time.

[24] At the third session of the Sixth Ecumenical Council the Papal legates charged that the correspondence between Pope Vigilius and Patriarch Mennas was fictitious. It was the Emperor and his staff who undertook a close investigation, acknowledged the forgery, which could not be attributed to any specific persons, and ordered the offending material excluded.

[25] Anastasius the Librarian (d.879) lived and worked in Italy, holding appointment under Pope Hadrian II, but he had connections at the Imperial court and was acquainted with Photius. Possevino is espousing the theories of Baronius (1538-1607), the first great Catholic historian, author of the *Ecclesiastical Annals*, which he based on systematic study of the material contained in the Vatican archives. Honorius (Pope 625-638) was frequently assailed for his initial failure to condemn Monothelitism, for which subsequent Synods openly condemned him as a heretic. This was offensive to Baronius, who developed several alternative hypotheses in an attempt to explain it away.

[26] This is merely what the Pope (*PL*. 119, Col. 930) and Possevino thought about the matter.

[27] The second Trullan Synod was convoked in 692 by the Emperor Justinian II. It issued 102 Canons, primarily concerned with church governance and administration. In so doing it tended to ignore the dispositions of Western Synods and disregard the enactments of the Popes. The Eastern Church has always considered this synod authoritative, but the Popes have refused to acknowledge it.

[28] A quaint legend is the story of Joan, who is supposed to have been Pope 853-855, when she was either killed or forced to abdicate after she bore a child.

Notes To Chapter VI

[1] Krzystof Warszewicki, whose brother, a Jesuit, was serving at the Swedish court, had shown himself extremely zealous in the Catholic cause. For this reason Possevino requested his inclusion in the Polish delegation as an observer. His lack of official standing caused some initial difficulty.

[2] Indiction was originally a Roman term used to denote the fiscal, as opposed to the calendar year. An Indiction comprehended a sequence of five consecutive years; thus, Ivan meant that he was in the tenth five-year sequence of his reign.

[3] *Prikaz* meant government bureau. It was originally a unit designed to administer the ruler's personal estate, but by the middle of the sixteenth century the Princely government of the Grand Duchy of Muscovy had developed a structure sufficiently complex to require rudimentary departments, in which both the functions and the personnel tended to shift in accordance with particular demand. The *Posol'skii Prikaz*, which had the responsibility of dealing with foreign envoys, came into existence in 1549.

[4] Sweden had taken advantage of Batory's successful campaigns against Muscovy to send her forces, commanded by an able French soldier of fortune, Pontus de la Gardie, to seize a number of fortresses in northern Livonia. Ivan did not wish to have the Swedes included in the negotiations because he planned to proceed against them after he had made peace with Poland. Sweden was unwilling to participate because John III was anxious to continue enjoying a free hand. Poland, however, desired Swedish adhesion to the treaty, as this would be an effective device to prevent further Swedish encroachments into the territory Poland coveted and had fought hard to obtain. Possevino's insistence on involving Sweden is one example of his attempts to serve the Polish cause.

[5] Jan Zamojski (1542-1607) was one of the most powerful men in Poland at this time. In Italy, where he acquired a liking for the ideals of the Roman Republic and a reputation as a gifted humanist, he studied at the University of Padua. On his return to Poland he was appointed Secretary to King Sigismund-Augustus in 1565, and began his rise to prominence. He sought to curtail the great power of the Magnates by increasing the involvement of the lesser gentry in affairs of state. He consistently opposed a Habsburg orientation for Poland and the presence of a Habsburg on the Polish throne. At the election of 1576 he advocated the elevation of a native ruler, but on Batory's accession he rapidly established good relations with the new king, whom he served faithfully. In turn he was rewarded with the office of Chancellor of the Kingdom in 1578, and Grand Hetman (Commander-in-Chief) of the Polish army in 1581. In this capacity he directed the siege of Pskov and supervised the truce negotiations. Something of his direct and forceful style emerges from his letters. Entirely devoted to Poland's interests, Zamojski was suspicious that Possevino might sacrifice Polish conquests to Muscovy in his pursuit of church union.

[6] Stanisław Żółkiewski (1547-1620) was a distinguished Polish military commander. A kinsman and supporter of Zamojski, he carried out a number of delicate commissions for the Chancellor. He assumed a leading role in affairs during the succeeding reign of Sigismund III Vasa, when he commanded the Polish army operating in Muscovy during the chaotic period of that country's history brought about by the activity of the Pretenders. He was killed in a battle with the Turks.

[7] Vladimir Sviatoslavich, Grand Prince of Kiev, not Muscovy (978-1015), who introduced Christianity into the Kievan State.

[8] Karamzin (*Istoriia Gosudarstva Rossiiskago*, SPb., 1892, Vol. IX, Note 601) has preserved an interesting anecdote that reveals Possevino's exhausted condition at the conclusion of the negotiations. According to the report of the Muscovite envoys, he lost patience with them and cried: "You have come to steal, not to negotiate." Seizing Alfer'ev by the collar, he spun him around, and shouting, "Go on, get out of here! " he threw him bodily out of the hut.

Summoning his Boyars and Antonio, the Pope's emissary, the Lord said: "A state of hostility and war existed between ourselves and Stefan, King of Poland and Grand Prince of Lithuania, and we sent a letter on the subject to the Most High Pope Gregory by our young courier, Istoma Shevrigin, since the war made it impossible to send a full Boyar Son. We therefore dispatched our junior Boyar Son to Pope Gregory XIII, Shepherd and Teacher of the Roman Church. We wrote that Pope Gregory should take advantage of his position as Teacher to write to King Stefan, directing him not to fight with us and shed blood, and Pope Gregory sent you to us, Antonio. You came to our kingdom and met with us at Staritsa, in the Grand Principality of Tver', and then proceeded to King Stefan. Following Pope Gregory's instructions you labored zealously to arrange a truce between our envoys and the envoys of King Stefan at a meeting; now Pope Gregory, the Emperor Rudolph, myself, and all the Christian Princes have made a splendid beginning towards concluding a friendly alliance. The only contention or argument that might arise would be on the question of faith; therefore, Antonio, you should not discourse with us on matters of faith, in order to prevent intrusion of any dissension in our quest for harmony with the Pope."

Antonio, the envoy of Pope Gregory XIII, said to the Lord: "Most Illustrious Lord, Tsar and Grand Prince, our Lord, Pope Gregory XIII, the Shepherd and Teacher, has ordered me to say: 'You sent your representative, Istoma Shevrigin, to us bearing a letter, and the letter you sent to us contained the statement that you wished to live in a state of friendly union with us.' Pope Gregory XIII, the Successor of Peter and Paul, desires to be united with you, Great Lord, in faith and friendship. The Roman faith is the same as the Greek faith; the Pope wishes soon to establish but one Church and one Faith, just as Christ said to Peter, the Chief Apostle, 'feed my sheep,' and gave Peter the Keys to the Kingdom. Pope Gregory, the Successor of Peter and the Apostles, wishes that there should be but one Church and one Faith, neither Roman nor Greek, throughout the whole world, and then we could go to Greek churches and confess our sins to Greek priests, while the Slavic people of the Greek faith could enter our Roman churches. Perhaps you do not have an adequate supply of Greek books translated in your kingdom: we have original Greek books, such as the works of St. John Chrysostom, written in his own hand, other Great Saints, the Teachings of the Apostles, the Seven Holy General Councils, the recent Council of Florence, which was attended by the Emperor, John VIII Paleologus, Pope Eugene, and many Patriarchs and Philosophers. There was dissension at the Council, but its members agreed to unite, and they provided that the Greek faith should be at one with the Roman faith. Since there is but one faith, the Greek church is joined together with the Roman church. You, Great Lord, will enjoy friendship and union with Pope Gregory, Caesar Rudolph, and all the other rulers, and you, Great Lord, will not only possess your ancestral patrimony in Kiev, but you will also be Lord of Constantinople. The Pope, the Caesar, and all the Great Lords will attempt to bring this about."

At this the Lord, Tsar and Grand Prince earnestly represented with Antonio, the Papal envoy, seeking to dissuade him from a discussion of the faith: "Only we have the right to initiate discussions with you, Antonio, and you will not like what we say; furthermore, even we, the Great Lord, dare not touch upon so awesome a topic unless we have received a blessing and a laying-on of hands from our Father and Intercessor, Metropolitan Dionisii, and the entire Sacred Council, and it is improper for me to discuss the faith in their absence. You, Antonio, are anxious to discuss it, and have been sent here by the Pope for this purpose. Since you yourself are a priest you can venture to speak of it, but we cannot talk about it until our Metropolitan has laid his hands upon us and we have received the advice of the entire Sacred Council."

The envoy Antonio stubbornly insisted on speaking: "I hope to avoid controversy; you are the Great Lord, and, like the humblest of your subjects, I must seek to avoid uttering contentious words, but, my Lord, I am obliged to expound the charge Pope Gregory laid upon me."

The Lord, Tsar and Grand Prince said to Antonio: "You and I will not agree on faith. Our Christian faith has been our own since ancient times, just as the Roman Church has been your own. We, the Great Lord, were born in our Christian faith, and by God's Grace have reached maturity and fifty-one years of age. We can no longer change, nor do we seek greater dominion. For the future we want but little, and we do not crave universal empire here on earth, for this is conducive to sin. Our faith is the true Christian faith and we want no other, nor do we need any other teaching besides the pure Christian teaching of our faith. Antonio, you say that your Roman faith is the same as the Greek faith: we uphold the true Christian faith, not the Greek faith. The Greek faith derived its name from the fact that many years before the Birth of Christ the Prophet David foretold that Ethiopia would stretch forth her hand to God. Now Ethiopia and Byzantium are one and the same, and the first Greek state in Byzantium was infused with Christianity; this is why it is called the Greek faith.[2] We, however, believe in the true Christian faith, and your Roman faith differs substantially from our Christian faith. We do not wish to discuss the question for the simple reason that you will be driven to utter harsh words in your annoyance at what we say, and so we do not want to talk about it, in order to prevent rancor and hostility from arising between the Pope and ourselves on this account. We wish to preserve and avoid impairing the friendship that has sprung up between Pope Gregory and ourselves. So do you, Antonio, desist from your course."

The envoy Antonio replied with great earnestness to the Lord:"I shall not become annoyed, but I am determined to speak to you, my Lord, about the faith."

The Lord said: "To save you annoyance we shall not discuss the great issues of the faith with you, but there is this one small point. We notice that you shave your beard, but neither priests nor members of the laity are allowed to shave or trim their beards. You are a priest of the Roman faith, and yet you shave your beard. Will you please tell us whose example you are following or on what authority you base your action? "

Antonio told the pious Lord and Tsar that he neither shaved nor trimmed his beard.

The Lord, Tsar and Grand Prince said: "Our courier, Istoma Shevrigin, told us that Pope Gregory sits in a chair and is carried about in this chair. The people kiss the shoes on his feet, and he has a Cross on his shoe. The Cross carries a representation of the Crucifixion of the Lord our God: now how can such a thing be right? Here is one of the prime differences between our Christian faith and the Roman faith. Our Christian faith considers the Cross of Christ the sign of victory over the Enemy; we revere the wood of the glorious Cross and esteem and honor it as enjoined by Holy Apostolic Tradition and the Holy Fathers in the General Councils. We are forbidden to wear a cross below the girdle; similarly, ikons of the Savior, the Virgin Mary and the Pious Saints must be placed in such a way that the ikons, when viewed by spiritual eyes, uplift the soul to their source. It is unseemly to place them on the feet. In our churches seats are built breast-high, because it is improper for any holy object to be below the girdle. Pope Gregory is acting in contravention of the mandate of the Holy Apostles and the Holy Pious Fathers in the Seven General Councils. The practices he follows are caused by pride.

At this point the envoy Antonio began to speak: "The whole Roman realm, including neighboring rulers such as the Caesar, the King of Spain, and many others, honors His Papal Holiness for his deserved greatness. He is the Father and Teacher of all rulers, whether western or northern, and, as chief of all rulers he sits in his capital, mighty Rome, as the Successor of Peter and Paul, and Peter was the Successor of Christ. The source of the whole Greek faith has resided in Rome since the birth of Christ, for to this day the bodies of Peter and Paul lie buried in Rome, as well as their disciple, Barnabas, the Apostle Mark, and the Apostle Andrew. The Relics of the Great Ecumenical Lords, teachers like Gregory the Theologian, are buried in Rome, as well as many other Great Lords, such as St. John Chrysostom and Nicholas the Wonderworker, and many martyrs. The well of martyrs' blood has been full since the days of the Caesar Nero down to the present, and Shevrigin saw all these places with his own eyes.

"All the holiness of the whole world has converged on Rome; thus, how could we, and all the people who come to Rome, fail to magnify and glorify the Great Lord, Pope Gregory, the Successor of Peter and Paul? In accordance with Christ's precept the Apostle Peter taught and proclaimed to the whole world that Christ had said to him: 'Feed my sheep' [John 21:17], and 'I will give you the keys to the Kingdom' [Matt. 16:19]. The Apostle Peter was the Successor of Christ; this is why the Pope is the teacher of everyone in the whole world, and this is why the Pope is honored. He is carried aloft because the Prophet Isaiah has written" -- (the envoy did not give the exact quotation). Then Antonio went on to say: "You are a Great Lord in your realm, as was your ancestor, Grand Prince Vladimir, in Kiev: how can we fail to magnify, glorify, and fall at the feet of such rulers as you?" So saying, Antonio bowed low to the feet of the Lord.

The Lord, Tsar and Grand Prince said: "Antonio, you are uttering words of praise of Pope Gregory, saying that he is the Successor of Christ and the Apostle Peter -- 'feed my sheep,' and 'I will give you the keys to the Kingdom' -- and that it is incumbent upon all to honor him, and to fall at his feet and kiss them. But the words you utter about Pope Gregory are said out of cunning, and not in accordance with the Lord's Commandments or Apostolic Tradition. Holy men should not give themselves such airs. What is written in the Holy Gospel? The Lord said to His disciples: 'But be not *ye* called Rabbi: for one is your Master, *even* Christ; and all ye are brethren. And call no *man* your father upon the earth: for one is your Father, which is in heaven. Neither be ye called masters: for one is your Master, *even* Christ. But he that is greatest among you

175

shall be your servant' [Matt. 23:8-11]. In the Gospel the Apostle Mark wrote: 'And he called *unto him* the twelve, and began to send them forth by two and two; and gave them power over unclean spirits; and commanded them that they should take nothing for *their* journey, save a staff only; no scrip, no bread, no money in *their* purse; but *be* shod with sandals; and not put on two coats' [Mark 6:7-9]. In his first Epistle the Supreme Apostle Peter says: 'Feed the flock of God which is among you, taking the oversight *thereof*, not by constraint, but willingly; not for filthy lucre, but of a ready mind; neither as being lords of *God's* heritage, but being ensamples to the flock' [I Peter 5:2-3]. You say that Pope Gregory sits on Peter's throne, and that is why it is proper for you to honor and exalt him so highly. He should blend humility with wisdom and follow Peter in all things, because Christ commanded it. He should not act as our courier, Istoma Shevrigin, told us he acts, and as you are telling us now. You also say that, besides esteeming the Pope, you are giving honor to us because it is necessary to honor Grand Prince Vladimir Monomakh, like ourselves a pious Tsar. This is the way of the world of men; in our Tsaric realm we honor all our brothers, the Great Lords, because of their Tsaric dignity. All holy men, the disciples of the Apostles, should display a fitting humility, not try to elevate themselves, nor seek in their pride to be mightier than Tsars, for a Tsar has his rightful honor, which is temporal, and holy men, Popes and Patriarchs, have theirs, which is spiritual. You yourself should remember how Tsar Uzziah conceived a desire to enter upon the spiritual life and forsake the temporal one, whereupon God visited him with misfortune. For this reason the strong-voiced prophet Isaiah did not prophesy for many years, which caused the Tsar shame. However, upon the death of Tsar Uzziah, Isaiah obtained the gift of prophecy [Cf. II Chronicles 16-21]. On the death of the Holy Apostles Peter and Paul in Rome, their Apostolic disciples upheld the Apostolic throne. The period from the convocation of the First Council in the days of the Roman Pope Sylvester to the Seventh, held in the days of Pope Hadrian, created, to take the place of the Four Evangelists, the Sees of the Four Patriarchs, the Universal Teachers; namely, Constantinople, Alexandria, Antioch and Jerusalem. This time witnessed the consecration of innumerable Metropolitans in many places; our Tsaric realm consecrated a Metropolitan and Russian Archbishops and Bishops in our Metropolitanate. A pious Tsar should receive the honor proper to him, while a holy man should receive his spiritual due. We honor our Russian Metropolitan for his spiritual prerogatives, call him our Father and Intercessor, bow down before him, esteem him, and seek his blessing when we meet him. But Pope Gregory XIII does not walk upon the ground; he has himself carried in a chair, calls himself the Successor of Peter, and calls the Apostle Peter the Successor

176

of Christ. But the Pope is not Christ; the chair in which the Pope is carried is not a cloud, and those who carry him are not angels. Pope Gregory has no business pretending to be Christ or His Successor. Peter was the First Apostle, the Chief Disciple of Christ, and he carried out all the behests and commandments of Christ in accordance with Christ's precepts, but it is not fitting to compare even Peter with Christ. After the Transfiguration of our Lord, at the Inspiration of the Holy Ghost the Apostles, Christ's Disciples, went forth into the whole world to preach; they cast lots for their preaching [Cf. Acts 1:26] in order to fulfill Christ throughout the entire world, and 'Do I eat the flesh of bulls,/ or drink the blood of goats?' [Psalms 50:13]. Make to the Lord a sacrifice of praise [Cf. Hebrews 13:15], and offer up your prayers to the Most High -- in spite of all this it is improper to equate the Apostles with Christ or to consider them the same as Him. The Apostolic Disciples in Rome -- Popes such as Sylvester, and the other great Popes, who were universal teachers -- followed Christ's teaching and Apostolic Tradition. They can properly be compared with the Apostles, but they must not exalt themselves through pride, have themselves carried in a chair, wear a Cross on their shoes, or allow the people to throw themselves at their feet. A holy man should manifest a humble visage, even as did Christ and his Disciples, Peter and Paul, and other Apostles. Any Pope who follows Christ's teaching, Apostolic Tradition, and his mighty predecessors, from the Great Lord Sylvester to the great Pope Hadrian, and other such holy men, who undertakes to profess their teaching and to preserve God's Commandments, Apostolic Tradition, and the work of the Holy Fathers in the Seven Ecumenical Councils, is a Successor of these great Popes and Apostles. The Pope who does not seek to live in accordance with Christ's teaching and Apostolic Tradition is a wolf, and no shepherd."

The envoy Antonio ceased speaking: "If the Pope is a wolf, I have nothing further to say."

The Lord, Tsar and Grand Prince said to Antonio: "I told you some time ago that if we discussed the faith it would be impossible for us to avoid harsh words. I am not calling your Pope a wolf; only the Pope who refuses to follow Christ's teaching and Apostolic Tradition do I call a wolf, not a shepherd. But let us now terminate our discussion."

The Lord placed his hand upon Antonio, thereby showing his favor to him, and dismissed him. He was escorted to his abode as before. The Lord ordered the *Great Pristav* Astaf'ia Pushkin and his associates to take fine foods and drink to Antonio from his own table.

[The Muscovite version of the sessions now differs considerably from Possevino's account. An exchange of communications ensued between Possevino and Ivan and his Councillors, headed by Nikita Romanov, dealing with the political issues Possevino had come to negotiate. Possevino submitted written memoranda on February 22, 24, 27 and March 4, and had audiences with the Tsar and his Councillors on Feb. 23, March 4, and March 11. They covered such questions as Possevino's desire to serve as mediator between Ivan and the King of Sweden, the projected league of Christian Princes, exchange of prisoners, the release of some Spaniards and Italians held in Moscow after escaping from the Turks, sundry complaints about the restrictions placed upon the envoys in Muscovy, and arrangements for Possevino's forthcoming journey to Poland. The section contains but one allusion to religion: on February 23 the Tsar reminded Possevino of his reluctance to engage in a discussion of the faith, as it could only produce rancor and ill-feeling, as it had done. There is no hint of the apology Possevino indicates Ivan tendered him at that time. Beyond this there is no further discussion of the topic until Ivan brought it up at the audience he granted Possevino on March 4.]

On Sunday, March 4 the Papal envoy Antonio Possevino appeared at the court of the Tsar and Grand Prince. His arrival at the Lord's court was as it had been before. On the Lord's instructions he was met at the head of the stairs by the Treasurer, Petr Ivanovich Golovin, and a secretary, Andrei Sherefedinov. When he entered the Lord's chamber he was announced by an Equerry, Prince Fedor Mikhailovich Troekurov. The Tsar and Grand Prince asked the Papal envoy Antonio to sit down. After he had been seated for a short time the Tsar and Grand Prince said: "Antonio, you have told our Boyars that you would like to visit the Cathedral of the Blessed Virgin to behold the service of our Orthodox Christian faith. We are presently about to depart for the Cathedral of the Blessed Virgin to confess our Orthodox faith. You may come to the Cathedral, witness our services and the piety of our Christian faith, and see how we honor the Metropolitan, our Father and Intercessor, ask his blessing, and esteem him and honor his holy office. But we do not deify him, as you told us earlier is the case with the Pope -- that he is carried in a chair, and has the people kiss his feet: this is pride, and not a holy thing. You call the Pope the Successor of the Supreme Apostle Peter, and say that the Apostle Peter took Christ's place, but even the Apostle Peter did not do what the Pope does -- be carried in a chair and have people kiss his feet: this is pride, not holiness. Christ's Apostle Peter did not ride on a horse and was not carried in a chair; he went about with bare feet."

178

Antonio said to the Lord: "Lord, I am anxious to visit the Cathedral and see the service, but concerning the Pope, Lord, I say to you that he is the Successor of the Apostle Peter and it was God Who placed him on Peter's throne. The Apostle Peter took Christ's place; Christ gave him the Keys of the Heavenly Kingdom, and Christ said to him: 'Feed my sheep' [John 21:17], and 'whatsoever thou shalt bind on earth shall be bound in heaven: and whatsoever thou shalt loose on earth shall be loosed in heaven' [Matt. 16:19]. The Pope now occupies the Apostle Peter's place, so how can we all fail to honor him or to render him the esteem due a Pope? He is the Father of all Fathers. Here, Lord, you have a Metropolitan, and look at the honor you pay to him -- he washes his hands during the service and then, Lord, he scatters you with the same water."

The Lord said to Antonio: "You call yourself a teacher and say that you have come to teach, but you do not even know what you are talking about. Have you not read the Interpretation of the Liturgy?" Antonio fell silent and did not answer the Lord.

The Lord said: "Since you do not know, I shall tell you. The Metropolitan washes his hands at Mass; next he hallows his eyes with the water, and then we hallow our eyes with the water, and the Metropolitan has the water carried about the entire church to the whole people. This is an imitation of the Passion of Our Lord. During the Passion, Our Lord Jesus Christ washed His hands and sprinkled His eyes; this is in imitation of the Passion of Our Lord, not in honor of the Metropolitan." The Papal envoy had no reply to this either.

The Tsar and Grand Prince ordered Astaf'ia Pushkin, Fedor Pisemskii, and Possevino's own *Pristav*, Zaleshenin Volokhov, with his men to escort Antonio to the Cathedral of the Blessed Virgin, and he instructed Astaf'ia Pushkin and his associates to wait with the envoy outside the Cathedral until he arrived, so that Antonio might see how the Metropolitan came out of the Cathedral, bearing a cross and accompanied by all his clergy, to greet the Lord, and how the Lord would follow the cross into the Cathedral. Antonio was then to enter the Cathedral behind the Lord; on this occasion the Cathedral of the Blessed Virgin had been magnificently adorned in preparation for the service. When the Papal envoy and the *Pristavs* reached the Cathedral, Antonio wanted to go in right away, without awaiting the Lord's arrival. Astaf'ia and his associates sought to restrain him and make him wait for the Lord, so that he might see how the Metropolitan and all his clergy would bring the cross out of the cathedral to greet the Lord. Antonio suddenly lost his temper, refused to wait, and decided to return to his quarters. The *Pristavs* tried to calm him, and Astaf'ia Pushkin and his associates told the Lord what had occurred.

The Tsar and Grand Prince sent the secretary, Andrei Shchelkalov, to Antonio, telling him to say that it was he, Antonio, who had begged the Lord to allow him to behold the service in the Cathedral, and the Lord, acceding to his request, had sent him to the Cathedral, merely asking him to wait a few minutes for the Lord so that he might see how the Metropolitan and all his clergy greeted their Lord with the cross, and then to follow the Lord into the Cathedral. Instead he had flown into a rage, refused either to wait for the Lord or to enter the Cathedral, and decided to return to his quarters. Antonio had behaved in an unseemly manner by refusing to enter the Cathedral. If he did not wish to do so, that was his affair; he was free to go to the chambers and negotiate with the Boyars concerning the issues that had not yet been resolved, but he should not return to his quarters at the moment. The secretary, Andrei Shchelkalov, followed the Lord's instructions and delivered this message. Antonio went upstairs to negotiate with the Boyars.

Notes To Appendix

1. Taken from *Pamiatniki diplomaticheskikh snoshenii drevnei Rossii s derzhavami inostrannymi*, SPb., 1871, Vol. X, Cols. 298-326. This is the Court Record, the thoroughness of which so greatly impressed Possevino.

2. Possevino would of course be familiar with the source of the Tsar's first reference, which is: "Princes shall come out of Egypt: Ethiopia shall soon stretch out her hands to God" (Psalms 68:31), but he may well have been surprised at Ivan's abrupt identification of Ethiopia with Byzantium. However, this too comes from the contemporary Muscovite ideological milieu. The *Communication of Spiridon - Savva* (Dmitrieva, *op. cit.*, p. 160), in speaking of the genealogy of Alexander the Great, says in part: "On Alexander's death his mother returned to her father Fola, the Ethiopian Tsar. Fola married her a second time to Viz, a kinsman of Akhtanovov [Nektaneb, the seer and legendary father of Alexander]. By her Viz had a daughter and called her Antiia, and he built a city at Sosveny and gave the city his own name, and that of his daughter, *i.e.*, Vizantiia [Russian form of Byzantium], which nowadays is called Constantinople."